Eric Clark is a former investigative reporter for the *Observer* and the *Guardian*. He lives in London.

THE REAL TOY STORY

Inside the ruthless battle for
Britain's youngest consumers

Eric Clark

BLACK SWAN

TRANSWORLD PUBLISHERS
61-63 Uxbridge Road, London W5 5SA
a division of The Random House Group Ltd
www.booksattransworld.co.uk

THE REAL TOY STORY
A BLACK SWAN BOOK: 9780552774062

First publication in Great Britain
Black Swan edition published 2007

This book is a work of non-fiction. In some [limited] cases names of
people, places, dates, sequences or the detail of events have been
changed [solely] to protect the privacy of others. The author has
stated to the publishers that, except in such minor respects
[not affecting the substantial accuracy of the work.
the contents of this book are true.

A CIP catalogue record for this book
is available from the British Library

Addresses for Random House Group Ltd companies outside the UK
can be found at: www.randomhouse.co.uk
The Random House Group Ltd Reg. No. 954009

The Random House Group Ltd makes every effort to ensure that the
papers used in its books are made from trees that have been legally
sourced from well-managed and credibly certified forests. Our paper
procurement policy can be found at:
www.randomhouse.co.uk/paper.htm

Typeset in 11/13pt Melior by
Falcon Oast Graphic Art Ltd.

Printed and bound in Great Britain by
Cox & Wyman Ltd, Reading, Berkshire.

2 4 6 8 10 9 7 5 3 1

For Marcelle, Rachael, Charlotte and Dan

CONTENTS

Introduction 9

1. If it's February it must be toy fair 15

2. The Inventors 46

3. What Hasbro wants 77

4. Barbie goes to war: battle of the dolls 105

5. The (vicious) business of toys 145

6. War of the aisles: the retail battleground 177

7. Grabbing them young: toy marketers 211
   lead the way

8. Santa's sweatshop 252

Afterword 287

Bibliography 291

Acknowledgements 299

Sources 303

Index 315

INTRODUCTION

'Play is the work of the child' – Maria Montessori

'The business of toys is anything but child's play' –
Toy Department,
Otis College of Art and Design, Los Angeles

Toys are wonderful. They inspire love, comfort the lonely, enrich experience, embody the best childhood memories. A bedraggled toy dog in bed can hold back the night. A red plastic fire engine can put out a tantrum. A tiny doll stems tears. They encourage learning, nurture imagination and creativity, and turn people into lifelong collectors.

Toys are special. They give a glow, years after they've been discarded. Remember the excitement of opening presents: the belled clatter of a xylophone, the slither of a Slinky, the waxy smell of Crayola Crayons. The feel of Play-Doh in your hands. That Fisher-Price aeroplane peopled with pop-in passengers. Toys are fun. More, they are a vital part of our lives, our culture, and our children's development. They are crucial for physical, emotional, intellectual and social interaction.

Good toys enhance play. Play is the work of childhood and toys are the tools of that work. They stimulate imagination, creativity, co-ordination. They let children experiment, discover themselves, solve problems, feel in control. They provide a two-way connection with adults. They help them make sense of the world and find their role in it.

The industry that produces these toys should also be special. It has to hold a singular place in our society: few others impact on such a critical and sensitive area of family life.

The American toy industry dominates not just the United States but the whole of the globe. It is now a $22 billion business, and although fewer than 4 per cent of the world's children are American, American children consume over 40 per cent of the world's toys.

This industry is massive and exciting. Every year it puts almost 3.6 billion toys into the home market alone, including 76 million dolls, 349 million plush toys, 125 million action figures, 279 million Hot Wheels and Matchbox cars...

Toys has never been a static industry: part of its genius has been a capacity to adapt with speed and flair. Today, though, the changes that buffet it are huge, the greatest for at least fifty years.

Kids are leaving their toys behind earlier and earlier. Partly this is due to the fact that they are growing up faster – the famous KGOY (kids getting older younger) syndrome, a trend ironically encouraged by the toy industry's own marketing methods of using sex and violence to attract kid sales. Another factor is the competition from all the other rivals for childhood time and attention, especially from today's new 'toys' like iPods and cellphones – electronics is eating the toy industry, laments one insider.

The industry that once drew vigour and innovation from the sheer number and challenging creativity of its range of companies is now corporate-dominated. Just two toy companies and three retailers control a huge proportion of the world's toys, determining which will be produced and which die. And their overriding concern is not the wonderful, special nature of toys – but the bottom line.

The fact is, the toy business is no longer fun and games. It's a harsh, corporate world, driven by social and demographic changes, concerns about stock prices and fierce battles between global brands.

The rewards for success are enormous: a top toy can earn billions. H. Ty Warner shot into *Forbes* World's Richest People list with his Beanie Babies. Likewise, the cost of failure can be catastrophic – the battlefield is littered with the corpses of once successful toy companies whose multimillion-dollar gambles did not pay off.

As a result, the toy business has become increasingly ruthless, willing to use 'gloves off' methods and exploit its young customers. In the struggle to adapt and to survive, our kids are regarded as walking wallets. Ever-younger age groups are constantly being targeted. Research companies work with children as young as two; by four, most are already making requests by brand name. One-year-olds attract increasing attention from researchers.

Marketers put into play the whole range of sophisticated research and selling techniques developed for adults, plus some extra (and sometimes dubious) techniques such as covert data collecting at child-oriented websites.

The impact of the US toy industry on children can hardly be exaggerated. It reflects, influences, stimulates and sometimes anticipates their wants and whims. Half the 40,000 commercials the average child views every year are for toys. Industry-promoted toy fashion fads condition toddlers for the wider marketing onslaught that will engulf them as they grow older.

Play has become too easy. 'A child loves his play,' wrote Dr Benjamin Spock, 'not because it is easy, but because it's hard.' Kids have a short attention span. A good toy is versatile: a cardboard box can be house, boat, fortress, tent, sledge . . . you'll never improve on a box. But the toys produced today too often do everything at the touch of a button. Vast numbers have computer chips and many come with pre-scripted storylines. Far from encouraging creative play, they stifle it: the action comes from the toy, not from the child. The play patterns that result are structured by the movies or television programmes that spawn them, or from the built-in electronics. No one says, let's pretend . . .

Today's big toy companies like to see themselves as being in the 'lifestyle entertainment' business. They are no longer selling playthings but promoting 'properties'. The only way to change the play with these toys is to discard, move on to a new one – which, for the industry, is the perfect commercial solution. Even better, these toys, once purchased, stimulate the sales of other toys and accessories in the line, promoting constant repeat buying. The industry's continued existence depends on selling instant gratification over and over again.

Today's toy men are not manufacturers. Most of the world's toys are made thousands of miles away in China by migrants toiling for a few cents an hour. The monstrous gap between the cost of manufacture and the selling price fuels the process to which toy companies devote themselves – the marketing. Throughout America – and throughout the world – the way kids play is increasingly determined by a tiny number of executives who could just as effectively be selling soap or breakfast cereals (and probably have, or some day will).

There are still toy men who care: lone, maverick inventors conjuring up captivating playthings with passion and ingenuity; persistent, daring entrepreneurs.

It is a business where losers far outnumber winners. The losses are monumental, the wins colossal. And it can happen in the space of a season: one longtime commentator on the industry memorably says, 'Every big toy company is just a stone's throw away from disaster.'

It is a high-wire act without a safety net. That's why the thrills remain.

Chapter One

IF IT'S FEBRUARY IT MUST
BE TOY FAIR

'What is the measure of a successful toy? Sales, sales
and sales'– Ralph Osterhout, toy designer

One is a New York City landmark, the other is the
contender. Two of the world's greatest toyshops stand
just sixteen blocks apart in midtown Manhattan. FAO
Schwarz, the Fifth Avenue flagship of America's oldest
toy retailer, calls itself the 'ultimate' toy store. The
competitor, Toys R Us, an upstart newcomer, is self-
styled as the 'world's biggest'. Rivalry between them
is given added edge by the fact that the Times
Square challenger was the brainchild of FAO's ex-
chief John Eyler after he moved across to the big-box
toy retailer.

None of that matters, though, not to the kids and
their parents as they flood through the brilliantly lit
stores. Both stores are, in their way, pure magic.

The glittering prime tourist destination that is FAO
Schwarz is the crème de la crème of the toy world.
This traditional stylish wonderland for the upscale
shopper sits almost in Central Park, and security
guards keeping order in line are as much a part of
the New York Christmas experience as the tree in

Rockefeller Center or the dancing Rockettes. Schwarz's dramatic showmanship has been exceptional for 140 years. Each year 3 million visitors throng past the toy-soldier doormen to wander through the plush toy animal jungle, wondering at the 20,000 computer-controlled LED lights that twinkle in a breathtaking variety of colours and patterns overhead. They watch actors reprise the memorable scene in the 1988 movie *Big* in which Tom Hanks and Robert Loggia picked out 'Chopsticks' with their feet on a 22-foot piano. They pose for photographs that shrink them to a doll-sized person sitting on the lap of a favourite toy. Schwarz marries prestige with product to market its own unique merchandise, from a doll's designer T-shirt set at $15 to a $50,000 child-size Ferrari. It sells 'chocolate volcanoes' at $100 a pop in its old-fashioned ice-cream parlour, and offers a chance to 'adopt' a doll in an area set up like a real nursery staffed by suitably dressed employees. From goodies that are either unique to the store or produced for only limited distribution, customers can select a polished maple rocking horse for $6,000, spend several hundred dollars on a one-off Barbie doll, or take home an American Kennel Club-certified plush puppy, complete with its own registration papers.

It's said that imitation is the sincerest form of flattery. Blocks away in Times Square, on the bow tie where Seventh Avenue crosses Broadway, on a heavily trafficked corner site that once housed two theatres, Toys R Us hypes their lavish flagship store as 'the Center of the Toy Universe'. A million and a half pedestrians daily see the glass exterior walls glowing like a light box, changing by the minute from transparent to an opaque billboard. Even from the outside, this vast open space is a fairground dominated by a 60-foot-high, four-storey, neon-flashing Ferris wheel with

fourteen cars inspired by toy characters and games –
an M&M's car, a Mr and Mrs Potato Head, a Buzz
Lightyear and a Pokemon. This, like the life-size
moulded-silicone T-Rex dinosaur standing at the
entrance to the Jurassic Park section, shaking its head
and tail and roaring, is a giant selling tool. As is the
4,000-square-feet two-storey walk-through Barbie
Dream House with its own elevator, and the miniature
New York City model built of Lego and including a
King Kong atop the Empire State Building. Here, the
prices are more moderate – this chain, after all, started
out selling toys from warehouses – but the razzle is
every bit as effective. Staff members wear scarlet,
making them easily visible. The store mascot is a life-
size Geoffrey the Giraffe. There is a real sweetshop
modelled on the Candy Land board game, complete
with giant gumdrops, and a sculpture with a skirt
made of lollipops.

The two stores fight it out: the Tiffany of the toy
business, and the Theatre District mini theme park.

Many of the toys they sell are tried and tested, the
winners proven over the long haul, the ones your
parents loved first, then you, and now your kids:
Barbies, Play-Doh, Monopoly, Etch-a-Sketch, Erector
Sets, Lego bricks. An ever-increasing number flash and
blink and perform, products of the electronic toy
revolution. Some are this year's crop of hopefuls, the
novice racers in this fiercely competitive field.

Behind every one of these toys stands an invisible
crowd. At the back is its inventor. For a few – a very
few – this might be a lone individual who quit the day
job, even mortgaged the family home for seed money
to make the prototype. More likely it will be a
company's in-house designer or one of the five
hundred or so professional inventors, sometimes

working through licensing agents. Next in line is the toy company. This would once have been among a thousand father-and-son family businesses, now almost certainly swallowed up by one of the few major companies. These giants could have spent big money acquiring the rights, and possibly millions in development and design. The product might be linked to a book, a film, a kids' television series. Then there is the manufacturer: the toy will likely be made in China, probably for even less than a dollar. Millions may have been spent on promotion, ads developed using all the wiles and expertise of several groups of professionals, from marketers to child psychologists.

And now the toys sit enticingly in their clever packaging on the store shelves. Lights flash, tunes tinkle, childish voices squeak. Look, press the shoelace on her trainers and Dora the Explorer shouts 'Ola! I'm Dora!' and dances wildly from side to side in her box. Furby murmurs, 'You Happy See Me.' From Shout Elmo's box comes the spoken message, 'You can shout with Elmo.' By the time the kids and their parents see them here, even if they're new designs, a lot of serious investment has tried to ensure that these objects are famous, familiar and infinitely desirable.

Here are classic toys. Hi-tech toys. Contender toys. Some that may make it big, others that will be dead and forgotten within a year.

This – writ large and theatrical – is the public face of the $22 billion American toy industry which today dominates the world.

Every year, a further eighteen blocks south, another toy world descends on New York. It's still a land of board games, plush animals, dolls, action figures, kites and stickers. But this time there are no wide-eyed children. The exhortations here are different. The chance to make money is what's on sale. The advertising message for Chicco's Sing Along CD Player, a toy for children four and older, is different here. Now it is 'Music to everybody's ears. Especially ones that like to listen to tunes of profitability.' This year's slogan says it all: 'Play Meets Profit.'

February and New York. It's not exactly the stuff of songwriters. It's Sunday, first day of the International Toy Fair, and the city is in the throes of the biggest winter storm in its history. After two months of near-spring-like weather, the day has begun with claps of thunder and lightning. Snow that will reach a record 26.9 inches before the day is over is falling at the rate of up to five inches an hour, obliterating everything more than a few feet away. Even when the snow eases, vicious winds will sweep across the Hudson.

With airports closed and other transport suspended or disrupted, many toy men have not made it this far. For several of those who do, it only confirms what they have thought for a long time: that Manhattan in winter is a lousy place to hold a big event. Even if the event in question is the International Toy Fair and, as the organizers keep saying, New York is the heart of the United States toy industry and thus, by implication, centre of the world toy industry.

Only about 400 make it to the opening – 2,600 were expected. But as the day goes by, more toy men and women struggle through. By the end most are pronouncing it a 'good fair'. Several quietly liken the heavy weather to the toy business itself: the going is increasingly tough – but everything is still alive and kicking.

Toy Fair in New York is 103 years old. It has come a long way from that February day at the turn of the century when seven American toy salesmen set themselves up in the Broadway Central Hotel to catch buyers travelling to and from Europe, then the Mecca for toys.

The fair is a microcosm of the industry, the only place to see it in one spot, to observe the annual gathering of the clan as its members try to feel the mood, sense the trend, sniff out the next hot thing. Today, with toys a global business, products may be conceived in Chicago, developed in Los Angeles, made in China. Uniquely, the fair brings together all the players – manufacturers, retailers, wholesalers, licensing companies, inventors, exporters, analysts.

Each year the toys on show, even the way they're exhibited, embody the industry's current hopes, fears and preoccupations. This year a new section, e@play, a commercial homage to toy technology, reflects the attempts to struggle with the digital reality of kids' lives. Overall, throughout the fair, there's less innovation, much concentration on licensing and on extending existing tried lines – all signs of an industry cautious and unwilling to take risks in times it still can't fully comprehend.

Mood aside, Toy Fair remains part of the potent mix of raw talent, energy, determination, desperation and know-how that has driven America to dominate the world's toy industry. The fair has seen toy men come and go, watched hundreds of famous-name companies thrive and fade. It has witnessed the changes wrought in the industry by television and the progression of plastic (to the point where one cynical toy man can now say, 'We're not in toys, we're in plastics'), looked on as many toys were stuffed with electronic chips that made them talk, dance and pulse with light. It has observed toy manufacturing's exit from the US to

China and contemplated the rise of the mega-retailers and their power over toy men.

The one-man entrepreneurs and the inventors who set up shop at the fair are as creative – and as full of hope – as ever, even if their struggle to launch their products grows ever harder in these days of the dominance of the big toy makers and mass retailers.

Alan Hassenfeld, chairman of Hasbro, the world's second largest toy company, and an inveterate toy fairs lover, reckons that whatever the state of the industry, whatever the climate, Toy Fair always represents spring. 'It's the only business that no matter how difficult it is right now or tomorrow or in November, we can't wait to show the buyers the new line for next year. Stravinsky would have had a field day with us, because it's *The Firebird*, it's *The Rite of Spring*, it's a new year, we're reborn. There are new toys. God, life's great.'

Hassenfeld stands astride the old and the new days of the toy industry. He is the last big figure whose family name is still over the door, and the nearest thing the industry has to an aristocrat. Immaculate but unconventional (usually tie-less and given to wearing rubber bands as bracelets), he is diffident, elaborately polite and softly spoken in the way of old money. He never sought the top job – previously he led Hasbro's international expansion, and it is said he preferred writing short stories and dating beautiful women – but was propelled into it by his brother's untimely death from complications of the AIDS virus.

'Then you finish Toy Fair,' he continues, 'and you basically say, oh God, what a terrible year this is going to be, but next year will be better. There's this eternal optimism. It's one of the things I love about this business.'

The toy industry is undergoing a revolution. Sales have been failing as kids abandon traditional toys; price competition has got keener; costs have soared, revenue has fallen; stores have closed – and the powerful shadow of Wal-Mart has loomed ever larger. In the carefully understated words of Arnie Rubin, chairman of the Toy Industry Association, the fair's promoter, 'It (2005) was certainly a year of challenges for both retailers and manufacturers.'

It seems a far cry from the almost hysterical optimism at Toy Fair's 100th anniversary just three years before. On that occasion, laughing, attendees donned special Centenary Year T-shirts and held hands to break a Guinness record for the world's largest ribbon-cutting ceremony.

But while everyone there sensed the rumblings, few could have predicted the extent of the imminent upheaval. Within a year FAO Schwarz had fallen into bankruptcy. Saved by a New York investment firm, the D.E. Shaw Group, it reopened later as an extravagant playground, more lavish than ever – but other FAO Schwarz stores, with the exception of Las Vegas, closed permanently. While the industry was still absorbing that, Toys R Us, too, under the onslaught of Wal-Mart, struggled and changed hands, in its case to two private equity firms and a real estate developer. In the wave of closures and conversions to baby stores, the only Manhattan Toys R Us store that now remains is the flagship Times Square building.

There are even question marks over the future of New York's Toy Fair itself.

For now though, for a few days, New York is the Toy Centre of the Universe, a magnet to retail buyers, toy manufacturers, sales representatives, inventors and up to a thousand of the world's press and TV looking to break the latest trends and the next hot thing. Buyers are about to view the industry's new lines. There's a bewildering variety – Toy Fair features 100,000 toys of which 5,000 are new; and there are thousands more never seen at the fair. Up for grabs is which of them a nation's kids will be demanding in a few months' time.

It's a unique feature of the toy business – a group of grown men and women deciding ten to eighteen months in advance what a three-and-a-half-year-old will want to buy when he or she is five. As Jay Foreman, president of Jakks Pacific Play Along division, says, 'It's up to all of us to figure out what's hot for next Christmas now. We're all throwing stuff out there and seeing what sticks.'

Everyone is searching for the must-have product with the 'wow factor' that will get the tills ringing – the Furby, the Tickle Me Elmo, the Cabbage Patch Doll. The sellers, especially the newcomers with dreams, pray their own new toy will be discovered and swept to stardom – or, at least, offered a deal. The buyers pant for the next big one.

Hasbro and Mattel, the world's biggest toy companies, don't play much part in the fair any more – they have previews for the Big Five retailers at their own venues or in exotic resorts. Mattel's takes place in the Oscarnight headquarters Renaissance Hollywood Hotel. Visiting retailers are flown in First Class or Business Class (depending on their company buying clout) and glad-handed around the company's own Toy Fair outfitted with separate Barbie and Hot Wheels Rooms.[1] But

[1] Another, much more recent Toy Fair is held every October in New York. Restricted to large companies, who have long lead times, its secrecy makes clams seem loquacious – at that stage no one wants publicity for the toys, often still in prototype.

their scouts are on the lookout. Hassenfeld says, 'I tell my people, "Nobody has an ownership of great ideas. In the farthest corner of the Toy Fair is a toy waiting to be found. Go forth, my children, and find it. And bring it back." It is like going after the chalice.'

On how well, or how badly, those toys and games fare (and many will never leave the fair), fortunes may be made or lost. Keith Elmer, head of an English retail-buying consortium, says the real task is sorting out which toys *not* to buy. Back home in the UK, the average independent toyshop can only stock 5,000 out of 66,000 items that are available to them.

As Maria Weiskott, editorial director of *Playthings* magazine, a toy-trade bible, puts it, 'For those of us in the toy industry, only one thing ever happens in February: International Toy Fair. The whole year sometimes hinges on that week when manufacturers bring out their best efforts and cross their collective fingers.'

Toy Fair in New York, confusingly, is in two places – a collection of showrooms in Chelsea, most notably the International Toy Center at the corner of Fifth and 23rd, and the Jacob J. Javits Conference Center, on the far West Side, an area that even in Manhattan manages to feel like the middle of nowhere. Transportation problems to and from Javits are one of the things the anti New Yorkers complain about. This is compounded by this year's blizzard, as the shuttle buses between the Toy Center and the hotels struggle and taxi cabs vanish.

Until Javits opened in 1986, companies without sales showrooms exhibited in booths in hotels. The Toy Center, two separate buildings connected by a bridge, has been the hub of the American toy business since the end of World War II, not just for the 300 individual companies with showrooms there, but also as the industry's spiritual heart. The companies represented are diverse. They include MGA of California, the success of whose Bratz Fashion Dolls has been delivering the first-ever real body blows to what is arguably the industry's most important and significant toy, Barbie. M & C Toy Centre Ltd, Hong Kong ('Toys at collectible quality but at toy prices'), and Radio Flyer Inc of Chicago ('America's Original Red Wagon since 1917') are also exhibitors. Other floors house importers or representatives. In all, it's fifteen floors with something to sell. Oh, and eight firms offering toy chests to hold it all.

It is a place with a rich history. In the eighteenth century a mansion was built on the site. It then became an inn and stagecoach terminal, next Franconi's Hippodrome and, in the mid nineteenth century, the lavish Fifth Avenue Hotel. As such it hosted millionaires, Presidents, visiting royalty – and a group of visiting toy salesmen who met to plan adjacent sample rooms convenient for visiting buyers. In 1910 the hotel made way for the Fifth Avenue Building, and toy manufacturers began to open salerooms. In 1925 there were 700 exhibitors and it officially became the Toy Center, then in 1994 the International Toy Center.

Most New Yorkers call the surrounding area the Flatiron district, after the distinctive wedge-shaped building located on the triangle where Broadway cuts across Fifth at 23rd. Toy men have always known it as the Toy district.

This year there is a marked contrast to former glory days. The trouble is that an area of New York that was once abandoned and desolate is now chic. The Toy Center has been sold and its tenants are leaving. Elevators are half empty; many offices remain dark;

eviction notices are taped to some glass doors. The building will be renovated into expensive condos and the industry is having to face the fact that the district could slide into history.

As Toy Fair opens, the search for a replacement centre is still on. At this stage, the only thing any of the toy men pitching or buying know is that this will be the last fair held in this building.

As always, new lines are viewed behind closed doors, strictly by appointment. Impromptu visits are not appreciated. The guys who look like bouncers probably are. The toy industry is fixated on secrecy. Visitors to company offices sign 'confidentiality agreements' and the industry doesn't hang about when it comes to sending in an attorney if such an agreement is broken. The paranoia about ideas theft isn't unmerited. Jim Silver, editor-in-chief of *Toy Wishes* and a member of the fair's Conference Advisory Board, explains just how quickly a new toy can get knocked off. New York isn't the only Toy Fair. It's not even the first. That's in January in Hong Kong. There, Silver explains, a manufacturer may get word of someone else's new item. Perhaps someone in one of the factories being shared by a number of manufacturers will tell him. The word circulates. Chinese plants can move fast. 'In a matter of thirty days you can see prototypes in three or four showrooms in New York,' says Silver. For that reason, some manufacturers with a big innovative toy may not show it at any of the Toy Fairs. Mattel kept its new My Scene Barbie (its riposte to its Bratz doll competitor) under wraps until May. But only a major company can get away with that kind of secrecy and still merit holiday shelf space.

At both buildings, there is massive security. There are checks everywhere around New York of course, but this is more than post 9/11. Every year there is the fear that someone from the public will get in, or even worse, one of the public's kids. As the organizers put it, 'Toy Fair is open to the trade only. Absolutely no consumers and no one under eighteen, including infants, toddlers, child inventors, demonstrators or "consultants" will be admitted.'

Children, the observer soon starts to realize, have little place in the toy world, except as objects for market research, actors in toy commercials, and, naturally, consumers. At Toy Fairs their role is restricted to photo opportunities and public relations. It's on those media-attracting occasions, carefully orchestrated and confined within time and place boundaries, that a closely chaperoned child or group of children may appear. At the London Toy Fair a few weeks earlier I'd watched a number of them lined up and marched away as soon as they'd fulfilled their role. There was no pretence: the Diary of Events had made a special point of the fact that on one stand children would be present all day and that on another a four-year-old could be photographed playing with a new Zapf Creations product. That was it. Even there, though, the children offered for photo opportunities were far outnumbered by television personalities, pop singers and models. The toy business, despite any protestations, is for Toy People. It's about sharp suits and power talk.

You need to step into Javits to get the full impact of Toy Fair. This is where most of the 1,500 exhibitors set up shop to be inspected by 11,000 buyers, another 7,000 licensors, analysts and reps, and 1,000 of the world's media. Fair organizers extol Javits as the place to go for inspiration, to see fresh ideas and to experience the excitement of the toy business in action. To gauge what's hot and what's not. To seek out gaps in the market and identify trends.

Buyers work the aisles of an area the size of three football fields, dragging rolling totes filled with literature. (*No wheeled luggage or sample cases will be permitted on the show floor except small empty cases to be used for collecting exhibitor material.*) 'What's new?' is a constant call. The speciality toyshops remember Beanie Babies that, for a while, injected new life into their struggling businesses. Despite blandishments, H. Ty Warner, inventor of the under-stuffed beanbag animals, would sell only to the small shops, turning down chains like Wal-Mart and Toys R Us. It worked for him: his privately owned company reportedly earned $700 million profits in 1998. It worked for the speciality shops too: for some of them the toy accounted for almost a third of the total revenue.

About a third of the exhibitors are very small-scale concerns, often one man or woman, with one idea. Everyone, it seems, wants to be a toy inventor, and this is El Dorado: come to Toy Fair, get discovered, strike gold. No one deters them — they provide the fair with its dynamism. In a business increasingly dominated by the big and the corporate, inventory levels, risk reduction and the demands of Wall Street, they fulfil two crucial functions. First, they give the business a more appealing image, a picture of toy-loving small guys achieving their ambitions through vision and guts and hard work. Secondly, the toy business constantly needs new product.

Many of the great ideas of the past have come from lone inventors. The massive success stories become legend. Barney, the purple dinosaur, went on to world-wide success after being introduced at the show in 1989. The deal between Xavier Roberts and Coleco that turned Cabbage Patch Dolls into one of the top sellers in toy history was struck at the 1983 fair. Rubik's Cube really began to take off here. Within a year, it was in the Museum of Modern Art. At its height, it is said, it was played with by an eighth of the world's population.

The Toy Industry Association, the body behind the show, reckons to get 4–5,000 approaches direct from the public each year. Of the 500 or so newcomers who make it to Toy Fair, a hundred disappear within twelve months, back to their 'real' jobs, wiser and poorer, never to be seen here again. One estimate is that less than one in every hundred new products is licensed from an inventor.

That doesn't stop the creating and the hoping. John Webb, from Delaware County, Pennsylvania, has spent $28,000 so far, including $1,000 to attend the fair. He has a patented toy and storage chest that doubles as a wrestling ring. Nearby, Gregory Hughes eagerly demonstrates 'Hip-Hop: The Game' to any potential buyer who will stop. Players move around a board answering questions about urban style and hip-hop music, picking up illin' (lose money) and chillin' (gain money) cards. Greg's nervous – he needs publicity but doesn't want his media employers to know he's moonlighting.

Sometimes the dream has survived for a long time. Jim Corbett, from Mukilteo, Washington, and a friend created a spelling game for kids, Spelling Beez, thirteen years ago. Jim, vice-president of a company sourcing court records, bought out his friend's share. He has had the game produced, sold it direct, but it has never taken off. Now he is looking for a licensing deal.

Geoff Beckett, from Buffalo, New York, who left his job in construction seven years ago, has already come a long way. His line is Shockinis, mini action figures with interchangeable parts. They already sell in comic stores and on the Web. He is aiming high here, hoping for a mass retail deal.

There is often serious money on the line. Dan Tibbs, a former polygraph officer with the Niagara regional police, and his business partner, reportedly spent $500,000 developing their invention. Liar Liar Pants on Fire is basically a lie-detector game for kids. A palm-size device is strapped to fingertips and measures blood-flow and skin responses to such questions as 'Have you ever farted in the bathtub?'

Lee Hae Gon brought over his educational toy from South Korea. It is his third invention. The first was a clip device to stop shoelaces coming undone. It was, he says proudly, taken up by Nike.

A few are risking their futures. Helmut Gutfleisch, from Nuremberg, gave up managing a chemical factory after he brought back wooden toys from holiday to sell at Christmas. They are Estonian, beautiful 'back to basic' artefacts that will, he volunteers through his English-speaking wife, 'last a hundred years if you want'. Manufacture in Estonia keeps the price down: he can sell a tractor at $34–$35.

What none of these hopeful exhibitors can truly comprehend until they set up shop is just how many toys there are, how great the competition, how tough a world it is. They have to contend not only with each other but with all the classic toys, many with updates to give them a new twist. Easy Bake Oven, introduced in 1963, now looks like a contemporary kitchen range and has a plug-in heating element that no longer requires a light bulb. Lego comes with FX bricks that add sound, light and motion. Board games like Candy Land, Twister and Clue (Cluedo in the UK) come not only in their original forms but also in DVD versions.

More Power Rangers are on call to protect the world from evil. Countless action figures range from Megazords through Hellboy and Samoa Joe to ones you can eat after playing with them. Bob the Builder and Care Bears are here in almost every conceivable guise, from camera phones to trikes. There are princess costumes, portable ant containers, flip-flops with secret compartments, levitating globes (all done by magnets), glorious peacock puppets, and Pretend and Play office sets with make-believe staplers.

Dolls, animals and other plush toys come in every manifestation. Dolls that just roll their eyes and talk are old hat: Baby Alive eats, poops and now has facial expressions. Amazing Allysen is programmed to learn a child's preferences, such as the names of best friends, and work them into conversations. Soysilk bears and bunnies, made from fibre extruded from soybean cake, are environmentally friendly. Butterscotch, a $300 life-size plush pony, whinnies, moves its eyes, ears and head, swishes its tail, nuzzles and 'eats' carrots. Large-scale animals from Hansa have titanium frames under the plush so kids can sit on their backs. Holy Folks presents 16-inch-high faith-based plush figures including Jesus and Moses, 'complete with magnetic hands and accessories'.

Electronics are everywhere. Digi Makeover is a product with a digital camera that allows little girls to photograph themselves, plug into the TV and try out different make-up and hairstyles. A build-it-yourself robot comes with a load of software programming tools for a cool $1,000. Thanks to a combination of infrared and radio-frequency technology, Barbie dances to music from the doll's base. The Fly Pen, a computerized pen that looks a lot like an electric toothbrush, speaks and translates words into foreign languages, and can even play music.

A handful of exhibitors work the aisles, trying to whip up orders. Frank Blumen and Ron Yoder urge passers-by to try their bungee balls. It's good, hard huckstering – buy on the spot with cash, cheque or credit card for $1.15 and sell at suggested retail $7.95. That's a 6–1 markup, they're quick to remind, and they say some retailers have made holiday profits of between $20,000 and $50,000.

Javits is more democratic than the Toy Center: it has open booths where potential customers can gaze, wander, ask questions, even make orders.

Stevanne Auerbach, a PhD from California known as 'Dr Toy', gets the big treatment as she tours. An established child-development expert with books, columns and regular TV shows to her credit, she's an industry consultant and fair-going veteran.

Dr Toy selects and evaluates the best of the new for her website. An endorsement from her can help any toy along. She attends the pre-fair preview days at the showrooms in the International Toy Center, an appointment every half-hour. Then at Javits she undertakes four days of walking. She is not looking for just another stuffed bear, another doll. What she's after are unique features, 'unusual products, creative, different. Educational toys that are really going to help kids learn something, that is my focus. I am always looking for the needle in the haystack.'

Dr Toy is wary. 'Hot does sell and it does bring up the curve in terms of sales and excitement. So one year it can be Tamagotchi, another it can be Yu-Gi-Oh, another time it can be Furby. Each child is different and these hot products – whether it's Spiderman or Hulk or Harry Potter – it's not for all kids.'

She cautions that however successful the book or movie, 'the products themselves do not satisfy, or do not last. I would rather look at the assortment of products from Marvin's Magic than the magic wand from Harry Potter.' She makes a dismissive gesture. 'You can use anything for a magic stick.'

At Toy Fair, you meet two types of toy man. *The Real Toy Guy* and *the new-kid-on-the-block-who-could-be-in-any-business-but-it-just-happens-to-be-toys.*

The Real Toy Guy has probably been around for a long time, though not necessarily. He may even be retired.[2] Real toy guys are entrepreneurs, trailblazers, quick decision makers, blunt speakers, often foul-mouthed, who take lip from no one. Bernie Loomis, former president of Kenner Products, was one.

It was Loomis who pulled off one of the industry's great selling stunts. Kenner (according to consultant Philip Bloom, toy industry insider and at that time buyer for Circus World, a chain of toy stores in malls) bought the original rights to make Star Wars action figures. Trouble was, the figures would not be ready for delivery until after Christmas. Loomis had the answer. 'His salesmen came round with pictures of what the products were going to be, and with empty boxes. As a buyer, I was asked to pay $6 for each box. The customers would then pay $9.99 retail for those same empty boxes.' The boxes were a form of IOU: when there was product, the customer would get it. 'People', recalls Bloom, 'were buying empty boxes like they were gold.'

Sy Ziv was a similar figure. Sy was at Toys R Us until Wall Street and the corporate suits began to call too many shots. They've all got a Sy story. Mostly they're permutations of Sy looking at a $10,000

[2] There are a good many retired real toy guys in Florida.

prototype toy someone's trying to sell him, screaming it's shit and hurling it across the room, smashing it into pieces. The stories are always told with nostalgia and affection: it's implicit that Sy wouldn't have done it if the toy wasn't lousy. He was allowed his eccentricity, his cursing, because he had a feel for toys, knew instinctively what sold. His boss Charles Lazarus, the man who founded Toys R Us and started big-box retailing, was another original.

For more years than anyone can remember, the name Fred Kroll has been synonymous with Toy Fair. The archetypal real toy man, the 100th fair was his sixty-fifth, and his long career virtually mirrors the development of the modern toy industry. At the Centenary Fair, Fred sits in the booth of Global Toys, the US distributors of Uncle Freddie's Toy Factory. He's immaculate in a blue blazer, salesman sharp. In front of him he's got his calendar, his new catalogue, and a calculator. Old friends stop to chat and swap thoughts, though they get sidelined fast whenever a potential buyer arrives: Fred, like everyone else, is here to do business.

He is straight out of a *Reader's Digest* Most Unforgettable Character profile. Tall, so you scarcely notice he's bald, he has a garrulous, abrasive charm: it's said of him that other men pick up people in bars, he picks them up in Toys R Us. He drives a 1992 Mercury Sable with a trunk full of toys and 'TOYZ' on the number plate. He knows everyone and everyone knows him. What everyone does not know is that, over the years, he has bought hundreds of thousands of unwanted toys in from Hong Kong to give away to needy children.

He's been in toys since he was twelve. He started work full-time in 1938, the introductory year of Fisher-Price's Snoopy Sniffer, a wooden pull dog with floppy ears and oilcloth feet, a toy that would sell 10 million units. Fisher-Price was an independent business then, one of literally thousands of small companies, many of them Jewish family firms which had begun as merchants and pedlars. The key figures were the toy wholesalers, most located within a few blocks of the Toy Center. Fred's father had a printing business, Whiz Novelties, that expanded into cardboard games.

As a boy, Fred would take orders, go to the family factory on West 35th, return with deliveries. Enrolled at New York University in the School of Commerce, he became known as an elevator chaser, taking classes, eating his 10-cent lunch and then doing factory shifts until 10 p.m. every weekday. 'I took a room for $2 a night, five nights a week, and went home to Brooklyn with my parents on the weekend.'

He flourishes an original catalogue from those days. 'All of our games were magnetic, shapes stuck on the magnetic board – a donkey party game, a racing game with reverse magnets pushing the cars, a magnetic doll . . . I devised most of them.' They had a forerunner of Colorola, individual sheets with wipe-off crayon: 'Forty-nine cents retail, which means our cost was 15 cents, we sold it for 25. Can you imagine retailing an item for 49 cents?'

During and after the war, magnets were unobtainable and raw materials scarce. Whiz Novelties turned to wood toys, but business was bad. The Krolls sold out to Jack Pressman of the Pressman Toy Corporation for $25,000. Fred, out of the army and newly married, went to work for him as a salesman at $150 a week. 'In those days the selling season was over by April because you got your orders at the Toy Fair. Well, every year I got a nice raise and stuff like that. After six years I asked Mr Pressman if I could buy into the business, and he said, "No, I have two boys and a girl."'

Fred almost went to work for Merrill Hassenfeld of Hasbro, but before he could do so, he was introduced to the Kohner Brothers – in those days everyone in the toy business was like family. 'They were doing at the time $600,000 a year total business. When I got done with them a few years later, they were doing $8 million.'

Fred was inventing and selling his own lines too. Television had come to the toy business and he embraced it. 'I was known as Mr TV in New York. A commercial in those days, 1963–64, black and white, made in our basement with a photographer and film, cost $3,000. I was on the three independent stations in New York at between $25 and $50 for a full minute, with a master of ceremonies giving a live lead-in. We were on programmes like Wonderama in New York with a budget of maybe $5,000.

'I took Kohner's Loonie Lynx, just a basic item. I went to our main customer in New York, the biggest wholesaler, and I said to Nat Greenman, Nat, we're going on TV, and he says, Fred, I sold 36 dozen last year. I said, Nat, you can open up with 72 dozen or you're gonna kiss my ass for deliveries, we're going on TV. He sold like 360 dozen and this was not even Christmas. You established an item on TV in those days, and it remained a basic almost for ever. It didn't die. If it was well packaged, well priced, good trade value, it sold for years and years. Today, the items are so overpriced that the minute TV is over they're either closed out or they don't buy them any more.'

Over the years, Kroll licensed designs and items from overseas companies, notably Hungry Hungry Hippos, a game that has sold more than 25 million units. He owned the international rights, sold to Hasbro, and says the interest alone from his share 'is enough for me to live on for the rest of my life'.

Fred is quick to curse the presence and power of the

big companies, notably the five dominating retailers – Wal-Mart, Toys R Us, Kmart, Target, and KB Toys. Even Fred, astute and experienced and well known as he is, finds it hard to deal with them. He excoriates the way their buyers behave, exerting their power over toy men such as him, no matter how much they like the product. 'If you're not a major factory they hardly give you the time of day. It's very difficult for the small guy.' Fred Kroll, like many others, stopped offering his inventions to the big companies and discount stores and deals only with independents. Still, he worries that 'young guys starting out today are facing a terrible situation.'

He used to know his customers, relying on friendship, personalities and trust. 'There's only a few companies who have that today.' He remembers Buddy L, Ideal, Irwin, Kenner, Kohner, Marx, Matchbox – most of which are lost names. He has seen toy factories disappear from New York, Brooklyn and the suburbs as well as from small American towns where they were often the major employers. He despises 'overpriced, poorly made action figures based on horrible action series' and the plethora of plastics: even that toy classic, the Fisher-Price Snoopy Sniffer dog, is now made in China, out of plastic.

Toy men like Fred Kroll – worldly, mature, and in the business all their working lives – are a dying breed. Their successors are often number crunchers, many of whom you frequently feel could equally well be making, marketing or selling almost anything else. All that matters is the bottom line.

Alan Hassenfeld, who faces the big retailers on equal terms, is convinced that 'You've got to come up with a plan for them, show not only that a toy is great but how they're going to make money from it.' Though he talks enthusiastically about gut feelings, he concedes, 'We have to be more sophisticated than we were in the past. The Ps are very important – product, price, promotion, package, public relations. Each is an ingredient that goes into making the many-layer cake. If anything goes wrong in the Ps, it can ruin a product.'

While he feels that some of the changes are for the better, he, like Fred Kroll, has nostalgia for the way they were. 'A great deal of the toy industry was family. The Parker family. The Handlers. Mettoy was the Katzes. Lyons Brothers was the Lyons family. Bandai was the Yamashina family. Tomy was the Tomiyama. As competitive as the business was, there was a collegial camaraderie, a specialness. I like the people in our industry.

'I guess what happened, some of the baton-passing to the next generation worked, some didn't. You had a time when bigger was better, when everyone began to consolidate. For a while, all people wanted was to take their company public, but they had no idea of what being a public company meant, the responsibilities, the bond you must have with different shareholders. I grew up in a toy industry of giants, of wonderful, larger-than-life people. I miss those days.'

Those people were frequently mavericks, and that was their strength. Today, as stakes get higher not only in the toy business but in all industries, gut reactions and fast decisions give way to consensus meetings, research, and risk reduction. The big companies now seek stability and predictability – one of the reasons they prefer dealing with each other. The problem, as Fisher-Price's Stan Clutton explains, is that they can't have it both ways. 'High innovation often means high failure rate. It's also where your biggest hits come from.'

There is a saying in the business: 'What toymakers

want is something that is totally innovative, ground-breaking, really, really terrifically new – but with a record of success.' Because costs are higher, targets have become infinitely larger. Industry veteran Philip Bloom recalls that in the 1960s, a goal might be to reach one million units of a toy. 'That would be a major, major hot success. Today one million units is nothing.'

One toy executive points out that for the consensus decision makers and research users at the big companies, the problem is that virtually every monster hit in the history of toys broke the rules. Rubik's Cube – too complex and too expensive. Cabbage Patch – kids don't buy ugly. Ninja Turtles – green things don't sell. Monopoly, one of the great toys of the twentieth century, could not find a home at first – its inventor had to produce it himself after Parker Bros decided it had fifty-two insoluble faults.

The toy business across the world is shifting, modernizing in ways that have it reeling and confused. But America is special. The United States toy industry to many observers is *the* toy industry. It accounts for close to half the world's toy business – around $31 billion (when video games are included) of $69 billion sales. Because its kids and their parents are the ultimate customers, what toy companies make for sale is mostly determined by American culture and tastes.

And this industry is hugely extending its grasp. It wants – needs – all those children out there. The big toy makers and sellers – Mattel, Hasbro, Toys R Us, Wal-Mart – girdle the world as surely and potently as McDonald's or Gap. And like them they invade, determine and permeate the culture of those places. Toys are very much part of the global Americanization that has consumers flocking to buy and protesters blocking the streets.

Toy makers in other countries struggle against the American onslaught. Germany, home of one of the oldest and proudest toy-making industries, has no native equivalents to withstand products like Barbie. In 2003 Poland had an astonishingly high number of toy producers and distributors, around 2,000 – but, with 85–90 per cent of toys being imported, the country seriously contemplated the end of the industry. The *Warsaw Business Journal* commented, 'Large factories in China filled with state-of-the-art equipment churn out patented designs for major-league global manufacturers, who then sell them to foreign markets at enormously inflated margins because of the benefit of low wages and taxes in the east.'

Today, the leading toy makers – Mattel and Hasbro – account for about a third of the US industry. They dominate the major store shelves and the licensing deals that are conducted to produce toys linked to star properties. They capitalize on economies of scale, maximizing the brands they have developed. They want hits, of course – but they can always acquire them by takeover.

The small *need* hits. They too can manufacture in China (possibly even at the same plant as their huge rivals) though their costs will be considerably higher and they will lack clout at the big retailers who mostly deal only with the major players. So they will probably go to the speciality toyshops who have only a tiny percentage of the market and who are themselves struggling.

With its constant product innovation and short life cycles this is an impatient world. The toy makers and big retailers, like the kids they target, require instant gratification. Thanks to year-round toy stores and other factors, the business is not as seasonal as it once was – until the 1970s up to 80 per cent of toy sales were in the six weeks before Christmas. Today 45 per cent of toy sales still take place in November and December. For some companies it's still as high as 70 per cent. All this conspires to make it an unforgiving industry. *Toy News*, a UK magazine, referring to both the UK and the US, commented, 'When it comes to wielding the axe and ruthlessly sorting out the wheat from the chaff, the toy industry takes some beating.' Writing about it, I encountered an unusual and disconcerting problem: the number of executives who vanish from companies in the short period (once, no kidding, fourteen hours) between making and keeping appointments.

It all adds up to a 'hit' mentality. This is an industry that must have big sales, low costs, constant high-volume product. Production matters only in so far as it is cheap and efficient. Eighty per cent of all toys and video games sold in the United States are now manufactured partly or wholly abroad. The once proud American toy-making business has virtually vanished. The present head of Mattel, Robert A. Eckert, is determinedly a new-breed toy man, a former head of Philip Morris Cos' Kraft Foods Inc. Ranking him in its 2003 Top 50 'best performers', *Business Week* referred to him as a 'voracious cost cutter'. As an early step, he closed the company's last American manufacturing plant, laid off headquarters staff, ended some high-priced movie licensing deals, ditched the loss-making computer-games division, and increased efficiency.

The smaller pure toyshops, the specialist businesses, strain to stay in operation; the small toy producers can often only hope to survive long enough to have a success that attracts one of the bigger players who will take them over. The losses may be inevitable, but each one brings sadness. Kids still play with glass marbles. A hundred years ago at Akron, Ohio, Martin Christensen made the giant step of designing a machine capable of producing perfectly round specimens. Not only were they cheaper and more colourful than what had gone before, they were far superior for shooting. Now they are virtually all made in the Far East.

There is a world circuit of toy fairs and Alan Hassenfeld is a veteran. 'We used to have the expression that on January 1 your wife became a toy fair widow: you were literally gone the first weeks of the year. You would leave on the first or second of January for Hong Kong. From there you'd fly to Milan. From Milan to Paris. From Paris to London. London to Nuremberg. Nuremberg to New York. New York to Valencia and then Australia and Japan.' He sighs. 'We got together and we drank at night and we told those lies. I loved it.'

Nuremberg is remarkable for its range of skilfully crafted toys. (The first doll factories here were founded in 1500.) The world's largest toy fair, it lures around 3,000 exhibitors of fifty nationalities who show a million products to 80,000 buyers from well over a hundred countries. Inner passages link twelve vast halls. One alone could easily occupy a visitor for a full day – it is filled with model trains that hiss and swish over the noise of the crowds. Stevanne Auerbach, 'Dr Toy', describes it as 'the best of all of the toy shows, it has the broadest reach. I see some wonderful high-quality products in Nuremberg that never reach children in the United States because they cannot afford to market and sell here.

The prices are higher than the US is willing to pay.'

The London Toy Fair, which precedes it, is a more domestic affair. Hasbro, Mattel and Lego all have big presences. The year the New York Fair was a hundred years old, the London Fair was fifty. There's a lot of grey hair, more bonhomie than New York, but an equal number of anxious faces. People on stands grab sandwiches without relaxing their eyes as they scour for potential buyers. Occasionally there is a piece of theatre – a group of young dancers mime a playground game; a couple on stilts hand out leaflets; life-size animals loom. But no one appears to notice. It seems very British until you realize that many of the people not noticing are foreign visitors.

Hong Kong is the fair that marks the official start of the toy year, giving the trade the first glimpse of what is new. All the big buyers like Wal-Mart send contingents. It is important because Hong Kong is the world's major toy exporter, and the Chinese production factories are nearby. It too knows its priorities. Jon Salisbury, a toy industry commentator, reported to his readers: 'No mention of fun, then . . . This was always about one thing and one thing only: money.'

For a time in the 1990s it looked as though Toy Fair in New York was heading for extinction. Advertising man Bob Moehl described it as 'a dinosaur wandering around in the woods'. Not surprisingly, the organizers of this fair have a strong interest in fighting this view: they are an entity in their own right, people, power and cash bases. The fairs are showcases, provide a focus of attention for a range of people from inventors to legislators, and, not least, they provide public relations opportunities.

Toy fairs, like the toy industry, are adaptable and resilient. As veteran toy man Norman Walker (Hasbro,

K'Nex) says, 'When push comes to shove, anyone who is anyone in the toy industry goes to toy fairs.'

So in the middle of a city strangely muted by snowfall, which empties even Times Square of traffic and turns the sidewalks into obstacle courses, just getting through to Toy Fair makes everyone feel part of something special. Even if, as a mass industry at least, it deserves the title bestowed upon it by one cynical but cheerful insider: 'the plastic junkyard business'.

There is one fact that must never be forgotten: most toys are designed for marketing needs. Once you accept that, it is easy to take Toy Fair for what it is – less fun land than a hard-nose, hard-sell marketplace. If toy men suddenly seem to have rediscovered some of their classic lines, their core brands, it is partly because spin-offs cost a fraction of the creation of new lines. Extending brands through licensing, as Dove and Tommy Hilfiger do, makes marketing sense and underpins the industry. Toy brands appear on anything from lunch boxes to clothes. Barbie is even into cash registers and ATM. Alternatively, toy makers buy in the rights on fads, movies or television programmes: two thirds of Fisher-Price products use licensed characters like Winnie the Pooh, Barney and the Muppets. At the same time continuous developments in technology allow for updating of products at very little cost: Little People, silent for forty years, now talk through electronic chips, Brio's wooden trains get infrared remote control and electronic sounds, Fur Real Pets communicate interactively with each other. Electronics not only allow 'new' toys at relatively low cost, but also ones that have a short life cycle. From the marketing standpoint, they have that extra virtue: inbuilt early obsolescence.

* * *

Despite the industry's problems, it is not all gloom. American families may be getting smaller, but they are spending more on each child – over $400 a year on average. Couples tend to become parents later in life, which means they have more disposable income available for the children. The present generation of grandparents were brought up without deprivation and are shopping and brand veterans. They love to spend lavishly, accounting for nearly 17 per cent of toy sales – a major reason why classic toys enjoy a renaissance. Even the high rate of divorce is good news for the toy men. Bryan Ellis, chairman of the British Toy and Hobby Foundation, says, 'Because you have got more broken families, children these days quite frequently have two sets of parents, so the expenditure per child is rising by more than enough to compensate for the falling birth rate.'

Toy men do have a gigantic asset: the Big Guilt Factor. As parents split or spend less time with their kids, they buy them more: it becomes a case of Money Can Buy Me Love. Guilt, worry about children getting on in the world and electronics developments have combined to create a massive new category: smart learning toys that help teach everything from reading to geography. And the biggest bonus of all, the obvious one: kids are a constantly renewing source.

Walk around New York's Toy Fair for four days, negotiate the noisy, crowded aisles, the enthusiastic inventors, the piles of gaudy plastic and plush, the giant television monitors endlessly reprising the product, and you start to ask yourself: do kids need all these toys?

They may not. But the toy industry certainly does.

Chapter Two

THE INVENTORS

Longtime toy man Fred Kroll's Rule Number 1 for toy inventors: 'Don't Give up the Day Job.'

Ron Dubren was on his way from New York City to a family event in Chicago when he realized his life had changed for ever.

For fifteen years Ron had been building a reputation as an inventor in the tough world of toys. Thousands of wannabe toy creators would envy what he had achieved – forty different ideas licensed to companies, half of them actually produced and on sale to America's kids. But, as Ron is the first to admit, it was a modest success. None of his toys had lasted more than a year before lines were closed, the products swept off toy-store shelves and consigned to clearance outlets. Nor – in a business where the decision to advertise can make or break a product – had he ever had a TV-promoted toy. Several times it was promised, but then plans were dropped at the last minute, a common happening in an industry high on empty hype. Ron had no illusions left. 'It's a novelty business,' he says today. 'They're always throwing a bunch of stuff against the wall to see what sticks. Very few items have any staying power.'

Nevertheless, recently things had been more hopeful. On the trip to Chicago, Dubren settled down to read the *New York Times*, opened the Business section and the words leapt out. Even today, a decade later, he can recite the key lines virtually word for word. *As just about anyone who spent last week on planet Earth knows*, it said, *Tyco Toys Inc. has shipped over a million Tickle Me Elmo dolls, and stores simply cannot keep them in stock.* 'What I knew was, here you have *the* paper of record and it was saying if you hadn't heard of Tickle Me Elmo you probably hadn't been on the planet. That's when I *knew*.'

What Dubren knew was that he had invented not merely a big selling toy but a phenomenon, something every toy inventor and manufacturer dreams about. He had created a toy that newspapers and television featured, that jaded retail buyers begged for, that had kids screaming and pleading – and parents willing to pay way, way over the retail value. His product transcended age and gender, and got analysts and investors jumping. The last time it had happened was in 1985 when thousands of kids and their parents had fought to get their hands on Cabbage Patch Kids. Soon after the *Times* article, Dubren saw his long-sought TV advertising pulled – this time because the commercials were only fuelling a demand that Tyco could not fulfil.

There are no more than a few hundred professional toy inventors in the United States. Insiders put the number at around 300, maybe 500 if you include games creators. Others pitch it lower. The two biggest toy companies, Mattel and Hasbro, each have about 125–150 names on their active lists. But nobody can be sure how many amateurs there are. The Toy Industry

Association in New York alone gets four to five thousand enquiries every year. Smaller companies, bombarded with ideas, joke that they have more inventors than customers.

Creating playthings is a universal and timeless dream, combining as it does two potent images – inventing and toys. The history of the United States to a great measure is a history of its inventors; the best of them are its heroes, a roll call of ingenuity and courage and progress, of triumph over adversity and rejection. Edison. Colt. Fulton. Ford. Gillette. Land. Birdseye. Bell. Add to that toys, objects that touch a deep, emotional spot. Together you've got childhood and a chance to hit it big.

Ron Dubren started as a doctor in research psychology, moving next to what he calls an 'eclectic career', embracing experimental video and writing screenplays, which he never sold, before chancing on toys. He's a polite man with soulful eyes and the look of a New Age ascetic.

It happened when he was playing Scrabble with his wife and a friend. 'I said to myself, someone must have come up with this game. I'm going to try.' He went ahead and invented one. 'I was in the Y in the locker room and I heard some guy say something about Toy Fair. I said, What's Toy Fair? And he said, That's where all the manufacturers gather and they show off new products. Why, are you an inventor or something? And I said, Yeah. That's how I got in the toy business.'

Dubren's new contact was willing to look at his inventions. 'I scrambled to create some stuff.' One idea was a game he called Chinese Chess with two sets of different-coloured pieces. Both players could move both sets of pieces, but one could only jump same-coloured pieces and the other only different-coloured pieces. Dubren eventually licensed it to a company called Gabriel Games. The boss of Gabriel was a chunky fast-talker named Stan Clutton. Dubren bombarded Clutton with new ideas, fifty or so over the next fifteen years. 'Over those years Stan went through several different companies and he never licensed another thing until Tickle Me Elmo. You have to have a really thick skin and it's all about being persistent. And if you're not persistent, if you take rejection personally or as a reflection of your inadequacy, you won't be able to sustain it.'

Over a period of ten years Dubren gradually became a little more successful, licensing products more frequently. After fifteen years inventing toys and games, he took stock. Statistics showed that out of every twenty products that come to market, only one of them enjoyed a second year's life. Trouble was, Dubren had sent far more than twenty products out into the market – and not one had outlived a year. Statistically, he reckoned one of his toys or games should have received TV advertising. None had. 'As far as I was concerned, I was due for a TV-promoted product that would sell big and that I'd make some money off. I was due. I just didn't know I was due in such a big way.'

There's often a eureka moment with toy invention. With Dubren it came as, strolling in New York, he watched two kids in a park. They were tickling each other, erupting with laughter. There was a surge of memory, the rush of what it had meant being tickled as a child. But most of all, he remembered the uncontrollability of it, how you couldn't stop. Now came the idea: a toy character with a built-in giggle, one that started gently and built up to manic.

Inventors often work in pairs or groups. For this toy, Dubren needed someone on the engineering side. He had met such a man, Greg Hyman, previously at Toy Fair. Hyman lived on the West Coast, Dubren on the East. Dubren bought and gutted a stuffed toy monkey which was sent back and forth between New York and California as the two men persevered with its development. Finally the toy emerged – Tickles the Chimp. Hyman was happy, but cautious. 'You never know if you're going to have a hit,' he says. 'Once you've submitted a concept, it's a long way from the bank.'

Basically, Tickles was a plush toy that laughed. What it didn't do was move in any way. Dubren's wife suggested it should shake as the laughter peaked. 'I said, no, no, no, it's too expensive, they'd never do it. So I never even made it part of the pitch.'

The pitch was not very successful; twelve companies turned him down. 'I couldn't get anywhere with it.' Pitch number thirteen was to Tyco Preschool, part of Tyco Toys, and to the man who had bought his very first invention fifteen years before. Stan Clutton was now vice-president of Marketing and Research and Development. Unlike the twelve potential buyers before him, he saw the possibilities but with one caveat: he didn't like the chimp. They had to find a better character. The trouble was, Tyco Preschool owned no licensing rights for plush toys. One of the Sesame Street figures would be perfect but while Tyco had the licensing rights in plastic for Sesame, Hasbro owned plush. Unable to buy the idea himself, Clutton thought maybe a colleague, Gene Murtha at Tyco's main company, who handled Looney Tunes characters in plush, might be interested. He was. Tyco decided to make the new toy as Tickle Me Taz.

Unknown to Dubren, Tyco Preschool's founder Marty Scheman had been thinking about Sesame Street. With the licences split between two toy makers neither company was pushing really hard, both reckoning any big promotions would only help the competition. This meant no TV, and without that the retailers were doing little with the products. Scheman approached the Children's Television Workshop to convince them that when Hasbro's licence ended it should be shifted to Tyco. He was successful. Suddenly Stan Clutton found he had Sesame Street with its Muppet characters like Elmo under his wing. Not only that, but he needed to deliver on Scheman's promise to produce a product that would be advertised on television.

As Dubren recalls: 'Stan remembers the tickle me thing. So he goes to Gene, You know that Tickle Me Taz? Any problems giving it back and letting us do it? And Gene says No, and that's how it became Tickle Me Elmo.'

Bob Moehl had been an advertising man for twenty years. He started his career at Ogilvy and Mather in Los Angeles, and was deep into toys before he realized it was an uncool area in the ad world. By then it was too late. Besides, he liked it. He had worked with the top companies, many of whom had defined toy advertising. Then, as creative director of D'Arcy Masius Benton & Bowles Communications, New York, he had the job of introducing Tickle Me Elmo to TV.

Moehl is a laconic, frequently smiling man with a hard-edged approach to advertising. He believes that a commercial is literally a product's one shot at living or dying. Moehl took a look at Elmo and said he would do the best he could, but made it clear he had reservations. Its selling point was its laugh, and sound doesn't have a major impact on the screen. He pleaded for the toy to have a visual aspect.

Marty Scheman, who was temporarily running Tyco's preschool division, liked to keep a close eye on toy stores. He visited one the following weekend and was fascinated by a monkey that jiggled when a motor inside the toy made it vibrate. This, he said, is what Elmo needs. He bought the monkey and placed it before Clutton and Tyco Preschool's marketing director. 'Let's try it,' he said.

Two Elmo prototypes were made, one that shook and one that did not, and both were tested on focus groups. The groups responded to both toys, but only marginally better to the shaking one. A motor added $5 to the toy's cost, meaning a Tickle Me Elmo without movement could be sold retail at $19.99, but to make it shake increased the price to $29.99. 'Tyco decides it's too good, let's leave it in, make it a $29.99 product and hope it won't kill it,' says Dubren. 'The rest is history.'

At Toy Fair the reaction from the trade was not great, warm rather than hot. A focus group of moms was distinctly cool. Nevertheless, Neil Friedman, who took over as Tyco Preschool's president, decided to produce 300,000 Tickle Me Elmos, a reasonably strong number for such a high-price toy.

The television advertising was not due to start until the fall, but by late summer Elmo was already the best-selling plush toy at both Wal-Mart and Toys R Us. The people who loved it were parents. 'They'd do it, they'd start laughing, immediately they'd want to show their kids. It didn't matter they were six months old . . .'

Tyco knew they had something that was going to sell. But Elmo still wasn't a phenomenon.

At first glance, Bruce Maguire looks like a sportsman. Only when he speaks – sound bites and staccato facts – does he come across as what he is, one of the best and most respected pluggers in the toy business. He is one of the few specialist publicists – toys is a minor sideline at the bigger public relations firms. He is a hands-on operator – his own outfit is small. Until he was banned from doing so, he would stand in the lobby at Toy Building handing out cards to get buyers into his clients' showrooms. The press and television like him; he's always good for a tip on what is soon to be the hottest toy, even when he is not handling it. Maguire was the man given the job of publicizing Elmo.

Maguire shares Moehl's one-shot philosophy: there is just one chance to make a media impact. 'So you want them to really say, Wow!' But his target differed from Moehl's. The commercials, Maguire reckoned, would get the kids. He wanted to reach the moms. He set his sights on Rosie O'Donnell's new talk show. 'Rosie was able to make women at home feel she was the one friend in the neighbourhood who knew all the cool things . . . Rosie happened to like toys and she had a kid of the right age and her kid happened to like Elmo.' It worked. Rosie O'Donnell kept Elmo on her lap throughout one entire show. But the real masterstroke came later. Maguire drummed up 300 Elmos, and O'Donnell went on air and announced that whenever one of her guests said the word 'wall', an Elmo would be thrown into the audience.

Dubren sees the O'Donnell show as a key moment – both for Elmo and for the 'queen of nice'. 'People always say Rosie was the one who made Tickle Me Elmo. Most people don't realize Rosie had just started. With Elmo she was identified with what eventually became a pop cultural phenomenon.'

Bob Moehl's commercials were finally playing. One was placed during the Macy's Thanksgiving Day Parade coverage, to be watched by millions of parents. The next day the toy sold out. 'They upped the manufacture; they even began to air-freight the stuff in rather than put it on a boat.'

To become a phenomenon Tickle Me Elmo needed just one more ingredient: scarcity. Now it had it. Newspapers carried a string of stories as the supply of Elmos dried up: Wal-Mart employees in San Antonio were fired for hiding Elmos to buy for themselves; crime boss John Gotti Jr reportedly bought (from prison) a case of Elmo toys; there was a theft of Elmos from a locked police storage area in New York City. A radio station in West Palm Beach auctioned one for $3,500. In Baltimore six contractors offered to build a wheelchair ramp for a disabled child free when they heard the boy's grandfather was hoping to raise the money for it by selling an Elmo doll.

It became a self-feeding frenzy. One toy buyer reported that some customers clamouring for non-existent Tickle Me Elmos didn't even know what they were. Tyco and Dubren watched as sales soared. They reached a staggering $30 million.

Tickle Me Elmo joined a long list of the toys inventors like to recite, all created by independent outsiders such as Dubren. Beanie Babies. Cabbage Patch Kids. Candy Land. Crayola. Etch-a-Sketch. Furby. G.I. Joe. Hungry Hungry Hippos. Lincoln Logs. Monopoly. Mousetrap. Mr Potato Head. Nerf. Operation. Othello. Pictionary. Pokemon. Rubik's Cube. Scrabble. Silly Putty. Simon. Trivial Pursuit. Twister. View-Master. Yahtzee. Yakity-Yak Talking Teeth.

The first great age of toy inventors began around the turn of the century, a few years after the start of mass production. In 1900, 22-year-old Joshua Lionel Cowen created a battery-powered train engine, and Lionel Trains were born. Three years later Edwin Binney and C. Harold Smith produced the first box of Crayola

Crayons. In 1913 A.C. Gilbert, former Olympic pole-vault gold-medallist and medical doctor, invented the Erector Set. In 1914 Charles Pajeau, inspired by watching children poke sticks into the holes of cotton reels, invented a similar toy for younger children, Tinker Toys. Just two years after that John Lloyd Wright, the son of architect Frank Lloyd Wright, devised Lincoln Logs. In Britain in 1901, a Liverpool shipping clerk, Frank Hornby, invented Meccano, construction kits based on mechanical engineering principles.

Halfway through the century, with the surge of inventiveness honed by wartime, coupled with a good economy, manufacturing capacity, new materials (especially plastic), after-hostilities euphoria, and the post-World War II baby boom, another Golden Age arrived. In the 1950s came Fisher-Price's Little People, Colorforms (when two art students discovered that vinyl sticks to semi-gloss paint), Mr Potato Head, Matchbox toy cars, the Ant Farm, Tonka, Frisbee, Barbie and Hula Hoops. The next decade introduced Etch-a-Sketch, the Easy Bake Oven, G.I. Joe, Hot Wheels, the Nerf Ball.

There is no doubt that toys exert a special pull for inventors. Part of it is the product itself and its connotations. Adam Kislevitz, of the New-Jersey-based inventing firm The Obb, says, 'I am a lucky son of a bitch. There's something rewarding about a toy because it has a cultural element about it. You see a kid with your product and you feel great.' But there are practical reasons too. Foremost, the toy business is unique in the way it creates new products. Most industries, whether cars, electronics, pharmaceuticals or housewares, rely upon large internal research and development departments. The toy business, on the other hand, has taken many of its biggest sellers from outsiders.

Added to this is the fact that there is a constant need for new product. Although there are a breathtaking 150,000 different playthings on sale in the United States, these constantly die or disappear and thousands of others emerge to take their place. A manufacturer typically introduces 40 per cent new product every year. There are good reasons for this: kids' attention spans are short; store buyers want novelty and newness; and the industry struggles for big toys to spark sales. Fads are serious business for retailers. They capture imagination and draw customers.

In an ideal world (for them), companies would create all these new toys internally. Many try, some succeed, but most know that it is impossible. Inventor Steve Schwarz points out, 'I'd find it hard to think of anyone but LeapFrog (makers of LeapPad) in the last twenty years who came up with a great internal idea. If you have a good idea the US companies can effectively market it. But they have a hard time coming up with exciting new creations themselves. The inventor is the catalyst, the excitement of the toy business.' It means that a surprisingly large number of toys are still bought in.

For inventors, money, of course, is a major draw. The right toy can transform an inventor into a multi-millionaire. Ty Warner, creator of Beanie Babies, is on the *Forbes* billionaires list; Xavier Roberts earned major millions from Cabbage Patch Kids and Play-Doh made Joe Clicker a millionaire before his twenty-seventh birthday. Dubren does not talk about his earnings from Elmo, but normal royalty rate is 5 per cent. As Elmo was a product licensed from the Sesame Street organization, that amount was probably reduced by about half. Plus co-inventor Greg Hyman had to be paid his share. But Tickle Me Elmo has earned a hell of a lot of millions.

Even advances on toys that never happen can be sweet. Mel Birnkrant says, 'One of the worst things about inventing toys is that you can work for weeks on something that will never see the light of day. One of the best things about inventing toys is that you can work for minutes on something that will feed your family for years.' In the wake of the enormous money-making success of the Cabbage Patch Kids, Kiscom, an inventing group, came up with a concept called Weenies. Mel was the designer. 'The best way I can sum it up is that it was Mickey Mouse and the gang reincarnated as hot dogs,' he says. There was Willie Weenie, his girlfriend Wilhelmina, a pup called Hot Doggie, a raft of other characters. The idea was presented to the president of Coleco. 'He said, "I'll take it!" on the spot. A deal was concluded there and then.' The presentation consisted of twelve drawings and about six pages of typewritten story sketches, Mel recalls. 'And they gave us $500,000. Those were the days.' Weenies was a toy that never made it.

These are exceptions, of course. Richard Levy, a veteran professional toy inventor, points out that one feature of the toy industry is that losers far outnumber winners. Most inventions never get anywhere, and advances against royalties are usually modest. (A rule of thumb for advances is a quarter or a third of royalties during the first year of projected sales.) Stan Clutton says, 'It's the person who invented Twister or Cabbage Patch that gets talked about. You don't talk about the guy who invented the little toy that made $10,000 royalties. The ones who are very rich? I'd say less than ten.'

There are those too who miss out when it comes to selling their invention. Stan Weston was a freelance licensing agent when he came up with the idea of G.I. Joe. Hasbro offered him a choice: $100,000 up front, or $50,000 with a 1 per cent royalty once sales passed $7 million. Weston chose the larger up-front figure. Over the succeeding years observers estimate it cost him at least $25 million. The point, though, is that the potential for wealth is there.

Money is not the only draw. An outsider sometimes gets the feeling that inventors – professionals as well as amateurs – just can't help what they do. It often starts young. Mel Birnkrant recalls taking apart a toy car and turning it into a mobile at the age of nine.

Befitting a business of lone creatives, toy inventors are individuals with little in common except curiosity and creativity. Their backgrounds are legion. Graphic artists, industrial designers, model makers and mechanical engineers not surprisingly feature large. David Fuhrer, whose inventions include Bounce Around Tigger, was a Hollywood talent scout. Erno Rubik, creator of the Rubik's Cube, was a professor of architecture. Mike Bowling (Pound Puppies) was a Ford plant factory worker. View-Master came from a piano tuner, Silly Putty from a chemical engineer.

Triggers for inventions can occur in strange places. William Gruber, a German immigrant, was in an Oregon hospital for minor surgery when he got the idea for what became the View-Master. The Frisbee was devised in a California basement. Trivial Pursuit was born in a cramped apartment in Montreal.

The trigger can be almost anything. John Lloyd Wright conceived Lincoln Logs after seeing the way his father designed the earthquake-proof Imperial Hotel in Tokyo. The hotel used interlocking beams. John's invention utilized sticks of wood with notches to interconnect. The first building he assembled reminded him of a log cabin, so he named his construction toy in honour of the President born in one. For Richard James, a naval engineer, the trigger was watching a large torsion spring fall onto a boat deck in 1943. He was fascinated by the spring's end-over-end walk after it fell.

He took the spring home. His wife Betty was equally captivated. They set out to develop it, to give it the right amount of coiling to produce the perfect walking effect. Betty named it Slinky. They began selling it in Gimbels', Philadelphia, during the 1945 Christmas holiday to immediate success. Decades later it would be immortalized in *Toy Story*.

Milton Levine was inspired by a fourth of July barbecue. In 1956, relaxing in his sister's garden in Southern California, he gazed fascinated at the movement of a colony of ants. From that came the Ant Farm. Levine enthused later, 'I love ants. They put my kids through college.'

Some toy inventions began as something else. Play-Doh first came onto the market in 1956 as a wallpaper cleaner. Joe McVicker, noting it was non-toxic, less messy than modelling clay and that it had a distinctive smell, realized it would make a toy. Toy aeroplanes evolved from detailed models used by manufacturers to sell their product to the military.

The best inventors are ingenious and adaptable. Tonka trucks were the creation of a group of Minnesota teachers who had been trying – and failing – to make garden tools. They turned to toy trucks and came up with the tough, virtually indestructible, plaything, naming it Tonka after the nearby Minnetonka Lake. Other toys were born out of love. Johnny Gruelle was a newspaper cartoonist in the early part of the century when his daughter Marcella found a battered old rag doll in the attic at their home in Silvermine, Connecticut. The doll's face was worn away and her father refurbished it. He named it Raggedy Ann, both words taken from poems by his friend James Whitcomb Riley – *The Raggedy Man* and *Little Orphan Annie*. Marcella died at the age of thirteen, and in 1918 Gruelle published stories he had told to her. Dolls were created to promote the book. The doll – the smile, the loops of red wool hair and the heart saying 'I Love You' – became part of American lore.

Matchbox cars grew from another father–daughter relationship. Rodney and Leslie Smith, two school-friends, went into business in London after serving in World War II. With their £600 war gratuities, they bought die-casting machinery to make industrial parts. Jack Odell, a skilled die-caster and mould maker, joined them as a partner. Toys became a sideline. Together the three wartime buddies designed a large toy, a diesel road-roller model, which was sold to a few local shops. Matchbox toys arrived five years later when Odell made a small brass model of it and put it into a matchbox for his daughter to take to school.

Other inventors recognized gaps in the market. Edwin Binney and C. Harold Smith had a company making pigments. They branched out into marking inks and black wax marking pencils. The company was the first to discover the secret of using carbon to produce strong blacks in shoe polish, printing inks and tyres. In working with teachers, they saw a need for better wax crayons. They experimented with making them smaller and adding more pigments to the paraffin. The result, in 1903, was their first box of eight crayons at 5 cents each. Binney's wife Alice named them Crayola – after *craie* (French for chalk) and oleaginous, a word that described their consistency. The firm still makes 12 million of the wonderful nostalgic-smelling crayons a day in Easton, Pennsylvania. Some of the greatest ideas have a simplicity that belies their ingenuity and appeal. Scott Stillinger, an engineer, set out to make a small ball that would teach young children to catch. He tied together rubber bands. Out of it came Koosh balls ('koosh' from the sound of the ball landing in a hand).

As for the inventors themselves, there are some who are prolific and others who invent once or twice and then quit. Eddy Goldfarb, a doyen among inventors, started after World War II. Sixty years later he had invented 750 products, not all of them toys, and held over 300 patents. He created his first product after seeing an ad for a container for false teeth. He found it funny – and came up with Yakity-Yak Talking Teeth. Another invention, his Stompers miniature battery-operated vehicles, has sold over 200 million units since 1980. Xavier Roberts who created Cabbage Patch Kids (originally called The Little People) stopped with just one invention. The dolls combined several elements of genius: each one was different; they couldn't be bought, but were adopted; and they were not made but 'born' in a magical cabbage patch. Legend has it that several companies turned Roberts down on the grounds that no girl would want an ugly doll. Psychologists now say that the ugliness was the great draw – little girls thought themselves ugly and were attracted to the dolls for that very reason. Whatever the motivation, Cabbage Patch Dolls became a phenomenon. At their peak Cabbage Patch Dolls comprised 10 per cent of the entire US toy market.

All those things said, inventors today have a big problem. The hurdles they need to overcome are enormous and constantly growing. The biggest problem is the most obvious – there are fewer and fewer markets. Steve Schwarz turned to inventing after holding major executive jobs. Today he works with an assortment of people and groups, depending on the project. He says, 'It's become incredibly hard. Back in the eighties, early nineties, mid nineties, even late nineties, we'd sell thirty, forty, fifty products a year. Today we're lucky if we sell two or three. Obviously we're not working as hard, but the problem is that there aren't that many people to sell to any more who can do serious buying.'

Producing a new toy is risky. Manufacturers, faced with a tougher marketplace and the need to constantly cut costs, have tried to lessen those risks. One solution has been to bring back old toys like Care Bears and Strawberry Shortcake, cashing in on today's nostalgia boom. These are toys that have a ready-made familiarity with parents. Tim Coffey, an industry consultant, points out, 'It's far easier to reintroduce a toy than to create a new one.'

They have also increased licensing, tying their toys to entertainment properties, characters and movies. Here the risks are great – the cost of licensing can be colossal and if a movie flops or if kids don't embrace it as 'cool', losses can be high. But manufacturers see it as a quick way to get immediate recognition, to piggyback on someone else's innovation. Agent Carol Rehtmeyer points out that about 70 per cent of new toys now have a licence. 'As licensing has grown to an all-time high in the toy industry, product innovation has suffered.'

Manufacturers too are less interested in single products than in extending lines of existing toys or bringing new lines into being. So when Zapf Creation launches its Baby Born range – a product with eight lifelike functions, 'with no need for batteries' – it is as a line of dolls complete with over seventy accessories.

The professionals had to adapt to this. Steve Schwarz reckons that half of his work ends up as licensed product – a brush-your-teeth Cabbage Patch Kid, a lot of Pooh products, the enormously successful Sing and Snore Ernie. One-off products have another problem. These days toy manufacturers want high returns – and fast. Once a toy could start small, be allowed to grow. Now a new product is expected to bring in perhaps $15 million in its first year. Inventors point out with some truth that under these rules some of the biggest toys there have ever been, including Barbie and Hot Wheels, would have failed to make the grade.

Companies range from inventor-friendly to decidedly unfriendly. Some prefer to avoid outsiders if they can. Jakks Pacific, one of the largest second-tier companies below the big two, relies mostly on its team of fifty in-house designers. Executive Genna Goldberg says, 'It gives tighter rein, product control, and it's also probably more cost-effective. We have 100 per cent of their talent available to us. There are no royalty fees. We have ownership of any ideas that come into play.'

Even though they may end up using fewer and fewer outside-inventor ideas, other manufacturers are welcoming – to professionals, at least. Elmo continues to thrive at Fisher-Price, which took over Tyco (and which in turn was itself gobbled up by Mattel). Stan Clutton is now senior vice-president in charge of inventor relations, licensing and new business. By most inventor accounts, it is top of their friendly list. How it handles inventions – and how few it ends up using – is therefore instructive. Like most majors, it deals only with agents or professionals. 'I think it is important to know the industry, or else you tend to repeat what other people have done,' says Clutton.

He spends about 40 per cent of his time out on the road looking at inventions; for his number two it's 75 per cent. Their trail takes in the main inventor hubs: New York, Boston, Providence, Rhode Island (because of its proximity to Hasbro), Florida, Los Angeles, San Francisco, Chicago, Cincinnati, London and Tokyo. In each place, appointments are set up with regulars. Ideas presented can range from sketches to models. Increasingly, companies want more detailed workings. 'If someone came to me and said they could give me an Elmo that could sing "The Star-Spangled Banner" and then stand up and do a back flip, I know you could make Elmo sing because I know what electronic chips can do, and I know he could probably stand up, but you'd have to show me he could do a back flip. In that case, the inventor might not care to spend $10–$20,000 to make a model to do a back flip before we have discussion. He might say, if I could make it happen, would you be interested?

'It's not easy to put your finger on what people are going to like and not like. We don't take back anything that's not unique or innovative or in certain categories – puppets have never sold in mass market.'

On average, Clutton would expect to bring back two inventions per inventor. In total, Fisher-Price will look at about 6,000 ideas in a year. Out of every thousand of these, about 600 will fall at the first hurdle when teams from Research and Development and Marketing examine them. A week later, after further study, the teams will kill another large batch – 1,000 possibles will drop to 160. 'We're looking for something exceptional; the more so the better. The Wow! You have to picture the aisle in the store with toys either side; there's ten of these to go down even in a Target. What's gonna make a toy stand out, make a consumer want to grab it? They're pretty jaded and they've got a lot of options and there's a lot of great toys out there already.'

Of each surviving 160, around seventy more vanish when they are costed. The rough rule of thumb is that toys are sold at four to five times what they cost to produce. If a toy is going to be retailed at $9.99 it must be brought in for around $2. Furthermore, at the end of the day it needs to *look* worth at least $9.99. Looking worth more is OK (though then marketing may recommend upping the retail cost), looking less, it's dead. There will be consumer testing too. The ninety ideas still left go into a pre-line review for scrutiny by high but not top management. Seventy emerge for the final selection, and of those perhaps six or seven of each original 1,000 will go forward to production. At Fisher-Price this means no more than thirty-five to forty of the 6,000 ideas that entered the system, although it can be as few as twenty.

There are always two major reasons not to go ahead with a project, says one insider. 'The first is that it's not really new, it's been seen before. The second is that it *is* new and therefore has no track record.'

The little companies are the risk-takers. Here decision making can be short-circuited: the person looking at the idea may also be making the verdict. In any event these companies are where the new inventor may end up anyway, because the majors will not even consider him. But it's a different ball game. Where the majors see a production run of a million units as commonplace today, a small company may be happy with a first run of thousands. Financially, though, there are obvious downsides. A small company can have a resounding success, but the odds are against it, not least because the major retailers are unlikely even to stock its product. For this reason some professionals will not even approach these small businesses. Steve Schwarz says firmly: 'We don't sell to little companies. Practically all we're showing to today is Hasbro companies and Mattel companies. My experience has been that, with one exception, in the fifteen years I have been doing this on my own, anything I've sold to a small company, nothing's happened to it. I generally never earn back the advance and they want us to do all the work gratis.' In the highly volatile world of toys, small companies are vulnerable. Fred Kroll, after a diatribe about big companies, admitted he'd recently licensed his toys to a small one. 'Unfortunately, they went bankrupt and they stuffed me and a lot of people for a lot of money.'

Even when an inventor and a company do have a working relationship, it is liable to be very different today from even a few years ago. James Kipling has enjoyed a unique vantage point in the toy industry for twenty years, as an attorney at Kenner and at Hasbro, and in private practice where he has a number of toy-related clients. One of his major responsibilities was the multimillion Star Wars licensing deal. Being the good lawyer that he is, he chooses his words carefully. In earlier days, he says, relationships were informal. 'In most cases written agreements were very simple and straightforward, the parties relied on one another's good faith. Highly successful products were licensed and inventors paid on a handshake.' If a manufacturer suddenly brought out a product that seemed very similar to one an inventor had presented to them, he would almost certainly accept their explanation of coincidence. For their part, manufacturers would sometimes suggest a royalty-splitting deal to any inventor whose idea was similar to one they had just taken from someone else.

Kipling says that, 'In most industries, an inventor without an issued patent or at least a patent application on file would not get through the door.' Yet at one time toy inventors could sell a naked concept and receive a 'full' royalty from the manufacturer who had to develop and engineer the concept into a marketable product. Those days are over, and today inventors need patent and copyright to protect their ideas. A major reason, Kipling believes, is the fact that control of 'the food chain' is now in the hands of a tiny number of retailers, putting intense pressure on manufacturers' profits. And the result? 'Like so many aspects of American business, relationships between toy inventors and manufacturers have suffered, reflecting increasing formality and stress levels. Inventors are much less likely to accept the explanation of "independent development" and much more likely to file suit. Manufacturers are much less likely to pay an inventor royalties unless a detailed licence agreement or an issued patent makes such payments unavoidable. Today, the licence agreement that is negotiated between toy inventor and manufacturer has become as important to both parties as the invention itself. The inventor is concerned that the company will try to avoid payments to the extent that it legally can do so, and the manufacturer worries that the inventor would "double license" if he could. Each believes the other may take advantage if given the opportunity. In other words, the toy industry has deteriorated to the point that it now reflects most other businesses.'

Another instance of recent change involved one of Kipling's old firms, Kenner. In 1976 the research and development team developed Stretch Armstrong, a wrestler whose limbs could be tugged to four times body width. They would then snap straight back into place. Stretch was made of latex rubber, and his secret was a 'miracle' dense fluid filling – in reality, corn syrup condensed by boiling. Stretch was a great success and stayed in the list for four or five years. He then vanished from sight until, in the early 1990s, an independent inventor suggested to Cap Toys that the super-hero figure was worth reintroducing. They agreed, brought back Stretch – and paid the inventor a royalty for his suggestion, behaviour unimaginable today.

If professionals find today's toy marketplace increasingly tough, amateurs face an almost impossible struggle. For them, using an agent will be the only way of reaching the major companies and, increasingly, the smaller ones too. The reason, say the companies, is that although amateur inventors might come up with a great idea, the chances are slim and time and risk involved in dealing with them is far too great. One executive recalled that his company used to accept submissions from any outside inventors. Then one day it took stock. It found that in a five-year period it had spent time examining 5,000 product ideas from amateurs. And it had licensed only one – which flopped.

SpinMaster is a go-ahead, much admired Canadian toy company that does make a point of operating an open-door policy cultivating outside inventors. This is not without risks. The 'little old lady' whose idea is turned down can create hell, using the right lawyer, five years later when she starts screaming that something newly produced is a rip-off. Yet it is a fact of life, say toy executives, that new ideas do not emerge in a vacuum: it is the nature of creativity that similar ones are likely to surface at the same time. Ben Varadi, one of SpinMaster's founders, says that very morning a man had shown him five items: four were like others he had already seen. He remembers one inventor showing his design and two years later claiming it was the inspiration for a toy SpinMaster had just put on the market. 'Absolutely not true, it came from another inventor. But this part blows my mind and it continues to blow my mind each day – how many ideas out there are alike.'

Many agents double as inventors themselves and have their own portfolio of products. A number are former executives at manufacturers or retailers. Their great advantage, of course, is that the good ones know the business and what is needed at any given time. They have working relationships with key company executives (who will share insider information with them, including their 'wish lists') and can take care of all the pitching, negotiation and money chasing. An agent can provide insulation against the pain of rebuff. David Berko, who has been on both sides of the process, says, 'Rejection is your life if you're trying to sell something. And it can hurt. When I used to represent people, a lot would leave and try to do it themselves. Within a year they'd usually come back because they didn't have the stomach for the constant rejection and the hassle of dealing with corporations.' There are the practicalities too. Many innovators are lousy businessmen and negotiators. 'It's not just sitting down playing with toys,' Berko says. 'You need to know things like when to make a phone call. Too many and you become a nut, not enough and you're being taken advantage of.' It comes at a cost, of course. A pretty substantial one. Agents take as much as 50 or even 60 per cent of an inventor's earnings. They can take as little as 25 per cent, but that is usually for a professional with a good track record and an idea that appears highly marketable and doesn't need much work prior to presentation. Still, as almost every agent I met points out, 'Fifty per cent of something is a hell of a lot better than 100 per cent of nothing.'

Jim Becker is president and founder of Anjar, the oldest and largest toy- and game-licensing agency in the world. It operates out of New York. During Toy Fair, as many as a hundred potential ideas buyers troop though Becker's office on militarily precise appointment schedules. He called the company Anjar after his four sons – Arto, Neil, Jonathan and Roger. Two of them work in the business today, looking for, developing and marketing games. Jim began in toys in 1945, working for small and large wholesalers who used to control the business before big retailers, and a range of manufacturers including Irwin Toys and Gabriel. He started to develop products himself – the magic milk bottle was one. He got the idea going home on the train, and tested it immediately. 'I stopped, and I went into a toy store. I bought a doll and took out the voice mechanism.' With it, he created a crying milk bottle. It sold over 6 million pieces.

Since he founded Anjar in the 1960s, the company has sold over 500 licences to toy manufacturers – Becker produces a list that runs through Barbie 'Really Works' Appliances, G.I. Joe Earthquake, Nerf Ping Pong to Super Balloon. Many, he volunteers, have become worldwide household names. Are inventors still needed? 'If it weren't for them, toys would become a static business,' says Becker. He remains upbeat. 'Eighty per cent of the products at Toy Fair are new items,' he says. 'Kids' fantasies don't last very long.'

Some toys owe their success to individual entrepreneurs who recognized their potential. One of toy history's greatest triumphs, Silly Putty, took that route. The toy resulted from the wartime search for a synthetic rubber. James Wright, an engineer with General Electric, tried mixing boric acid and silicone oil. The result was of no commercial use – but it bounced beautifully. A New Haven, Connecticut, toy-store owner acquired some of the compound. It was not a great success, however, and it was ultimately dropped. A marketing man, Peter Hodgson, whose ad agency job and marriage had both collapsed, had been hired by the store to publicize its catalogue. Now he acquired the rights, renamed his purchase Silly Putty and took it to Toy Fair. Again, as on countless other occasions, the reaction was zilch. He was advised to dump it and quit. Hodgson decided to market it himself. With a borrowed $147, he bought a batch from General Electric and managed to interest some outlets. One was a Doubleday store in Manhattan where a New Yorker writer chanced on it. In late August Silly Putty was featured in *Talk of the Town*. Within three days legend has it that there were a quarter of a million orders. Still, Hodgson's success was not a smooth ride, even when Silly Putty did take off. The Korean War shut off the essential raw materials. When they were available once more, demand for Silly Putty was dead. Hodgson and a team of representatives toured every state demonstrating their product. Growing success brought new worries – there had to be changes in the composition, a problem that took years to crack. Nevertheless, it was solved, and when Hodgson died in 1976 he left $140 million.

Another similar success was the yo-yo. The yo-yo is age-old – it has been found with mummies in pyramids and was also a plaything in ancient China and Greece. In its original form it was totally simple, no more than a piece of wood, or even rock, and string.

In the late 1920s a Filipino bellhop called Pedro Flores started selling wooden yo-yos in Santa Monica where he worked. Flores's yo-yo was different. Unlike earlier ones it had a string hooked around a dowel between two halves, so it could do tricks. Flores also coined the name 'yo-yo' (previous names included, for example, jon jon). Ice-cream salesman and entrepreneur Donald Duncan was fascinated by the newly refined toy. He bought it – and its name – and propelled it to its massive and global success.

Frisbees were another example. Inspired by a Yale students' game of throwing empty pie plates, Walter Frederick Morrison produced a plastic version in 1948. He toured country fairs, demonstrating how it could fly through the air. He called his invention Pluto Platter, the Pluto meant to denote space. The real breakthrough came when Morrison teamed with two men, Arthur 'Spud' Melin and Richard Knerr. They owned a company called Wham-O that had begun as an import-export business, moved into making sling-shots, and was now edging into the toy and novelty business with cap guns. Melin and Knerr immediately saw the potential of Pluto Platter, although at first they envisaged it as a sporting object, not a kids' toy. It was improved – engineers developed a system of ridges to keep the disc stable. Finally, in 1957 it was patented and named after the Frisbee Baking Company of Bridgeport, Connecticut, which made the original pies.

The most powerful and influential toy inventor the American toy industry has seen was, ironically, a man who never did any hands-on creating himself. He didn't sketch, he didn't sculpt, he didn't make models or put anything together. Instead, he had a whole team to do that. What Marvin Glass, a legend among toy inventors, brought to the mix were breakthrough ideas, often bordering on surreal genius. Glass – powerful, loyal and generous, a ranting bully, sexually voracious, and a workaholic – was the spark. At his height, it was said that one in twenty of all the toys sold in America had their beginnings in his Chicago design studios. Such was his power that he became the only inventor ever able to insist that his logo be printed on boxes containing his toy inventions.

Glass's start was near-disastrous. In the 1940s he sank money into making stained-glass windows as Christmas-tree ornaments. They flopped, leaving him $300,000 in debt, a figure that would translate into nearly $4 million today. He immediately borrowed more money to restart. This time he made a vow: in future, he would supply the ideas, others could carry out the manufacturing.

Glass's first great stroke of luck came when he met Eddy Goldfarb, back from World War II and canvassing for a job. Three things immediately came together: the inventive skills of Goldfarb, the flamboyant sales and ideas genius of Glass, and the new system of injection moulding. Previously, metal toys had been made using molten liquid poured into moulds. With plastic this was impossible, it was too viscous. Injection moulding provided the answer: the plastic was forced – or injected. The process would revolutionize toy making because identical parts in plastic could be produced very cheaply. The toys flowed. Mr Machine was a 17-inch-high take-apart plastic robot, complete with top hat, swinging arms, a chomping mouth and a noisy bell. Purchasers got a plastic wrench to take it apart and put it back together. Then, on the turn of a key, Mr Machine would walk as its colourful gears turned. Every ten seconds a siren in his belly would go off. The toy's success helped to establish the Ideal Toy

Company as a major player in the industry until it closed in the 1980s. Mousetrap, which followed, was even more bizarre. This time Glass was inspired by Rube Goldberg's cartoon, 'Inventors', that began in 1914. What Mousetrap, a skill and action toy, did was utilize maximum effort to achieve minimum effect. It was a game in the sense that there was a winning goal – to be the last mouse on the board. But Mousetrap was far more than that, one of a new category of toy that Glass invented, sometimes called three-dimensional games, sometimes toy games. In Mousetrap, a player turns a crank which rotates brightly-coloured gears. These snap a lever that in turn slaps a shoe hanging from a lamp post. The shoe kicks a bucket, a ball rolls down a set of stairs and along a twisty drainpipe. The ball jerks a pole, and a hand pushes a bowling ball off its perch. This ball drops into a bathtub, falls through a hole in the bottom, hits a diving board, making a diver leap up and land in a bucket. The bucket jolts a cage on a post. And the cage falls on the mouse! Glass, whether seriously or not, was said to have regarded the complex futility implicit in Mousetrap as a representation of the depersonalization of modern American life.

The money poured in, allowing Glass to emulate his friend and role model Hugh Hefner. He worked hard – fourteen-to-sixteen-hour days – and played equally hard. The sybaritic charms of his house were pictured in *Playboy*. Parties were attended by belly-dancers and Bunny Girls – one of them became one of his four wives (he actually married five times, including one woman twice). Pictures by Chagall and Picasso hung on his walls. Although he ate sparingly, he employed two chefs, one just to prepare oriental meals.

Erick Erickson, now a sculptor, worked for the Glass

studios for twelve years. It employed about seventy-five people, including six partners, designers, artists, model makers, a lawyer and the Asian chef. The building, recalls Erickson, was a fortress. Glass's own office was double-walled and set on the inside of the building so that he could not be spied upon from the Moody Bible Institute across the street. 'Marvin also installed two giant room-sized safes, like bank vaults. He would insist that the model makers put the toy models in for the night.' Closed-circuit television guarded doors. At the time, such surveillance was a rarity mainly restricted to intelligence-organization buildings. Triple locks were changed regularly, guards patrolled, and employees were sworn to secrecy. In the work area, windows were papered over. No one has ever agreed on how many of these precautions were due to genuine fear and how many were for self-publicity. Some touches – like Glass delivering inventions to Toy Fair in an armoured truck or handcuffing his case to his wrist – smack of the latter. Erickson certainly believes the security was 'more hoopla than anything else. It made for good publicity and Marvin loved it.' Others disagree. Burt Meyer, one of the studio's most prolific inventors, says, 'You're dealing with a product that is worth your entire year's income . . . you need to protect it.'

Glass died from cancer in 1973 at the age of fifty-nine. The studios kept going until 1988. For all his success at reaching children with his inventions, Glass was curiously open in his contempt of what might now be regarded as the political correctness of toys. He thought 'play value', that much bandied-about term among today's toy makers, was a myth, a verbal crutch, an abstract concept used by buyers to justify themselves. Kids were simply the end user – not people to be consulted, studied, or observed along the way to see what toys they preferred. Of toy designers in general, he once said, 'It helps if (he) is emotionally retarded.' More personally, he said, 'What does it prove if I'm the foremost toy designer? I sometimes regret not being able to create skyscrapers or symphonies . . .'

Many of Glass's toys had batteries and *did* something. One suspects he would have been in his element in today's world, where 80 per cent of new toys have an electronic component. A toy designer describes standing in a toyshop 'watching bemused as a child prodded, pushed and shook an old-fashioned teddy bear, unable to comprehend that it wouldn't actually *do* anything.' Within the development, however, are aspects that further threaten the traditional toy inventor. More and more ideas now come from non-toy designers, as toy companies have realized that they can create what is to all intents and purposes a different product simply by adding or changing it in some way, using new technology. It is no longer the idea that is the driving force, but its fresh conception. Where toy-company buyers would traditionally scour toy fairs for products, now they look far beyond.

Times may be tougher for inventors. There are, sadly, far fewer outlets for out-of-the-box originality in these days of corporate ownership and marketing dominance, of licensing and line extensions, and of stripped-down versions of adult electronic gizmos.

What is heartening – what must offer hope for the toy industry – is how many individuals still contrive to flourish, striving to produce ideas and excitement with their creativity. And their obsession.

Chapter Three

WHAT HASBRO WANTS

'What do game inventors have in common? Unending hope!' – Mary Couzin, games inventor and founder of the Chicago Toy and Game Fair

It is the stuff of dreams. Over the years it has developed a mythic quality and, like all myths, there are variations in the telling, but this is how it runs . . .

Saturday 15 December 1979 in Montreal is cold and wet. Chris Haney, hippyish with long, scraggly dark hair and a luxuriant moustache, has spent much of the day with his friend Scott Abbott. Both are thirty and newspapermen, Haney photo editor of the *Gazette*, Abbott a sports editor with the *Canadian Press*. Where Haney is tall, Abbott is short and stout, hair receding, his sideburns and moustache beginning to grey.

The two friends' personalities complement each other well: Haney has a madcap sense of humour, reflected in his amused eyes, and Abbott is a detail man, a trait echoed in his more watchful look. They have much in common, not least a taste for beer-drinking and ribbing each other. Both love playing Scrabble, a game in which each regularly announces he is the champion. But when they decide to challenge each other that day, Haney's Scrabble game is unplayable – pieces are missing.

As the two men recall the number of replacement Scrabble sets they have had to buy over the years, they speculate that there is a lot of money in selling games. Haney suggests, 'We should invent one.'

It is the start of a forty-five-minute brainstorming session. By the end of it they have most of the basics of a new game. It will involve questions and answers, have six categories, and be played on a round board. They even have a name: Trivia Pursuit (Haney's wife suggests adding the 'l' later). Within five years it will revolutionize the games business, be outselling Scrabble's best annual sales performance sevenfold and make them (and others) untold fortunes.

The great, classic games are right at the heart of the toy business – much loved, part of our culture – and for the industry itself an excellent revenue source.

Their qualities are enduring. They incorporate fantasy, imagination, entertainment, excitement, distraction from the day's mundane problems. For children, they are not only fun but aids to development, mentally and socially. The best games span sex and often age barriers, providing engaging meeting grounds between generations.

Their creators exhibit endless ingenuity. Because manufacture does not rely on intensive cheap labour, production remains at source long after the rest of the industry's production has moved thousands of miles away.

The cruel irony is that those qualities that produced them – imagination, innovation, the readiness to take risks, persistence and belief to the point almost of mania – are precisely ones the big players so singularly lack today. That is left to the loners and small operators; for the majors, the priority is milking the cash cow.

Changes in the games business reflect those of the toy industry as a whole. Vast amounts of energy and resources are poured into what marketers call 'sweating the brand': squeezing every last drop of revenue by using it in every conceivable way. New games owe their existence more to TV or movie links than to play value. Vast numbers are gimmick-driven, designed for immediate – and very short-lived – amusement: white-bread sandwiches with no filling. The customer to be pleased is not the games player, but the Wal-Mart or the Target, outlets that insist on immense and instant returns. Even the very best games need time to establish their presence, build an audience and create demand. And time is the last thing they have these days.

And still there is always a glimmer of hope that, against all odds, something will break through. For small games companies and for inventors, Trivial Pursuit is living proof of what every gambler believes: that individuals can occasionally crack the system, beat the odds, win the lottery. Because every now and then, a lumbering behemoth of an industry is forced to lower its blinkered gaze and watch a winner coming from behind.

In retrospect, most great ideas look obvious. At the time though, Haney and Abbott's new game seemed to many a no-hoper. This, after all, was the age of PacMan and computer chips, not old-fashioned board games and definitely not one aimed at adults who, as everyone knew, didn't play games.

Unlike many ideas, this one remained strong the next day. The two friends realized they would need help and capital to bring it to fruition. They recruited

Chris Haney's older brother John, then working backstage at the Shaw Festival at Niagara-on-the-Lake, and Ed Werner, a lawyer, who – as developing and marketing the game progressed – earned the nickname 'The Dobermann' because of his tough bargaining. Three weeks after the original idea was born, the four gathered. A company name was agreed – Horn Abbot, a combination of Haney's nickname and Abbott's surname minus the final letter. (The spelling 'Abbot' was chosen so they could use a logo of an abbot blowing a horn.) The new company was divided out: Chris and Scott would own 22 per cent each; the other two, 18 per cent each. The remaining 20 per cent would be sold to raise funds. Less than a week later $700 was handed over to obtain a patent.

By the summer of 1980 the four were at work trying to raise funds from friends, relatives and colleagues by selling shares for $200 each in minimum blocks of five. It was not easy. At the *Montreal Gazette* everyone passed – except for one copyboy who raised the money by borrowing from his mother and cashing a savings bond. Within four years his $1,000 investment would be worth $2.5 million. Some accepted shares for services, including an unemployed eighteen-year-old artist who developed artwork. Others, like a cartoonist who designed posters, spurned shares and demanded cash. To gather information on how to launch a new game, Chris and Scott attended the Canadian Toy Show, using their press passes, and conducted phony interviews with games experts. Chris quit his job. He took his family to Spain to concoct the questions they needed. Scott joined them on vacation. All the questions used the journalist's five Ws: who, what, where, when, why.

Thirty-four shareholders had put in $40,000. With this and their own money, Horn Abbot had 1,100

Trivial Pursuit games made up. It cost them $60,000, almost $55 a game. They then sold the games to retailers in Canada at a loss – at around $14 each, so they could be sold for $29.95 (at the time a horrendously high retail price). These sales, pre-Christmas 1981, would fuel the real orders they confidently anticipated at the 1982 Montreal and New York Toy Fairs. At Montreal they hoped for anything up to 8,000 orders; they got 100. New York was no better. Potential buyers told them the box was ugly, the price too high, and trivia had been done a thousand times before and always failed. At one stage, it looked as though one company might order 50,000. That sale evaporated. Then to top it all their product was stolen from their booth. Haney by now had exhausted his savings, sold everything but his cameras and was suffering bad anxiety attacks. Still they persevered. Abbott's father helped; they got a line of credit. They produced 20,000 more sets that they got into stores. That didn't yield any profit, but they did break even. Then Chieftain Products, a Canadian company that had been watching Horn Abbot's progress, made them a distribution offer. After much discussion, the four men said yes. It had been almost three years since that first Montreal Saturday.

A big customer of Chieftain Products was an American games company, Selchow and Righter. Its national sales manager was Kevin McNulty, a man for whom games were more than a job. He was fanatical about them and had himself designed them since the age of eight. As a boy he had set up a shoeshine shop in front of the International Toy Building just so he could polish the shoes of the toy men who worked there. He started work for Selchow and Righter in 1971, first selling games on the East Coast. Among the successes that led him to the top sales position at the company was persuading Barnes & Noble to stock Scrabble. In 1983, he heard of a game generating a buzz north of the border. 'The first time I saw the game I knew it had the It factor. It had what other games at the time were missing. Despite being viewed as a huge risk, I wanted to sign it immediately.'

First, he had to convince his bosses at the staid, cautious American company that this was going to be a hit. The trouble was that it broke all the rules. At the time games were marketed for children and sold at around $5.99. This one was aimed at adults, and it retailed at $40, twice as much as the next most expensive game on the market. Furthermore, the box was too big (important to retailers for space reasons) and the game itself too intellectual. Additionally, there was a massive royalty payment to Horn Abbot involved. 'Despite Selchow's hesitancy, I knew this game would take off, and I put my reputation behind it.' Once Selchow's did the deal, a lot of money and a clever public relations campaign went into effect, sending Trivial Pursuit to hundreds of celebrities and generating endorsements from famous names. In the next five years Trivial Pursuit would sell 45 million copies. Its inventors – whose brainchild is now professionally managed with as much skill and business ferocity as is involved in marketing a Procter and Gamble soap powder – became enormously rich, able to pursue their own diverse interests from thoroughbred horses to owning ice hockey clubs.

In the long history of games, Trivial Pursuit is important at many levels. Like many good games, its birth reflected the times – a passion for trivia depended on the television age and baby boomers. It brought something that didn't exist before. It showed the industry that adults would buy and play a traditional board game. Before then, adults played games like bridge, cribbage and Scrabble, but there was nothing actually called the *adult* game. 'It wasn't a category that existed in the industry,' says Rob Daviau, a senior designer at Hasbro Games. 'It really helped forge board games as a serious part of home entertainment.' Adult games, it is now accepted, differ markedly from children's games, partly because winning is not a major factor. 'They're a facilitator for a social experience,' says Daviau. 'It's something to do with another couple or on vacation with friends, where the act of having a good time eclipses who's winning. You still want to win, but as long as you're having a good time while you're playing then the game is a success win or lose.'

Games, even more than toys, attract wannabe inventors. Like the inventors of Trivial Pursuit, most are amateurs. Vast numbers put their own money on the line, often producing their own games, convinced it is the first step towards the big breakthrough. The sad truth, though, is that the failure rate for games is even greater than for toys, and according to insiders is as high as 97 per cent. One major reason is that the classic games remain. Whereas new toys are frequently competing mainly with other new toys, new games are always up against the standards like Scrabble, Monopoly, Pictionary, Clue (Cluedo in the UK) and, of course, Trivial Pursuit. Not surprisingly, the marketers of those game brands do everything they can to keep them refreshed and alive. Companies work hard to make sure they are constantly updated and repackaged. They develop special collector's and anniversary editions, cross-brand them with TV- and movie-licensed product. Monopoly went through over 200 different editions in its first seventy years.

There are huge international promotions and stunts. Monopoly's seventieth anniversary was celebrated with 'Mr Monopoly' and Hasbro executives ringing the opening bell at the New York Stock Exchange. On the thirty-ninth birthday of the game Operation 'hundreds of thousands' of Americans voted to choose a new disease for Cavity Sam. (They decided on Brain Freeze, represented by an ice-cream cone in his head.) The 20th Anniversary Edition Game of Trivial Pursuit in 2004 was given such an aggressive marketing campaign that according to NPD Group, the retail-tracking organization, it became the number one new product introduction in the toy and game industry that year. Names of games are licensed out, yielding wider and more continuous brand reminders: Scrabble-tile letters feature on cufflinks, bracelets, and money clips.

Hasbro Games' Head of Product Acquisition Mike Hirtle enthuses, 'Our games have such tremendous staying power. I played them when I was a kid and they just go on and on and on because they satisfy that need. They just don't get old. It's good news and bad news. I'd like to see more innovative new stuff, energize the inventors. We want them to be satisfied they've got a good chance to be putting new games in the market. But at the same time we don't want to be shouldering aside things that have been selling for many years and have become part of the culture.'

Games for amusement, like toys, go back thousands of years – a board and peg game was found in an Egyptian tomb of about 2800 BC. Dice are said to have been invented in Greece about 1400 BC. Backgammon, originally called tables or tabula, emerged around the first century AD. Its players included the Emperor Claudius. Chess first appeared around the sixth century AD in India. Cards probably originated in China, perhaps as a result of sorting paper money, between the seventh and tenth centuries AD. Checkers (draughts in the UK) probably first appeared in France about AD 1100. The US games industry is relatively young. Imports, mainly from Europe and Asia, began dribbling in during the nineteenth century, and American inventors started producing their own designs. The popularity of games in both the United States and Britain was driven by increased prosperity, more leisure time, better production techniques, improved distribution methods, and the ethical climate. Games often made moral points. Snakes and ladders (chutes and ladders in the US) represented the rewards and punishments for good and bad deeds. By the early part of the century there were thousands of board games. The J.W. Spear company in England was advertising 114 different ones by 1910.

The game that stands largest in popular consciousness – Monopoly – came later, a product of the Depression. During its lifetime, it has produced scores of stories and legends: the Great Train Robbers in the UK whiled away time in their hideout playing the game with real (stolen) money; silk escape maps, compasses, files – and real banknotes – were inserted into modified Monopoly games delivered by the Red Cross to POW camps in Germany in World War II; two thirds of American households with children aged eight to seventeen own and play the game; jeweller Sidney Mobell created a gold, ruby and sapphire set of the game worth $1 million.

Monopoly was one of the games that helped Parker Brothers, started in 1883, become one of the dominating companies in the history of the modern game. Today the great names all exist only as brands, units of companies that have absorbed them. Hasbro has both Parker Brothers and the other great American name, Milton Bradley.

Milton Bradley died in 1911 but his name still lives, not just as a logo on a Hasbro box but as a thriving manufacturing plant in Massachusetts. Bradley was not the first major games manufacturer in the United States. That distinction belongs to the company W. & S.B. Ives of Salem, Massachusetts, which produced over two dozen games in the mid 1800s including the 'Mansion of Happiness', once claimed to be the first American board game. Bradley, though, was a trailblazer, credited by many with really launching the games business in the US. He brought to the industry most of the virtues of the toy business: ingenuity, a passionate regard for children and their education, resilience, and tenacity. Born in Vienna in 1836, Bradley's first incursion was into printing, setting up the state's first colour-lithography shop in Springfield. He enjoyed early major success with a lithograph of Abraham Lincoln, who had just been nominated for the presidency. Unfortunately, once in the White House, Lincoln grew a beard, dating Bradley's portrait and leading to demands for refunds.

Like the inventors of Trivial Pursuit, it was the act of playing a game – in Bradley's case probably an imported European one – that gave him the idea of devising his own. He also had a waning business as added incentive. He came up with the Checkered Game of Life (still selling today in updated form as the Game of Life). The aim of the game was to avoid financial ruin and proceed to the enjoyment of a happy old age. Pieces on the board were moved according to a numbered spinner; squares were good, bad or neutral. By 1861 Bradley had sold over 45,000 copies. He formed Milton Bradley and Company to produce others. He also printed manuals and wrote books on childhood and education, and he was a forerunner in the movement to establish kindergartens in the US.

The Milton Bradley plant in East Longmeadow, Massachusetts, is a rare sight, a place where a toy company actually *makes* something. Here, on a 20-acre plot, game manufacture lives in a million square feet of plant. Hasbro bought Milton Bradley in 1998, seven years after it took over Parker Brothers, the other giant games company. Now it is the manufacturing and assembly centre for all of Hasbro's games.

Most of the great names on the boxes here are those Hasbro owns not by its own development, but by having gobbled up other companies. That does not lessen the pride in the plant's existence. Ninety miles away, at Hasbro's Pawntucket headquarters (where nothing is made and which, apart from the displayed toys and the observational market research funlab, could house almost any kind of operation from insurance to environmental planning), they exchange chat about the wonder of East Longmeadow. Even a casual examination of Hasbro's history makes it clear, though, that the unit does not survive solely for nostalgic reasons. Another part of the Milton Bradley operation, its wood products company in Fairfax, Vermont, had been churning out millions of wooden Scrabble tiles when Hasbro took over. The company was the only industry in a town of 2,500 people. Hasbro lost little time in shifting manufacture to China. Hasbro was no less hard-headed with the Parker Brothers factory in Salem which it closed, ending a legacy of 108 years.

East Longmeadow survives not because it embraces over 150 years of Milton Bradley history and 100-plus years of Parker Brothers past, but because it works.

'This is the world head office for games,' says Pedro Caceres, the senior vice-president of operations. The reason is that games making and assembly is highly automated, needing little of the cheap labour that usually makes China so attractive for toy companies. East Longmeadow can deliver low cost and the flexibility that only home manufacture can provide. 'What's brilliant about our facility,' says Mark Morris, the PR face of Hasbro Games, 'is that the way it was set up long ago was very brilliant. It's a model that still works.' The plant is organized vertically, with raw materials coming in at one end and finished product emerging at the other. In between there are twelve core processes, from injection moulding to printing. 'It's like running twelve small factories,' says Caceres.

Machines clatter, water is sprayed from overhead pipes to keep the air moist and stop stacks of paper sticking, a paint-like smell of paperboard permeates the air. The scale is enormous – the forklift trucks manoeuvre an elaborate indoor road system complete with traffic signs. The assembly process is a mix of sophisticated automation and what must be boringly repetitive physical work. Bagged items are checked by sensitive weight machines, rerouted to discard trays if they sense pieces are missing. At one end of the operation, a machine makes a box bottom before starting it on its journey down a conveyor belt. As it proceeds, women workers drop in all the appropriate parts. At the far end, a machine makes the top which is dropped onto the box before it is automatically shrink-wrapped and placed into a bar-coded master carton which can be automatically directed to the right spot in the warehouse. The plant is one of the largest in New England. Its printing presses alone turn out more money than the US Bureau of Printing and Engraving.

The dominance of Hasbro is awesome. Its purchase of Milton Bradley in 1984, ending 124 years of family ownership, brought it Battleship, Mousetrap, Operation, Twister, Yahtzee (which itself had been acquired when Bradley bought the E.S. Lowe Company). The takeover of the Tonka Corporation produced a host of other games, notably Monopoly. Tonka had itself earlier swallowed Kenner which had bought from General Mills the legendary Parker Brothers. More games, including Scrabble, came when Hasbro moved in after Coleco went bankrupt. Coleco had earlier bought Selchow and Righter.

Therein lies a problem. What games come to market in quantity now depends to a major extent on what Hasbro wants or does not want. (Mattel is also a big player, but much less dominating.) The impact is not confined to the United States. Jack Jaffe, a London-based Scottish game inventor, complains, 'Ninety per cent of the brand games in the UK are from Hasbro or Mattel. They gain shelf space by their enormous advertising.' Furthermore, he feels the big two have killed the indigenous UK games industry: 'Waddington was swallowed by Hasbro, Spears by Mattel. The consequence is that these two companies do nothing to try to broaden the base of the industry.'

The crucial fact is that for Hasbro to be interested in a game, its potential sales need to be huge, a minimum 250,000 in the first year. Secondly, any game has to fit into Hasbro's three-pronged business. The first prong – the classics – is mainly about keeping the existing range refreshed. The second is games linked with licensed products, such as Star Wars or Lord of the Rings. Sometimes there is co-branding – Hasbro's Operation, for example, was married to Shrek 2.

It is only when it comes to the third prong that totally new games emerge. The scope is not large. At

Hasbro, Mike Hirtle and a colleague reckon to look at 1,500–1,600 new ideas a year. Some are from agents and professional inventors, others are existing games in other countries or being marketed by smaller US companies. Hirtle says they will get interested in about 200 of them – 'enough of an interest that we get other people here involved in taking a look at them, doing some play evaluation. The vast majority are just sort of, yeah, that's pretty neat but it's not for us. We have to pass on the vast majority.'

What Hasbro does not want is what most people think of as games. 'Most people on the outside, even some of the professional inventors, think of the game business and they think of board games, card games, word games, strategy games, dice games,' says Hirtle. 'But there's not much new product being developed in those areas because the kind of thing that we're looking for is promotional, television-driven games. We haven't introduced a new word game in probably twenty years because we own that category. An inventor will bring me a word game and it will be wonderful and clever and engaging, and I'll say, Well, it's just not quite good enough, it's got to be fabulous, it's got to be drop-dead tremendous – the letters have to levitate off the board – for it to have a chance to get space. It's got to be something that really stands out and first grabs me and my partner and then design has to have that same kind of excited response and then from us it goes to the sales and marketing team and you've gotta have that thing, Yeah that's tremendous – and from them it goes to the trade and then trade has to have that same kind of response. Maybe twenty, twenty-four of those games we see end up on the shelves. It's very funnelled, very broad at the top, very narrow at the bottom.'

Ayers Concepts, a Houston inventing and agenting company, urges inventors to go for 'what we call a "skill and action" game. This is really a toy mechanism around which someone has built a game.' Or what one disillusioned inventor called 'battery-run games that look and sound "cool" and sell well on television.' It means games like Hasbro's Bulls Eye Ball, a tabletop action arcade target game where players bounce steel balls onto a mini trampoline in order to hit one of the three targets built into the backboard of the game unit. A later electronic version offers music, lights and sound effects, even an internal announcer commentating on moves. Or games like Fred Kroll's Hungry Hungry Hippos where competing players operate a lever on the back of their hippopotamus to consume as many of the twenty white marbles on the playing field as possible. With its plastic tray and brightly-coloured plastic hippos, it looks like a toy, but the fact that players compete and there are rules makes it a game.

The changing market conditions for games has at least one ray of hope for inventors. The major companies may buy fewer games each year, but as with toys, most games now have a short lifespan and there is a constant turnover. Only a rare new game will last eight or ten years. Successful new product from major companies, backed with heavy promotion, will be big at first, but fall away after two years at most. Of the fifty to sixty new games introduced by Hasbro each year, only about ten last longer than twelve months, and perhaps two reach a third year. This is partly because they are gimmicky, 'feature-driven' games that get played for a while and then dumped. It is the opposite end of the spectrum from games like Monopoly. Hirtle volunteers that he does not think Monopoly would make it now if it didn't already exist as part of the public consciousness. 'If some inventor brought it to me today, I would reject it. The way the marketplace is nowadays, the requirement of something developing over time, getting seen and played with, our marketplace doesn't allow that any more. From the new product introduction standpoint, it's complicated, it's a difficult game, it's got a six- or seven-page rulebook, it's hard to explain. If people didn't know how to play Monopoly would they take the time? Just imagine trying to explain it to the trade: "Here's this game, you roll dice, you move tokens, you may or may not buy this property, and you may build some buildings . . ." And imagine a TV commercial to drive sales of Monopoly: from the point of view that nobody's heard of it before, what do you do?'

Although breakthrough games break rules, there are some rules that inventors – and games companies – disregard at their peril. Today especially the first two are that it should be playable straight from the box and that it should be fast. Jim Becker, a toy-industry veteran and strategy-game lover, introduced the Japanese game Othello to the United States and the rest of the world in 1976. Over 40 million copies had been sold by 2004 in a variety of formats including boards, hand-held and tabletop electronic games and CD-ROMS. In the process, it helped make him a rich man. A great key to the game – and other success-ful games – is simplicity, he believes. 'It's always important. I say of my game Othello that it takes a minute to learn, a lifetime to master. On one hand, it can be played almost straight from the box; on the other, a lot of top chess players use it to warm up.'

Mattel, a big player in games as well as toys, uses a lot of market research in developing 'rules' for its new games. Interviews with parents showed a need for a game that ended promptly and didn't cause squabbles among the kids. So a game called Break the Safe was created in such a way that players would have to work together to achieve the game's aim – to thwart a plot to end the world – before the game's timer ran out after thirty minutes. Phil Jackson, Mattel's marketing vice-president for games and puzzles, explained, 'Parents want to be able to say, "Finish dinner, play a game, and go to bed."' A major reason for the success of the children's games from the Cranium company is that they are short-lasting – so even if a kid loses he quickly has a fresh chance at winning.

One constant fault of amateur games inventors, insiders agree, is that they do not test their creations enough. Mary Couzin, inventor and organizer of the Chicago International Toy and Game Fair, says, 'I always tell people when they are starting out, you have got to get a working prototype. You have to get it play-tested at the minimum a hundred times. Then you take it to a retailer and you ask him what he thinks.' Cranium tests its new games for what it calls CHIFF – clever, high-quality, innovative, fun and friendly. Four prototypes are tested with observers watching outsiders play. They note everything, from how well questions work to whether players remain engaged in the game even when it is not their turn. With each prototype test, features vanish or are added until a final version emerges. It is vital that rules are unambiguous and cover all eventualities. 'You can't have a situation where someone says, "OK I'm here, now what do I do, it's not in the rules?"' points out Rob Daviau. Mark Morris of Hasbro adds another key rule: 'You don't want to be able to do what we call break the game. You know, if I go here at every turn and I do this, I win every time.

Or I lose every time, or the person who goes third always loses . . .'

The games inventor has two choices – to try to get the game licensed to a company or to produce it themselves. For real games enthusiasts, self-publishing has advantages – they retain control over their brainchild and in touting the product themselves they have great opportunities to meet speciality shop owners. Inventors and would-be inventors freely share information about the mechanics of self-production. Thus inventor Tom Jolly writes on the Web: 'My decks in Wiz-War were printed onto brown cardstock in black ink, 125 cards to a deck and weren't super-durable. Still cost me about $1 a deck, and I had to sort them by hand, but I could also get away with printing only 500 at a time. Boxes' cost would be about $1.30 each, and were a two-step process; first, I had to have a printer make the wraps for the boxes, then the chipboard-box maker had to make the boxes and glue the wrap sheets on. The minimums here were 1,000 . . .'

It is a high-risk business though. Mike Hirtle says of games he and other companies have turned down, 'A lot of times people believe in them so much they'll go on and they'll make them themselves and occasionally somebody will have a hit doing that. But more often than not it fails or they're able to sell enough to pretty much break even. When you're doing as few as they would do, maybe ten thousand, they don't have much economy of scale so costs are high – it's real difficult.' Mary Couzin took the risk with her first game. A first run, she reckons, costs seven to ten dollars a game – 'though it's true that Hasbro producing Monopoly is probably down to a dollar or two a game.' For her first game, she put $35,000 at risk. 'I had a partner who had some money and I took line of credit against my house, but I was able to pay it off. Even so I didn't make as much money as I'd hoped to make.'

Many quit their jobs to get their games off the ground. Tim Graf did so to work on ScandalMonger, a trivia game in which players pose as reporters gathering salacious stories. Development cost $75,000, including graphic designer, printer, legal and marketing costs, though not his time working stores coast to coast. Scott Pardee started when he sat down to play a game with his father but could not decide which game. His father suggested he make up his own. He did and in 2000 presented it at Toy Fair in New York, renting the cheapest 10ft × 10ft booth for $2,200. The game, Chebache, a blend of chess, backgammon and checkers, had cost $100,000 of his own and friends' money to develop, patent and produce. Years later he was still waiting for a big company to license and distribute it.

The alternative is to get it licensed from the start. The inventor may lose control, but he also passes on the risk in return for a royalty, usually 4–7 per cent.[3] Wannabe inventors immediately run up against problems, including the fact that most major game manufacturers only accept submissions from non-established inventors through an agent. Carol A. Rehtmeyer, president of Rehtmeyer Inc., a Chicago firm that helps bring toys and games to market, says the odds of getting licensed with a major toy company 'are slightly better than playing the lottery'. Her company receives twenty-three enquiries a day from toy and game inventors, of which fewer than 1 per cent are licensable.

Whatever the problems and the difficulties for inventors, new games pour forth. The range and variety is mind-boggling. There are games that ask

[3] In the case of Trivial Pursuit, very considerably more.

players to judge if urban myths are true or not, others where points are scored by diverting the flow of a river during a flood. Sometimes the titles tell all: So Sue Me! Stock Rush! A Week on Wall Street. There are countless twists on perennials: Take Four is a cross-word game in which everyone plays at the same time. Trivia recurs in innumerable guises: in Whad' Ya Know? the player has to persuade others the answer is right, even if it isn't. No Sweat, from Dan Thompson, a chaplain at the Sacramento County Juvenile Probation Department, is a mix of exercise and health education aimed at tackling the problem of overweight children. Patriot Challenge, from a former sales and marketing executive, uses reproductions of postage stamps to test players' knowledge of the USA. Legends of Abraham, complete with 'Faith cards' and 'Hope cards' has a 'custom-designed box inspired by Isaiah: 52:7'.

The ingenuity is extraordinary. Howling Monkeys, from a California mother and daughter team, has four card decks covering topics about relationships, celebrities and creativity, and instructions to players like 'Explain a new yoga position for Madonna' and 'Act out being a strawberry'. In Marry, Date or Dump? featuring movie stars, athletes and rock stars, players choose who to marry, who to date, and who to ditch while the other players guess what the choices will be. In Destination, from a Portsmouth, UK, ex-cab driver, players are cabbies aiming to clock up the highest takings while trying not to lose the cab's licence and avoiding hazards such as traffic lights.

The ultimate dream must be to create one of the Greats. The stories behind the classics range from romantic to sad. Candy Land, once described as 'the perfect first game', was designed by Eleanor Abbott, a retired schoolteacher, while recovering from polio in

San Diego. It still sells a million sets a year. Cluedo was dreamed up by a British law clerk, Anthony Pratt, whiling away his time on fire patrol in England during World War II. 'Between the wars,' he said, 'all the bright young things would congregate in each other's homes for parties at weekends. We'd play a stupid game called Murder, where guests crept up on each other in corridors and the victim would shriek and fall on the floor.'

Pratt died in obscurity at the age of ninety, having dropped out of sight. What the British press termed Cluedo's final mystery was solved when Waddington's, the company that first published the game, issued a public appeal to find its creator as the 150 millionth sale of the game neared. They received a call from the superintendent of a cemetery, saying Pratt had been buried there in April 1994. The man who had turned death into a game across the world had died peacefully of natural causes in a nursing home.

Pictionary, where players try to identify words that their teammates draw under time pressure, came from Rob Angel, a Seattle waiter. Angel would sketch words from the dictionary, and he became obsessed with the idea it could become a game. At first he self-published, borrowing $115,000: just three years later North American annual sales totalled a stunning 9 million.

Scrabble, another of the games that came out of the Depression, originated when Alfred Butts was laid off his job as an architect with a New York firm. Realizing that in hard times people seek cheap distractions, he decided to try to invent a game. It would use chance and skill and combine features of anagrams and of crossword puzzles, two of his great loves. A major inspiration for the word game came from the plot of the Edgar Allan Poe short story 'The Gold Bug'. In it a cipher is solved by comparing symbols to the alphabet, based on the frequency with which letters appear in words. To determine actual frequency, Butts worked through newspapers and magazines, totalling how often each letter appeared. Finally, he had his game – Lexiko, from the Greek 'of words' – with a hundred letter tiles and the aim of making a nine- or ten-letter word. Milton Bradley, Parker Brothers and the publishers Simon and Schuster all rejected it. Butts decided to make and sell sets himself. By August 1934 he had sold eighty-four – at a loss of $20. Finally, weary of the work and lack of success, he quit.

It might have been the end of the game but for another figure, James Brunot. In 1947 Brunot was also weary, but in his case it was because of the two-hour daily commute to New York. Looking to start a small business at home, he chanced across Butts's game and offered the inventor a small royalty to let him make it. Butts accepted. Brunot introduced more changes, including making the centre of the board a double-word-score square. He also came up with the name Scrabble, which he trademarked. Like Butts, Brunot self-published. For four years he struggled: in 1949 he made 2,400 sets at a loss of $450. However, sales rose gently until, in 1952, they suddenly soared to 2,500 in one week. The reason was probably that Jack Strauss, the chairman of Macy's, played the game on vacation and inspired a large order, promptly copied by other stores. The following year the game was licensed to Selchow and Righter, and within two years had sold nearly 4 million sets. According to Butts's biographer Stefan Fatsis, his total proceeds from his invention were just over $1 million – a tiny sum compared with the returns enjoyed by Brunot and the game's corporate owners, Selchow, Coleco and now Hasbro and Mattel. Butts, though, seems not to have had any regrets. He continued playing Scrabble with friends and family almost to the end of his life at the age of ninety-three. 'Alfred may have been content,' wrote Fatsis, 'but I see him as another exploited inventor.'

Erno Rubik, the creator of Rubik's Cube, was a lecturer in the Academy of Applied Arts and Crafts in Budapest, the Hungarian capital. He devised what was to become one of the most popular toys of all time as a teaching aid for his design students. The idea was to move a mixture of colours around the cube's axis until each side was a solid colour. (It is claimed that the number of possible combinations involved is 43 quintillion – the number that is represented as a one followed by 18 zeros.) For its inventor, engineering a 3×3×3 cube that would stay in one piece while it was manipulated was a major problem. Various methods of construction simply could not cope. According to the cube's official history, inspiration came when Rubik was beside the Danube. His eye was attracted by some pebbles, whose sharp edges had been smoothed to rounded shapes. He realized that the interior mechanism of his cube would have to be basically cylindrical, utilizing the same rounded architecture. Finally, the fifty-four outer surfaces of the individual elements were given their colours. Towards the end of 1977 the first cubes appeared on the shelves of Budapest toyshops. Another Hungarian working in Vienna 'discovered' the cube on a Budapest business trip and tried to find a German toy distributor. Instead he met up with Tom Kremer, a Hungarian-born toy and game inventor based in London. The two men developed a marketing plan and persuaded an Ideal Toy Company executive to place an order for 1 million cubes. Sales skyrocketed in 1980, and by 1982 'Rubik's Cube' had even entered the Oxford English Dictionary. Rubik became Hungary's richest private citizen while still in his thirties.

The inventors of another classic game, Yahtzee, the world's most popular commercial dice game, remain anonymous. They created it on their yacht to play with guests. In 1956, in response to requests for copies, they asked Edwin Lowe, manufacturer of bingo, to print some copies for gifts. He saw possibilities. The Canadian couple, who seemingly had no interest in benefiting from their game, sold the rights in return for 1,000 copies.

A remarkable fact about the games industry is how resilient it has been. Mike Hirtle says, 'When the first wave of video games happened there was word that, oh, that's the end of board games. And of course it wasn't, it wasn't even much of a decline. Our part of the biz is very healthy. The reason is very simple: we call it face-to-face fun. It's an interactive experience – people, families, adults, kids, getting around a table and playing a board game. It's not an experience you get with the PlayStation, video games, computer games.' Traditionally, games do well in tough times. During World War II Winston Churchill insisted the production of cards and board games should continue with as little interruption as possible, because he felt diversions for the British people were vital. Sales were reported to have increased after 9/11, and to have been helped by a troubled economy. Eric Poses, founder of All Things Equal, a California board-game company, knows why: 'Board games are a cheap alternative to a movie and dinner. If you serve some drinks and some food, it's a good evening.'

Mary Couzin thinks there is another reason: that parents have discovered games as a way of teaching kids, and of spending more time with them. Jeremy Young, founder of the game company Uberplay, agrees: 'Getting families to turn off the TV and sit down for an hour and play a really fun game. That's what these games are all about.' It is a message the industry likes, and it does all it can to promote it. There is a National Games Week in the fourth week of November each year, sponsored by a number of games companies. There are claims that playing games with kids makes them better people. Lew Herndon, president and CEO of Talicor Games company: 'The game-playing experience offers a chance to teach concepts of fair play, taking turns, following rules, respect for other players and, of course, competition. In addition, children can learn math concepts, statistical probabilities and vocabulary skills at the same time as they are learning social skills.'

For the industry games are not only big business,[4] they produce big profit margins. Some insiders estimate profits on games at five times that of most toys. On Trading Cards they are appreciably more, though, as one of the most boom-and-bust fickle areas of the industry, that carries exceptionally high risk. The biggest threat to board games is the growth of tech toys, but here again, the industry has found a silver lining, adding technology to its product. Editions of games like Trivial Pursuit and Twister come with DVDs and CDs, others like Cluedo come with voice chips. Mattel's trivia game Scene It? uses real movie clips. For companies, this has the great advantage of pushing up the perceived value – and the price. Cardboard and plastic generally have a selling range of $11.99 to $19.99, interactive $24.99 to $49.99.

Like inventors, smaller companies can make the big time. A single astute move can propel a company

[4] $2.7 billion in 2003, according to the Games Manufacturers Association.

upwards. Upstarts!, the largest independent games company in the UK, was formed in 1988 by two men who worked for Horn Abbot, the owners of Trivial Pursuit. Its moment came in 1998 when it decided – fortuitously – to pursue the UK distribution rights of Who Wants To Be A Millionaire?, a game that became 2000's biggest-selling toy brand in that country.

Cranium has been called the Ben and Jerry's of the games world. The Seattle-based company was founded in 1998 by two former Microsoft computer-programmer executives, Richard Tait and Whit Alexander. They dismissed thoughts of inventing a computer game: 'We realized that while no computer game has ever made more than half a billion dollars, several board games have,' said Alexander. There is a big difference in startup costs too: a software company would have taken $2 million, Cranium was set up with $100,000. In the way of many legendary games, Tait came up with the idea when playing other board games, first Pictionary and then Scrabble, while on vacation. 'I asked myself, why isn't there a game we can all play and shine at?' He sketched out the idea on the flight home from the Hamptons. The game that emerged combines skills, talent and knowledge. It is like a conglomerate of successful games, incorporating charades, drawing, trivia, word puzzles and sculpting. There's a Data Head category which tests knowledge; another in which a player might be asked to draw or sculpt (clay included with the game), another that can involve whistling or impersonating, a fourth that concerns spelling. Within a few years Cranium was in over 10,000 outlets – speciality and mass – in twenty-two countries and was said to have been played by 30 million people.

It was its early marketing, though, that was so

revolutionary. It happened almost by accident. Tait and Alexander got their new game ready too late for that year's New York Toy Fair. At that point they realized their potential customers were the same people they sat with each day in Starbucks. So Tait and Alexander made some calls and persuaded Starbucks to carry Cranium. It became the only board game there – and a massive success, the fastest-selling independent board game in history. Amazon.com and Barnes & Noble also became distributors. 'We really changed the rules on games distribution with our original games partners,' said Tait. 'In our business, distribution is very tightly held and the market is dominated by two large players so you have to change the rules to break through.' Cranium was the industry's first 'breakout hit' for two decades, and it inspired several other startup companies, especially in the Seattle area. In one six-month period in 2003 three Seattle game makers, including Cranium, raised $30 million in venture capital financing. In the process, board games have joined aircraft, software and bio-technology as a Seattle industry.

In today's toy industry, good games have to struggle as strongly to materialize and to survive as the rest of the industry's products. It is sad – but not surprising – that of those that do emerge, the vast number are consigned to oblivion and landfills within months.

Yet board games are still a part of American life, as they have been since the 1800s. Their durability is testament to the inventiveness (often bordering on fanaticism) of their creators. Their demise has been prematurely forecast many times – first, TV would kill them off, then video games, most recently the combined onslaught of all the other competitors for our cash and leisure. It is a tribute to their qualities and to the way they satisfy our needs that they have fared most strongly in America's hardest times.

The great games classics remain seemingly timeless billion-dollar brands. Only one other item ever produced by the industry enjoys that position – at least until now. And that is an 11.5-inch-high doll.

Chapter Four

BARBIE GOES TO WAR: BATTLE OF THE DOLLS

'I think every Barbie doll is more harmful than an American missile' – Masoumeh Rahimi, Iranian toy seller

Barbie is in trouble. Deep trouble. And when Barbie is in trouble, everyone at Mattel, the world's biggest toy company, has got problems. Because Barbie, the world's most famous toy, a genuine American icon, is their meal ticket. In the words of analysts, 'As Barbie goes, Mattel goes.' Barbie – over three sold somewhere in the world every single second – brings in around $3.6 billion a year in retail sales. She represents over a fifth of all Mattel sales and more than a third of the company's profits. It doesn't end there – there are also all the licensing spin-offs, everything from clothes to bedroom furniture, software and electronics to cosmetics, towels, bedding, and sporting goods.

If there is one toy that stands for the modern toy industry it is Barbie.

Of all toys, she is extraordinary. Mattel boasts with justification that she is not just a toy; she is a 'lifestyle brand'. As such, she is high maintenance, requiring hundreds of personnel, including fifty designers, a dozen hairdressers, almost a hundred workers just to handle licensing her name. It's been claimed there are more Barbie dolls in America than there are people. She is the subject of innumerable academic papers, the centrepiece of countless artistic works – not all flattering – and the focus of longtime feminist screams. A Barbie is so quintessentially American that she was included in the 1976 bicentennial time capsule. She is sold in 150 different countries. An advertisement selling the latest Barbie is showing somewhere on the globe every day of the year. There are Barbie conventions, clubs, websites, magazines, collectors' fairs. Most important for those who depend on her, she is the most valuable toy brand in the world, the only plaything to enter the list of the world's top 100 brands.[5]

Except, now sales are suffering. For the first time in Barbie's fifty years another doll (and a pretty sleazy one at that) is stealing her sales. Because the toy industry is not growing, sales that go to one company come from rivals. In Barbie's case, it means that every dollar spent on Bratz dolls comes out of Mattel's pocket.

None of this, though, is apparent as I step out of the elevator on the 10th floor of Mattel's El Segundo, California, headquarters, known internally as the Pink Floor. Outside the elevator, the solitary small Christmas tree is indeed pink. It has taken me months to get this far. One longtime Barbie observer has likened getting into Mattel to crashing the Kremlin in the days of the cold war. Security is tight: I am told toys are carried from floor to floor in boxes closed with

[5] In *Business Week*'s 2003 Global Brand Scoreboard, Barbie ranked 97, one below Fedex and above the *Wall Street Journal* and Jack Daniel's.

numbered seals. A copywriter on the Mattel account recalls attending a meeting at which he was told to face away from windows because spies with telescopes might read his lips. Over at the even more tightly protected design building, a sign at the entrance exhorts: 'Keep Em Guessing. Remember to keep Mattel secrets under wraps.'

I have lost count of the unanswered emails, un-returned telephone calls, broken promises, excuses, and requests for information and assurances and question lists to satisfy the lawyers I have encountered in the course of researching this chapter. You enter a special Mattel universe. 'Welcome to our world,' says one chirpy Mattel apparatchik, cancelling yet another meeting (only meant to determine whether the next one will take place). This is Toyland meets Kafka. But suddenly, after weeks of keeping me hanging around, Mattel relents – provided I can make an 11,000-mile round trip immediately. And now it's nearly Christmas, and on the surface everyone is upbeat and full of excited Barbie-future talk. It's the same a few blocks away in the Mattel design centre where the current key figure in Barbie's life, designer supremo Ivy Ross, shares her thoughts and plans. Barbie, in adversity, can be a jinxed – albeit lucrative – product with which to become attached. A succession of high-flying figures pass through her life. Ivy Ross is no exception. Within a month there will be a 'revamp' of the management team that runs Barbie's division, and Ms Ross will have moved to Gap. Mattel will also be back to its fortress mentality.

In the meantime, it is Ivy Ross's watch and, after a brief clash over my signing a secrecy agreement, all is sweetness and light. I find myself recalling that old saying: if you can keep your head when all around you are panicking, maybe they know something you don't.

But in tough corporate Mattel land you fix a smile and don't admit weakness to outsiders. And besides, Barbie has been under attack before, and has always seen off contenders with the ease of a pit bull facing a rabbit. We talk about how Barbie has constantly adapted to be up to the minute – Ms Ross master-minded major innovations for the millennium. The hovering but unspoken suggestion is that this time Barbie just didn't adapt fast enough.

Twenty-two miles away in North Hills, on a gritty trading estate, Isaac Larian sits in his first-floor office. In line with the difference between the two toy com-panies, this also happens to be the building's top floor. Unlike Mattel with its corporate sense, here there's a cottage industry feel. Reception is an apologetic girl – 'I'd get you a coffee but I can't leave the desk.' Larian is relaxed when he talks about Barbie. He can afford to be. It is his doll, Bratz, that is causing all the problems. Similar to Barbie in size, she has a cartoonish look with huge eyes and exaggerated features. She is hip, ethnic, and she too comes with endless accessories.

Larian, youthful-looking with a shock of black hair, reminds me of Michael J. Fox, with the same ready smile. There are family portraits on his huge, half-circle desk, piles of boxes on the floor, Bratz dolls on shelves everywhere. He has become the little guy in a classic David and Goliath clash. Coming out of nowhere in the best toy industry tradition, he has gambled his own cash (over $5 million, he tells me) on something no one else thought could fly – and in the process has turned the industry upside down. From nothing he has taken Bratz to a billion-dollar-plus property. (In one week, picked at random, the three top-selling toys in the US for five- to seven-year-olds at Toysrus.com were Bratz. Barbie was down at nine and ten.)

Larian loves goading Mattel in public. 'It's too late for Mattel. They're not going to stop this train now.' 'Mattel's boss comes from the cheese industry. They don't see that selling cheese and toys are very different.' Today Larian is more dismissive than vicious about his rival. 'Mattel can't even say our name,' he assures me. 'They call us "our nearest competitor". I'm thinking of changing our company name [from MGA Entertainment] to MNC Entertainment – Mattel's Nearest Competitor.'[6]

There's a great touch of the actor about him, and he grins winningly before stressing that while other companies have red tape, he stays personally involved, approving everything. That he's done it all against Mattel, who many think of as a mean, unlovable, corporate bully of a company, makes it all the sweeter. Many in the toy business still cannot believe it. They tell me it cannot last. He is too dependent on one product, they say; when that crashes (as hot toys invariably do) the big chains will drop him and his other toys too. Those who once forecast Larian's doll could never take off now tell me why it simply had to succeed. Just as their predecessors did nearly a half-century before, when Barbie was born.

Barbie, even more than Bratz, was the creation of one entrepreneur. The doll's birth, her subsequent often stormy history, the scale of her success, the size, expertise and ruthlessness of those who safeguard her, all tell more about changes in the modern toy industry than almost anything else.

Like Bratz, it all began in California, and like Bratz it was a product of its time. Before the fifties, girls

---

[6] Mattel fervently denies that executives have ever refused to speak aloud the name of MGA – though they say nothing about the tone they use.

cradled and cuddled baby dolls. Most women still remained at home, cooking, cleaning, and caring for children. But *their* daughters were becoming a hitherto unidentified group: teenagers. Times were good, and it was a pampered generation. Barbie, with her freedom and purchasing power, reflected the new culture. Like other Americans revelling in a strong postwar economy, Barbie would seek her fulfilment in goods and gadgets.

Ruth Handler had already noticed that her daughter Barbara preferred playing with paper cutout dolls. Ruth had begun to contemplate a new doll, grown-up-looking, that would allow girls to project fantasies of adult independence and glamour. After all, these girls did not need to stay home. They could be models, career girls, wear fashionable clothes, and teeter on high heels.

All this was in the future. Ruth, the tenth child born to Polish immigrants in 1916, moved to California after graduating and married her high-school sweetheart Elliot Handler. A penniless artist, the housewares he made for their apartment proved popular and sold from their garage. They moved into jewellery, and business flourished until the war. In 1945, with their foreman Harold Matson, they formed Mattel (merging the men's names) to make picture frames. They found bigger profits in making dolls' houses from picture-frame scraps – and doing so discovered the toy market. Interviewed in 1998, Ruth told *Forbes* Small Business, 'We didn't know how to run a business, but we had dreams and talent.'

Elliot's contribution was visionary product development, Ruth's was as a marketer and salesperson. Matson was forced out by stress, while the Handlers virtually created the modern, professional toy industry. Their innovations were numerous: they

110

became the first company to make toys from a variety of different materials. Starting with a music box, they produced toy mechanisms that could be used in a variety of products year after year. Ruth was credited with the then revolutionary decision to aim advertising directly at the child rather than the adult buyer.

What some observers have called the 'single most important moment in the history of the American toy industry' occurred when, on vacation in Switzerland, Ruth Handler saw a very adult doll called Lilli. With curves perched above high heels, it was based – though Ruth did not know it then – on a prostitute from a German adult cartoon and aimed at men. M.G. Lord, author of *Forever Barbie: The Unauthorized Biography of a Real Doll*, wrote, 'Lilli isn't just a symbol of sex, she is a symbol of illicit sex.' Vitally, though, this doll had the grown-up physical characteristics Ruth had envisaged for her doll – long legs, a tiny waist, a bust.

Back in California, Ruth had to overcome the resistance of engineers ('too expensive to produce'), advertising men ('too sexy') and of other insider sceptics (she had never designed a toy). For economy, Barbie was manufactured in Japan out of injection-moulded vinyl. Charlotte Johnson, a fashion designer, worked with a Japanese stylist to develop clothes that minimized the sewing process, then contracted to Japanese housewives. Finally, after three years, Ruth's doll was launched at the 1959 New York Toy Fair, named Barbie (after the Handlers' daughter) and labelled 'Barbie Teenage Fashion Model'. The source was unmistakable: like Lilli, there was overstated make-up, exaggerated shape and a ponytail – but, unlike the German doll, no nipples. (Ken, introduced later as Barbie's boyfriend and named after the

Handlers' son, is similarly desexed, his genitals a mere bump under his briefs.)

The new doll was totally out of sync with the sought-after toys of that year – large plastic playthings like Ideal Toys' Mr Machine. Buyers hated it. They found Barbie's breasts particularly disturbing; no doll had looked like this before. Sears, the key toy-buying company of the time, would not place an order at all. The minority who did order bought small. Market research proved disappointing: mothers hated the doll too. She had 'too much of a figure'. Mattel lowered its sales projections of 20,000 dolls a week and 40,000 clothing items, and cut factory orders. But one finding in the research had been underestimated – no matter what mothers thought, their daughters loved the doll. And soon they began to make their wants known.

By the end of the year over 350,000 Barbies had been sold. Mattel needed a department just to deal with Barbie's 20,000 letters a week. As a result of her success, Mattel went public in 1960, its shares selling at $10. A decade later those same shares topped $500. By 1963 Mattel was on the *Fortune* list of the 500 largest US companies. Ruth's genius was not just that she had sensed an unrealized and therefore un-exploited gap, but that what she created was a merchandiser's dream. It allowed girls to be part of the new world of fashion that had emerged after the shortages of World War II, beginning as couture and then filtering out to department stores. It was always part of Ruth's philosophy that Barbie could be what-ever her owner wanted, that she had no predetermined personality. In crude marketing terms, this opened the way to scores of play accessories and clothes, each a money earner. And, as girls might want to project themselves differently in different moods, there was room for more than one Barbie in each girl's life – the average American girl, it was later estimated, owns ten. (Only one Ken, though: for most of his life he has been regarded as an accessory.)

'You get hooked on the doll, and then you buy the rest,' acknowledged Elliott Handler. 'I know a lot of parents hate us for this, but it's going to be around a long time.'

Barbie's – and Mattel's – life has been turbulent. At the end of the day Mattel's genius has always been its ability to reinvigorate its biggest earner. By the 1980s Barbie, although still a mainstay of the business, was looking passé. Mattel, hit by the failure of its diversification tactics, faced bankruptcy. Another woman entered Barbie's life – and saved both doll and company. Jill Barad joined Mattel as a product manager in 1981. Her starting salary was $38,000 a year; she was later to become arguably the highest-paid woman in the world. She earned a reputation for being as tough within Mattel as she proved in dealing with competitors. A past colleague described her to me as 'a killer – and that's the kindest thing you can say'. Her former boss, Judy Shackelford, Mattel's first female vice-president, told *Business Week*, 'It's a shark pond. You throw people in and see if they can swim fast enough to stay alive. For Jill, it was a fit.'

Reincarnated under Barad, Barbie entered a golden age. Her earnings soared from $200 million to $1.9 billion. Barbies were segmented, sold for a variety of different play patterns. Day to Night Barbie – executive and party girl – led the way. Instead of three new dolls a year there were now dozens, all accessorized. Barbie, who had enraged feminists for encouraging girls to regard themselves as mannequins, sex objects or housekeepers, was now presented as a symbol of female empowerment with an advertising campaign, 'We Girls Can Do Anything'.

In 1997, the year Barad became CEO, she earned a remuneration package of $26.3 million, had the building repainted in bright colours and, extending both arms, told the company's 25,000 employees on video, 'I love you all.' Throughout nearly two decades, she became synonymous with her product. She dressed in Barbie-pink suits and signature high heels. Her Bel Air mansion fittingly displayed a six-foot model of Barbie by the stairs and an Andy Warhol painting of the doll. Her 'anything is possible' philosophy might have been Barbie's. Something her mother had said had made an impression on her. 'She told me, "Aerodynamically, bees shouldn't be able to fly. But they do!"'

Barbie's ability to adapt, to be contemporary, depends on an intelligence machine that would have chilled George Orwell's blood. Insiders boast of its size and scope, its ability to feed exclusive information. Teams of research scientists take a constant flow of data collected internally and brought in from third parties and manipulate it with sophisticated software. There are sales figures, trend and demographic information from five or more market-research companies, interviews in malls, anecdotal material culled from buyers about the competition, and material gathered from websites. There is a mass of 'psychographic' data about girls of different ages, how they play, their hobbies, the television programmes, music and clothes they like, their favourite singers. The data pours in from focus groups worldwide, including Mattel's own test centre where children are observed through one-way mirrors. Mattel researchers visit children's homes to watch girls play. Barbie's position in a room is noted. On the bed or on the floor next to dolls' clothes is good: the first indicates love, the second active play. Out of the way on a shelf, unless it is a Collector Barbie, is bad – this Barbie isn't played with any more. For years research persuaded Mattel not to try to update the notorious Ken, outdated though he might look. Young girls found a more contemporary Ken too scary – they wanted him clean-cut, unthreatening, more like dad.[7] Barbie designers videotape girls' birthday parties and what they shoot is examined and analysed.

And Barbie has altered over the years – her looks, lifestyle, jobs and fashions. The first Barbies had a sidelong glance, a closed mouth, what Mattel calls 'a little more mysterious' look. Later she became more youthful, outdoorsy, carefree, smiling; later still there was a big grin, very bright eyes, lots of blue eye make-up, big hair. The ponytails gave way to bubble cuts and pageboy hairstyles. Barbie started as a model and over the years has had more than ninety careers. She has been fashion editor, ballerina, stewardess, astronaut, doctor, nurse and veterinary surgeon. Her other careers have included those of palaeontologist, firefighter, Marine Corps sergeant, concert pianist, aerobics instructor, rock star, fashion designer. She has run for President three times and competed in the Olympics. Barbies have been Italian, Parisian, British Royal, Eskimo, Japanese, Korean, Jamaican, Native American . . . Her clothes have been designed by many great names: Armani, Givenchy, Calvin Klein, Donna Karan, Christian Dior, Ralph Lauren, Gianni Versace, Bill Blass, Vivienne Westwood. After the Beatles invasion she adopted the Carnaby Street look, then

[7] In 2006, to coincide with Toy Fair and as perhaps another sign of Mattel's desperation to keep pace, Ken finally did emerge with a new look, made over by Hollywood stylist Phillip Bloch to be 'more arm candy'.

went mod. She took on the 'prairie' look, and the glittery styles of the disco years. Her varied wardrobe is such, says Ivy Ross, that 'we're bigger than any garment maker in the world.' All in all, 92 per cent of Barbie dolls are designed new every single year. 'We're not in the business where you carry over last year's Barbie,' says Ms Ross. It is like fashion: 'You wouldn't have the same slacks of that colour sitting in Macy's for more than a season.'

Barbie's family and friends have been developed – and exploited. Mattel helpfully has a Barbie Family Tree, listing them all with a separate column for pets, including several (named) horses, dogs, and kittens. (There have been failures. Barbie's little sister Skipper was engineered so that when her arm was twisted she grew breasts. Later Barbie's best friend Midge came pregnant with a protruding rounded belly; when this was lifted off, a baby dropped out. Pregnant Midges were not universally welcomed – a Wal-Mart pulled them off the shelves after complaints.)

By the time Jill Barad went, the world around Barbie was shifting faster than ever. 'She reinvents herself over and over again,' says Julia Jensen, director of public relations for Barbie. Wasn't she, at heart, still the same old plastic princess . . . ?

Meanwhile, Isaac Larian was also contemplating dolls. After emigrating from Iran to Los Angeles in 1971 at the age of seventeen with $750 in his pocket, Larian washed dishes at a diner and eventually earned a civil engineering degree from California State University. After college he started a company importing consumer electronics, and in 1987 scored big with a line of hand-held games featuring characters licensed from Nintendo Corp. The company, which had started as ABC International Tradings, became Microgames of

America, and then later simply MGA Entertainment. It developed its first doll, Singing Bouncy Baby, in 1997. Bounced, the doll sang, squeezed, it giggled. Larian says it sold 1 million pieces.

My Dream Baby, introduced in 2000, was interactive, grew from infant to toddler, learned to crawl and walk, to speak, sing and play games. The price was a hefty $99.99. The following year, it morphed into a scaled-down version called Toddler Tabitha. Whatever their success, none had that Wow factor. They certainly had nothing to worry about over at Mattel.

Exactly how Bratz was born runs to a number of versions. Some are no doubt the stuff of attorney conferences. Larian told *License! Europe* that it all started when a Wal-Mart buyer told him that if he could bring in a doll that would compete with Barbie, he would take it. 'Finally a designer came up with the Bratz look. We tested it and found it worked.' The story Larian told me was: 'One inventor showed us sketches of what are Bratz dolls now, in the September or October of 2000 and I felt in my gut it was a good thing.' The name of Carter Bryant, a former Mattel designer, features several times. 'In 2000 . . . Bryant walked into his California office with a drawing of a Bratz doll . . . Larian commissioned a prototype . . .' (In April 2004, Mattel filed a lawsuit in Los Angeles County Superior Court alleging that Bryant 'aided and assisted' MGA while he was employed by Mattel. Bryant asserted counterclaims, in some of which he sought to invalidate Mattel's Confidential Information and Propriety Inventions Agreements with its employees. The battle took a new and spectacular twist in November 2006 when Mattel filed documents with the US District Court in California arguing that Bratz dolls rightfully belonged to them, an argument based in part on its allegation that Bratz's designer did initial drawings for the doll while employed by Mattel. The lawsuit claimed that 'Emboldened by the success of its illegal conduct, MGA had repeated – even expanded – its pattern of theft on numerous occasions.' Larian told the *Wall Street Journal* that the claims were 'a bunch of nonsense', and added, 'The last time I checked, it was not illegal for people to leave one company to go to a better company for a better job.') According to the London *Times*, it all began with Paula Treantafelles, a product designer who moved from Mattel to MGA in 1999. 'Executives moaned that girls were getting older faster, so they couldn't be blamed for Barbie's diminishing age profile. I didn't agree. I'd heard about this crazy Iranian guy who could challenge their taboos. So I came here.' Within six months, she had brought Larian her idea of a fashion doll targeted at seven- to ten-year-olds. The name Bratz was suggested by Carter Bryant, who provided initial drawings.

One thing is beyond dispute: Larian liked what he saw. 'It was different . . . it was about fashion. Actually that day my daughter Yasmin who was ten years old at that time – one of the dolls is named after her – was here, so you know I asked what do you think? And you could see the sparkle in her eyes and she said, "Dad, this is really good." Always I've found kids are very honest. You know, if they don't like something they tell you, "Oh it's crap." So I said, Let's take a risk, let's go.'

Mattel's intelligence machine had long been picking up signs that older girls were losing interest in traditional Barbie. It was the toy industry's great dread: the KGOY – kids getting older younger – syndrome, in Barbie's case writ large. In the sixties and seventies girls played with Barbie until their early teens. Now her core fans were aged from three to six. It was extra frightening that the group abandoning Barbie was such a key one in marketing terms. Not long ago, the youth market divided neatly into twelve-and-under and teens. From the mid 1990s, the famous tweens emerged (a vague term, but generally defined as seven to twelve), and have been increasingly coveted. Tweens are valuable because of their own spending power – they control $1.7 billion of their own money. But beyond this is their influence on what others buy, and their own future buying: brand loyalties that will last all their lives are formed now. Two thirds of tweens live in single-parent or two-parent working households, which means they often take crucial household decisions themselves. It is a group that has grown up with MTV, computers and electronic gadgets. Some claim they are cynical; they are certainly media-savvy. But they are also young and impressionable, greatly influenced by their peers, tele-vision, music and fashion. Their attention span is short, their desire for topicality constant. In the mid nineties, a trend could last three years; a decade later, it was down to months, a year tops. And as tweens have become ever more sophisticated consumers, they have become harder for the toy industry to attract.

Mattel knew Barbie was in urgent need of a major revamp, and pulled in Ivy Ross to head up this project. She grew up with design; her father designed the Studebaker Hawk; she herself has created products from handbags to watches to jewellery (her work is in several major museums). She was just settling at Calvin Klein as president of the men's accessory division when she got a call inviting her to make Barbie a modern woman. 'Literally my heart began to pound. I played with Barbie when I was a kid and I know exactly what she did for me.'

Sipping tea in her green-carpeted office with Collector Barbies regarding us from the shelves, Ivy Ross is immediately likeable. Animated in tight trousers, slashed black velvet shirt and drop earrings, she explains how she took the job and 'arrived with two suitcases'. Once in Mattel's long white design-centre building, she found fifty Barbie designers all working on their own, almost competitively. 'People would design in a vacuum and they'd kind of come out when it was done and present their idea of the doll ... And we'd recover their designs at night ... they were very possessive.' She set out to change the culture, make it more co-operative, more conscious of outside influences. 'It was a sort of like mind flash: what were modern women doing, aspiring to do, today?' Before new Barbie dolls were started, collages were regularly put together from girls' magazines to show what they were seeing and reading, what their influences were. 'I mean [once] you had long periods of time when French couture clothing was what people aspired to for ten years. Now what they aspire to this month could be different two months from now.' Barbie's body shape changed. 'My mind immediately went, oh my God the poor doll can't even do yoga, she's not designed to even bend.' Barbie also grew wider hips, a thicker waist and smaller breasts, to better display midriff-baring fashions like crop tops and hipster pants. Her look became what Mattel called 'more subtle' with a less toothy grin, no more bright aqua-blue eye make-up. The new millennium Barbie came with softer pink packaging, and hot fashions like knit tops and bootleg pants, activity sets that allowed girls to create their own lipgloss and nail hues. She had hi-tech products like a scrapbook with talking stickers and voice-activated locks, and a compact that allowed users to record a secret message. Mattel trumpeted its updated creation: 'The Barbie doll has done it again, she's reinvented herself to fit with the fast-paced, ultra-modern world of girls today. There's no mistaking Barbie for last millennium's doll . . . the line has a fresh feel to secure at least four more decades on top.'

Mattel might have come up with a reinvention, but in North Hills, Larian was mounting a coup. His new doll went into prototype. Although a gambler, Larian is a great believer in consulting kids and focus groups. 'I can't make decisions for eleven- or twelve-year-olds. I didn't have many toys when I was a kid, my wife says you're living your childhood. Maybe I am. I communicate with children very well, and sometimes it's hard for adults to do that. I bring myself to their level, I'm like a four-year-old kid. I listen to them. They will always tell you the truth because their mind has not been poisoned yet.' He says if kids don't like a product, he will drop it no matter what designers and buyers say. This time his gut reaction was confirmed. What the girls saw was a lavishly made-up doll with a bored expression, its eyes heavy-lidded and larded with colour. The lips were bee-stung, the body curvaceous. Oversized heads were emphasized by the skinniness of the rest of the body. The clothes were skimpy, ultra-fashionable, perched over pert little bottoms. Next to his doll he put Barbie and then asked what Barbie reminded them of. 'Our mothers, they replied.'

It was not the first time Larian had been convinced he had a major winner. He'd tried Magic Touch Ponies – when they were brushed, electronics lit up their eyes or set them galloping. Only they didn't sell. Larian claims he lost millions. The amount he was gambling on Bratz was even greater: $5 million 'just to get it out of the gate – the tooling alone was about a million dollars.' Within three months samples were ready in Hong Kong. He launched Bratz in Spain where sales were good. 'Then we put it in the USA in August and we thought it was gonna be huge by September.' Sales were not great. Those early days, he says, were a 'big-time' struggle. He toured buyers. 'I was persuading them, begging: "Please, this is good, I believe in it, give me one chance, if you don't sell it, I'll take it back." It's a hard thing, selling, and you get rejected every time. I have learned, I don't take no for an answer, I'm very persistent. Buyers have thrown me out of their office and I have come back the next day. They say, "Didn't I throw you out the door yesterday?" I say, yes you did, but . . .' Toys R Us cancelled a large order. 'I remember thinking, "Oh shit! Here we go again, another Magic Touch Pony, we're gonna go out!" But we had done so well in focus-group studies and the kids really liked it . . . so we kept on the TV advertisement and pushed it more, and three weeks later . . . boom! All of a sudden it was like horses coming out of the gate! Toys R Us had cancelled by the middle of September and by, I think, the end of September, early October they came back and they wanted to buy all of those back and more, and by end of December it was the number-one-selling fashion doll in the industry and it's been there since then.'

On the surface, life for Barbie was looking good as the new century opened. *Barbie in the Nutcracker* was the first of a series of videos. Even if sales were down domestically, international markets showed double-digit sales growth. In the words of M.G. Lord, Barbie's unauthorized biographer, 'Barbie's challengers do not tend to last long.' They had all been 'systematically annihilated'. An early casualty was Miss Seventeen, from Marx Toys. Louis Marx had acquired rights to the Lilli doll and sued Mattel for patent infringement, claiming they had copied her and perpetuated a fraud by leading the public to believe Barbie was an original product. The suit was unsuccessful. Britain's big challenger, Sindy ('the doll you love to dress'), brought out the Mattel cavalry after Hasbro acquired the manufacturing rights from Pedigree Toys, updated her look and packaged her in Barbie pink. Legal battles raged in country after country, from Belgium to Australia. Finally, Hasbro dropped the pink and agreed to give Sindy a different head, one cleared with Mattel. (In 1996 Sindy left Hasbro and two years later became a Vivid Imaginations product.)

Dolls offering something new and attention-grabbing have often found themselves confronted with a fresh Barbie, featuring those same features backed by all Mattel's clout. They trashed Hasbro's blonde, busty Miss America doll by introducing American Beauty Queen Barbie. Likewise, Tyco Toys' Little Mermaid doll initially skyrocketed, but eventually sank under a shoal of mermaid Barbies. Hasbro's Jem, in 1986, was a rock-star fashion doll, and for a time looked like a very serious threat. She was launched complete with television show, books, posters, T-shirts and tape recorder. Mattel struck back with an MTV version, Barbie and the Rockers, and outgunned its opponent with superior marketing power and faster to-store shipping.

Underpinning Barbie's triumph over rivals has been Ruth Handler's original brilliant decision that the doll should be a blank canvas for a girl to make her whatever she wants. 'She isn't anything in particular, so she becomes a vehicle for their dreams, their aspirations, their frustrations – their dress rehearsal for everyday life,' says Ivy Ross. 'Even when she's in a new movie,

Barbie acts Rapunzel, it's not Barbie *as* Rapunzel.' And here, she believes, lies Barbie's secret. Hasbro's Jem, for example, failed because she was presented as a rock star. 'That's all she was and you can't backtrack. They play with her only when they want a rock star. With Barbie you just buy the rock-star fashion.' It is a fundamental mistake of their competitors, she says, that they produce dolls with such fixed roles. 'It's too narrow a focus.'

Barbie has always been discussed within Mattel as though she were a living being.[8] 'We all sit around and do this exercise about if she was a person,' Ross and PR Director Julia Jensen tell me. 'How would she be emotionally, would she have problems?' Her personality and core values are preserved with extreme vigilance. There are strict limits as to what Mattel will allow her to do or to be. 'When she ran for President, there were very serious dialogues. We realize the responsibility that comes with it when we put her in these roles. Is it right for her?' Ross insists this 'is not weird, it's empowering. I recognize it's toys so there's something fun and light-hearted about it, but this particular toy comes infused with a lot of baggage because it is an iconic symbol.'

And icons, it seems, get the storybooks rewritten. Barbie can never be the traditional damsel in distress – she has to be involved with her own rescue. This is also reflected in her clothes. 'A confident woman knows exactly what she should wear,' opines Ms Ross. 'We carry this line we use in training, *Barbie's unapologetically all girl*. That's where the confidence comes from. She is not going to apologize about being

[8] In commercials, she is always portrayed as a person. An early copywriter Cy Schneider has said, 'We never mentioned the fact that she was a doll.'

a woman, being a girl. If high-heeled shoes are in, she's going to be wearing them.'

These core Barbie qualities must endure: therein lies her strength. But they are also her weakness. How, at a time of fast and drastic cultural shifts, can you alter Barbie dramatically without losing all those qualities that make her not only all girl but also uniquely great?

Larian had no such problem. From the start, Bratz was aimed firmly at the seven- to twelve-year-old-girl market, Barbie's deserters. And he succeeded where Mattel and Barbie had failed – he got tweens to play with dolls. After the initial struggles, Bratz quickly became one of the best-selling toys in the United States. Before Bratz in 2001, Mattel was estimated to have about 90 per cent of the US fashion-dolls market. Within three years it was down to 70 per cent. In the UK, marketed by Vivid Imaginations, Bratz accounted for 4 per cent of all toy purchases by Christmas 2004. 'Other toy brands have been trying for thirty years to topple this iconic grand dame,' enthused Vivid's CEO Nick Austin, 'and now her throne has finally been taken.' Larian, delighting in his triumph, volunteers his explanation: 'It's the look in the eyes of each doll: go to China and take a look at the face-painting – it takes sixteen layers by hand. And the kids are attracted to that, the amount of detail in the clothing, the fashion. It is what the girls want and we're giving it to them.' Another selling point is that the dolls are multi-ethnic. 'You could be in South America and look at Yasmin and say, OK it's a South American girl, or you could be in the Middle East and you could say, Oh she's from the Middle East. But she's the same one. We decided at the beginning the key thing was to keep the characters ambiguous. Not everybody is blonde, 6-foot, 2-inches and has perfect proportions: we're gonna make these dolls multiracial, mix and match, that's the way society is. It was a risky decision because a lot of retailers are gonna say, Oh, African American dolls do not sell in our store or Hispanic dolls do not sell in our store. It took us two years to convince everybody.'

This time around, it took more than a year for Mattel to hit back. It conducted a global, ethnographic research project, designed to understand how girls at different ages spent every minute of the day. It emerged that the same qualities that made Barbie appealing to three- to six-year-olds also made her unappealing to older girls. The play patterns of younger girls and tweens are very different. Preschoolers are discovering the world and want fantasy, tweens are trying to determine who they are and desire more realistic play that reflects their increasing social interaction and their concerns. The result was My Scene, a sort of anti-Barbie Barbie doll line, all with exotic faces, pouty lips, oversized eyes and edgy wardrobes. The commercials had urban settings, storylines concentrated on shopping, dating, music and fashion, and were shown on networks like MTV, Teen Nick and WB, rather than during Saturday morning cartoon shows. 'Think *Sex and the City* without the sex,' commented the *New York Times* ad columnist. Richard Dickson, Barbie's licensing supremo, claimed they were inspired by illustrations used to sell licensed merchandise which showed Barbie with a larger head, sulky expression and a hip, city attitude. Larian dismissed them as 'a cheap knock-off' of Bratz. *Business Week* noted they were 'dressed suspiciously like those of street-savvy Bratz'.

The hope was that girls would 'graduate' to My Scene at six-plus (but no earlier: Mattel doesn't want to cannibalize its main doll). That way Barbie would keep younger and older girls. 'Now that these girls are growing up quicker, an older sister won't play with the same thing their younger sister is playing with,' says Ivy Ross. 'Yet they all love Barbie. We were finding out that they were really closet Barbie fans. At nine and ten they didn't want to admit that they were still playing with Barbies . . . In some of the in-home research we have videotapes of girls going, OK fine, come to my room. They pull out these dolls and say, I only bring these out when I'm alone or playing with my baby sister. They're just beautifully maintained so you can tell an older girl is caring for her. We realized a seven-to eight-year-old is never going to play with what a four- to five-year-old plays with because that's baby.' Yes, says Julia Jensen, 'We had to give them something to graduate to, a reason to come out of the closet.'

Ironically, a rethink for the Barbie range seemed to fly in the face of the wisdom that had made Barbie such an enduring success over the years – which in itself suggests an element of desperation. Mattel insisted they turned product development and marketing processes upside down. Now 'the Barbie world will come to life through storytelling,' raved Matthew W. Bousquette, president of Mattel Brands. Different lines of Barbies would inhabit themed worlds. Russell Arons, vice-president of marketing, enthused, 'We're going to write a story first, then see what products naturally evolve from this story.'

Mattel's attempts to retaliate led to a spectacular flop. Tattooed, hip-hop-styled Flavas were introduced in 2003 complete with exposed midriffs, bling bling, baggy pants and a cardboard cut-out wall with graffiti. Flavas – meaning 'personal style' – were again aimed at the seven-to-twelve group. Mattel was convinced they had caught the moment – hip-hop had moved into the daily consciousness of the tween generation.

Critics thought the dolls too edgy, too bad-girl. On the Web, an anonymous poster asked, 'What the hell is Mattel smoking? . . . my little sister better not ask for one of these dolls.' Isaac Larian, never one to pass up a good shot, commented, 'The only thing missing is a cocaine vial.' Critics were right. Flavas were discontinued within the year.

As rivals, Bratz and Barbie have at least three characteristics in common. Their makers see them less as dolls than as the centre of lifestyle merchandising. They excite controversy, especially over their role in the premature sexualization of young girls. And their companies are utterly ruthless about protecting and defending their billion-dollar properties.

'Lifestyle merchandising' means Barbie and Bratz exist at the centre of two vast global empires with products ranging from picture frames to bedding, digital cameras to cosmetics, designer clothes to sports goods. Both Mattel and MGA have extended their franchises into music, movies and DVD. The sums involved are vast: Barbie licensed goods in 2004 were unofficially estimated to generate $2.2–$2.4 billion sales at retail.

In a corner office with two glass walls on the Pink Floor of the Mattel HQ building, Richard Dickson keeps a tight rein on the Barbie licensing empire. Stylish in a black sweater, he was brought in to overhaul the machine. It meant some blood on the carpet: he mentions in a gentle voice that 'we had a lot of people who are, unfortunately, not with us.' Under him, business has doubled. Previously, Mattel simply reacted to requests for licences. Now there are over 800 licensees around the world and an overall, proactive global strategy in over thirty categories. 'For instance, Barbie has the perfect name and heritage to be a fashion brand. So what does that really mean?' He takes a sip from his bottle of mineral water, and explains why Mattel has pursued fashion tie-ups: data from fifty-five countries show that tweens spend their money on what Dickson terms 'apparel and accessories'. Consequently, this has become bigger than the toy category. Hard work has had its reward. 'We now rank as the number 1 apparel brand in some countries. It's a very big piece of our business. Probably exceeding, at this point, 400 million dollars.' He flourishes a paint-fresh sample, a bathing suit by the trendy Brazilian designer Rosa Cha.

Dickson straightens his leather jacket, considering the balancing act in which he is constantly engaged. 'Licensed product can enhance the doll and the over-all brand image, assist in difficult times and some would say ride the wave in good times.' But licensing, while lucrative, 'is also a potentially dangerous endeavour. There's a very fine line of oversaturation and destroying the halo effect if done improperly.' Hence the tough control. Some areas have been dropped – food products, it was decided, diluted the doll's fashion image – and others pushed: a limited-edition lithograph of Barbie in evening dress (think 1950s fashion sketches), elaborately framed, signed and numbered, costs $200.

Mattel runs Barbie licences with missionary zeal. It controls not only the look and feel of products that carry the famous name but also the marketing. Richard Dickson arrived to find '700 licensees around the world, all advertising, promoting, doing special events with their own perspective, interpreting the brand image without the proper tools. Imagine.' He put a stop to that. 'So we basically set the rules of engage-ment and now have everything funnelled through our creative office, so that no matter what country you are in, no matter where you land, if you see a Barbie ad or a Barbie product it is consistent around the globe . . . Now there's a feel to everything we do that is so consistent and powerful that the perception is that we spend millions on advertising when all we really do is control the creative of our licensees . . . If you looked at my sales at a billion two and then took 15 per cent of that, it's a pretty significant number being spent by the licensees on advertising, so you have over 100 million dollars in additional brand impression on top of what Mattel spends.'

So say I've got a licence, what do I have to clear with Mattel? 'The product interpretation, the communications of the brand on all levels. If you're communicating to the trade or the consumer, to the retailer or the salespeople, all the materials need to feel branded consistently. The speak also needs to be consistent – what are the inherent messages when dealing with Barbie? Fashion, Fun, Friendship. Friendship is a big part of a little girl's life between three and eight years old, so fun, fashion and friendship become key traits and words that we use throughout everything we do.' In practice it means a licensee – especially a new one – must submit everything for approval 'to make sure that you're up to speed with our expectations. After a series of successful events we probably will become more lenient because there's already a learning process you've gone through that allows us to give you more flexibility.' But the indoctrination goes further yet. 'We put your item in a melting pot with what is happening around the world, around the country, around the category with the brand. Because in isolation a licensee doesn't know what is going on in the macro format of the brand, whereas we can see everything everyone is doing and then in some cases synergize people. We can say, "Oh my goodness, do the backpack people know that the shoe people are doing an event that same week? If we put them together and provide merchandising we can make a much bigger event." So we pull all this information together to keep the brand consistent from a creative perspective, and from a business perspective the information is powerful because we're able to then feed back out ways to either maximize that event, expand on that event, or just acknowledge the event with – there's an event!'

Successful licensing grabs a girl very young and holds onto her. Julia Jensen enthuses, 'You look at a little girl like she's three years old, she loves Barbie, she's playing with fantasy dolls. She gets a little older, she's five or six and she's playing with fashion dolls now, and all of a sudden she's going to first grade. She can't bring her Barbie because that feels kinda weird, like "people will think that I'm little", there's all kinds of stigma attached, but she can carry her Barbie back-pack. So there's this emotional connection to her best friend: Barbie is going to school with her. A lot of what we see is that girls will still play with the doll at home, but in the outer world it's the Barbie T-shirt, it's the backpack, it's the hand-held game . . . It's like a brand that's gonna hold them together.'

How far can you keep going – to what age group? Dickson tells me he thinks the Barbie name can be used to sell products well into adulthood, say forty-five. He claims Barbie is the first designer name a little girl knows. Not all find this so commendable. Commenting on a Julien Macdonald Barbie-branded designer range for girls, the *Financial Times* wrote, 'Mattel is behaving like a distiller that markets a limited-edition fifty-year-old whisky in the hope that the glamour rubs off on the cheaper blend drunk by the masses. This strategy may be fine when aimed at middle-aged drinkers, but is it right to encourage children to want products that in the vast majority of cases, neither they nor their parents can afford?' A fashion collection for adult women debuted first in Japan where Mattel has stand-alone stores. Globally, Mattel teamed up with the Italian clothing company to create a Barbie loves Benetton line with an introductory fifty garments and accessories.

Barbie's role as a doll representing woman as sexual object has been supplanted by Bratz. (Interestingly, mothers whose own mothers squirmed at Barbie's impossible shape now see her as the traditional safe doll.) Bratz is the doll of the Britney Spears generation, with her skimpy clothes, thick make-up, and crazes for boys and fashion. The spin-offs reinforce it: *The Bratz Superstyling Funktivity Book* for six-year-olds has 'luscious lip tips', 'design your own sexy skirt', and 'tips on being an irresistible flirt'. An advocacy group, Stop Commercial Exploitation of Children, protested outside Toy Fair in New York about the 'heavily sexualized' Bratz dolls 'at the forefront of a toy trend for girls that promotes stereotyped and sexualized behaviors that children cannot understand. They make the way bodies look a focus of play . . .'

Logan Bromer, writing in the college newspaper the *Cornell Daily Sun,* described her shock at coming across Bratz in the toy aisles of Target. 'I was, to say the least, disturbed by the fact that this is the most popular doll on the market for 9-12-year-old girls.' Saying she does 'not consider myself conservative', she added, 'There is clearly a fundamental problem with young girls playing with dolls who are sluts. What next? Bratz Frat Party, with girls being date-raped? Whatever happened to innocence? Barbie may have led girls to have harmful body images but she didn't show them how to sell their bodies.' 'The Bratz doll toy package trumpets proudly: Toy of the Year,' said an editorial in *The Times Herald-Record*, Middleton, NY. 'Chosen by whom? *Penthouse*?' Lauren Beckham Falcone, in the *Boston Herald*, felt the same way. 'Is it me, or does the doll section at Toys R Us resemble the Friday night stripper lineup at the Foxy Lady? . . . Plus the accessories look like a pimp's laundry list . . . I understand dolls are fantasy play for kids, and I know fashion dolls have always been a bit controversial – well, at least since Gloria Steinem came along. But when girls have their whole lives to play with this kind of fire, why give them the matches now?'

Syndicated columnist Froma Harrop calls Bratz dolls 'brazen', 'trampy', and 'appalling'. Patricia Leavey, a sociologist specializing in gender issues at Stonehill College in Easton, Mass., finds them repugnant and hypersexual. New York psychologist Dr Sheena Hankin dislikes the cultural trend of earlier sexualization of little girls. 'Overexposure to sexuality at a young age can lead to sexual dysfunction later in life.' Robert Verdi, senior correspondent for the *Full Frontal Fashion* television show, commented on Yasmin, 'Slutty, that's the only word for it.' Teens and twenty-year-olds in a class at New York's Fashion Institute of Technology were reportedly shocked by the doll's see-through thong underwear. One student said, 'If kids are really playing with this I would be concerned.'

It is all part of the sexualizing of younger target groups for marketing reasons. Always a selling instrument, sex is now aimed firmly at tweens. It is meant to make them feel older, more empowered, more likely to demand successfully what they want. Toys are not the only villains. The bombardment also comes from the wide range of industries so cleverly linked to them: clothes, video games, music. At its extreme, there is racy clothing, make-up, lingerie – bras for girls who don't need them, thongs (in the UK) for ten-year-olds with the image of a cherry and the words 'Eat Me' on the front. As one Canadian columnist put it, 'Innocent six-year-olds are not as profitable as sophisticated ones.' Small children are being cultivated to be consumers and to be consumed.

Unsurprisingly, no one will admit to this strategy. Larian, of course, disagrees – and, no doubt, relishes the publicity: 'Children are growing up faster than ever, but I just don't agree that my dolls are so "sexualized" . . . This is not to do with sex, believe me. And it will not be as long as I am in control of my company. This is about giving children what they want.' He says of complaints from mothers about the clothes, 'That's the fight I always have with my wife.' But their disapproval is the reason for Bratz's great success. Kids are 'little rebels. If mom doesn't like something, then they like it.' And, 'You know, it's always adults who make these claims about sexualization. Ask the kids, and they say they don't like Bratz because they're sexy but because they're fashionable.' He is not alone in his protestations. Mattel has a Barbie perfume for young girls. Denying that it would project an adult sensuality onto children, Richard Dickson told the *Financial Times* that Mattel was trying 'to help girls discover their sense of smell'.

Some countries have reacted to the sexy figurines with real anger. Barbie is banned in Saudi Arabia where the religious police declare her a threat to morality. 'Jewish Barbie dolls, with their revealing clothes and shameful postures, accessories and tools are a symbol of decadence to the perverted West', shouts a poster. In Cairo officials at the Arab League have headed efforts to create local dolls to oust Barbie. Dr Abla Ibrahiem explained, 'Barbie wears a bikini and drinks champagne. We need to prevent our children from feeling torn between their Arab traditions and the lifestyle that Barbie represents.' In Iran, the grandly titled Institute for the Intellectual Development of Children and Young Adults, a government agency affiliated with the Ministry of Education, developed two Muslim dolls, Dara and Sara, to compete. Each of the four models of Sara came with a white scarf. A toy seller, Masoumeh Rahimi, told the BBC, 'I think every Barbie doll is more harmful than an American missile.' The Iranians did not leave success entirely to conscience. The new dolls, manufactured in China, were priced at 125,000 rials ($15) compared with 332,000 rials for a genuine Barbie or 25,000 rials for a copy.

Another Arab doll, Fulla, has skirts that fall below the knee and her shoulders are always covered. In the eighteen months after she was conceived in Syria in 2003, she became the biggest-selling doll in the Middle East, complete with several outfits, luggage, and friends. There were also Fulla umbrellas, watches, bicycles, CD players, swimming pools and breakfast cereals. Fawaz Abidin, Fulla brand manager for the parent company, New Boy, said, 'She's not only a sexy lady, but she's honest, loving and caring, and respects her mother and father – things Arab parents would like for their kids.' Like Barbie, Fulla too is made in China, the accessories often in the same factories as Mattel's. She will be allowed to be a teacher or a doctor, but beyond that her life revolves around home and family. Nor will she have any boyfriends.

Religious Jews have produced their own doll, Shimmi. Said to outsell Barbie in ultra-Orthodox areas of Israel, it avoids the biblical prohibition on creating idols by having only four fingers on each hand and a clown's red nose. Instead of the latest fashion, Shimmi wears tzitzit, the fringes on the prayer shawl worn by Orthodox Jews, and a yarmulke. Press his hand, he recites prayers in Hebrew. In Los Angeles, Monica Garcia, a convert to Judaism, built up a (very) small business with a line of modest Barbie clothing she designed and sold on the Web. 'Barbie is a slut,' she said, and her customers 'want a doll that's dressed appropriately'. In Russia, where Barbie dominates the doll market, there have been attempts to ban her on the grounds that she has harmful effects on the minds of young girls. The doll has been accused of awakening sexual impulses in the very young, and encouraging consumerism among Russian infants.

The third characteristic MGA and Mattel share is the ferocity with which they safeguard their golden geese. Mattel has been vicious not only with Barbie's competitors, but in defending her honour – i.e., image. The company has pursued what the *Wall Street Journal* called 'one of the corporate world's most aggressive trademark wars'. Dr Michael Strangelove, a Canadian scholar specializing in corporate power and the Internet, has said, 'The Mattel Corporation exercises almost complete control over the representation of Barbie within mass media systems . . . through the legal system of international copyright and trademark law. Mattel is able to use the threat of lawsuits to control how its symbols are used.' Christian Crumlish, publisher of the e-zine EnterZone, points out that 'As a trademark or copyright, as the intellectual property of a corporate entity, Barbie enjoys better protection against legitimate criticism and inquiry than would a human being.'

Sometimes the 'defence' of Barbie verges on the ludicrous. The Great Lakes Chapter of the Barbie Collectors' Club held an annual fund-raiser called

'Barbie Grants a Wish Weekend' where it sold the dolls in aid of critically ill children. Mattel sent a cease and desist letter, demanding Barbie's name be removed because the event was not officially sanctioned. An Ohio Barbie collector and dealer Paul David wrote in his catalogue that 'if there was an ugly contest, Elizabethan Queen Barbie would definitely win.' He also forgot to put ® on some Barbie photographs and in advertisements. After a long battle with Mattel, he signed an agreement promising future catalogues would only portray Barbie as 'wholesome, friendly, accessible and kind, caring and protecting, cheerful, fun loving, talented and independent'.

Apart from anything it sees as intellectual property infringements, Mattel also pursues what it considers 'libelous or objectionable matter particularly for our target audience of girls 3 to 11'. Two professors delivering a paper on trademark wars to the M.I.T. Communications Forum found over 1,250 items relating to Mattel lawsuits and Barbie in a Google search, 'including sexual appropriations, critical commentary, and creative cultural reworkings of the cultural icon'. There is certainly no shortage of targets for Mattel lawyers. Barbie detractors emerged early, unauthorized Barbie art began to proliferate by the late seventies when the first generation of Barbie owners became adult. Although some artists and commentators were deferential, many used their work to convey their strong views on race, consumer, culture or gender roles. Barbie was lambasted as a sexist role model because of her obsession with looks and her unrealistic measurements. (Finnish researchers claimed in 1994 that a real Barbie would not have enough fat to menstruate. Just what the original doll's measurements represent in real-woman terms has been disputed. One of the most quoted suggestions came from a Yale researcher of the mid nineties in the *International Journal of Eating Disorders*. He claimed that Barbie's measurements projected to human size would make her 38-18-34.) Her original shape probably owed most to the need for her to be a clothes horse for the Paris couture fashions of the day. Barbie, claim detractors, encourages girls to be dissatisfied with their own bodies, causing eating disorders: the 1965 version of Slumber Party Barbie came with a book called *How to Lose Weight* that included the advice 'Don't Eat', and a bathroom scale set permanently at 110 lbs.[9]

Barbie is the woman who has everything and every year receives more. The plastic princess of capitalism, with her cars, houses, pools and clothes, invites attack as a programmer of little consumers. Opponents have created Exorcist Barbie, Drag-queen Barbie, and Sweatshop Barbie. Trailer Trash Barbie, on sale in San Francisco, came with platinum hair revealing black roots, a dangling cigarette and a baby slung on her hip. Big Dyke Barbie displayed a pierced nose. The Web has produced an 'Anti-Barbie Club' ('Let kids be kids and let's be honest about what Mattel really cares about: getting your money!'). There is a 'Mistress Barbie Bitch' site: 'Remember the doll you used to make fun of with your friends, undressing her, pulling off her limbs and head. Now that Barbie doll has come to life . . . Now it's time for HER REVENGE . . . I won't

[9] It should perhaps be noted that in a study reported in the *New Scientist* in 2004, a research team at Jagellionian University, Krakov, who investigated 119 Polish women found that the Barbie shape with large breasts and a small waist was a good one, biologically speaking. Women with these shapes had larger amounts of female hormones and were about three times more likely to get pregnant than women of other shapes.

be happy until I've reduced you to a whimpering mass of jelly.' Her detractors have included the self-styled Barbie Liberation Movement which, memorably, switched voice boxes of Barbie and G.I. Joe in a toy store. The next day G.I. Joe started mouthing, 'Let's go shopping' and Barbie uttered, 'Vengeance is mine'.

In one of its most famous pursuits, Mattel kept after Tom Forsythe for five years in an attempt to stop him publishing photographs of Barbie in ovens, under food mixers and bathing in Martini glasses. Forsythe, a self-taught Utah photographer who produces images with social and political overtones, believes that the dolls instil 'gender-oppressive values' in girls, and said he purposely made some of the images 'overtly sexual to (take) Barbie completely out of (the) context Mattel intends. I thought the pictures needed something that really said crass consumerism and, to me, that's Barbie.' The pictures, amusing yet disturbing, went on display in 1997 although, as the court noted, his 'market success was limited'. Two years later, he received a writ claiming trademark and copyright infringement. Forsythe's case was taken up by the American Civil Liberties Union. Five years later, a federal judge in Los Angeles said Mattel's action was 'groundless' and awarded the artist $1.8 million legal fees. He said the case would be a warning to companies who tried to intimidate individuals for minor copyright infringements. The toy company, wrote Judge Ronald Lew, had access to sophisticated lawyers who could have determined 'that such a suit was objectively unreasonable and frivolous'. Instead, it appeared Mattel 'forced the defendant into costly litigation to discourage him'.

This is not the only case Mattel has lost. It sued MCA Records for a hit record by Dutch band Aqua calling Barbie 'a blond bimbo girl', and Nissan cars for a commercial featuring lookalikes Barbie and Ken. In the MCA case, at issue was the title of the song 'Barbie Girl' along with suggestive lyrics that included Barbie telling Ken, 'You can brush my hair, undress me anywhere . . . you can touch, you can play.' The courts concluded the song's parody was protected speech and that First Amendment protection outweighed Mattel's property interest as a trademark owner. The court's decision ended with the words, 'The parties are advised to chill.'

In Germany, Mattel tried to prevent Simba Toys marketing a doll called Steffi Love. Mattel claimed that the company was exploiting its good reputation, systematically copying its ideas, and misleading consumers. Germany's Federal Court of Justice ruled against Mattel, saying that it was obvious there would be similarities among themed dolls and that the concept of a doll with accessories could not be copyrighted. Mattel also tried to stop a small specialist store in Calgary, with virtually no US sales, using the name Barbie's Shop. Ms Anderson Whalley, always known as Barbie, sold fetish wear and gothic-influenced designs. A Mattel spokeswoman said, 'You have to go after everyone who steps on your trademark.' The shop's owner retorted, 'I was around before Barbie (the doll) was – maybe I should sue them over the name.' To bring an action in the United States, Mattel's private investigator placed an order to have items sent to him in New York. However, a US District Judge in New York finally granted a motion by Ms Anderson Whalley's lawyer to dismiss Mattel's suit, based on a lack of jurisdiction. Apart from paying her lawyer, it cost her $10,000 in legal fees,

Mattel has won other cases. The company sued Barbara and Dan Miller, producers of *Miller's Magazine*. The suit claimed, 'Each issue of this magazine is replete with articles, photographs and captions [of Barbie] which infringe, disparage and/or dilute Mattel's trademarks, copyrights . . .' Supporters claimed the magazine commented on designs and marketing while promoting the doll itself. Challenged at Mattel's annual general meeting, Jill Barad said a photograph showing Barbie with alcohol and pills put the doll in an unflattering light: 'What I do, first and foremost, is protect Barbie.' Mattel proposed an agreement allowing them to review the magazine before it was published. In Mexico, Mattel managed to ban the film *Barbie Gets Sad Too* which was 'spoiling Barbie's image' by depicting her as a lesbian. The threat itself is usually enough for Mattel to triumph: arguing is expensive. Artist Steven K. Smith replied to a Mattel legal letter requesting the removal of satirical material from his internet site. Although he believed he was protected by free speech he said, 'I am not a stupid person. I realize that Mattel has much deeper pockets than I do and do not wish to be involved in a legal battle regardless of the outcome. I have removed the page at your request.'

In Isaac Larian, Mattel seems to have come up against an opponent as bellicose and litigious as itself. A Bratz-themed licensing supplement to the *Hollywood Reporter* included five ads from law firms congratulating Larian. He has clashed with George Lucas over rights to Star Wars hand-held games and won. McDonald's sued MGA after he challenged the company's design for Bratz Happy Meal dolls. That case was settled. Larian also filed a suit against Nordstrom claiming it sold unlicensed Bratz shoes, and he and his brother, Farhad, became engaged in a dispute over the price Farhad received for his stake in MGA.

He made it clear to me he bowed to no one. Talking

about the enormous power of the retail chains that have most toy companies quaking, Larian vowed he would never compromise. He had taken to heart the advice of one of his mentors, Minoru Arakawa, then president/CEO of Nintendo America. In the US, unlike Japan, retailers are far more powerful than manufacturers. Arakawa reasoned that success lies in making the best possible product because if the consumer wants it, then the retailers have to comply. Demand gives the maker the upper hand. 'So this is the formula we use for Bratz – we make products frankly for girls. If they're buying it, then Toys R Us, Wal-Mart, Kmart, have no choice, they have to buy it.'

It was inevitable that Mattel and Larian would square off against each other legally as well as commercially. After Mattel filed a lawsuit against their former designer Carter Bryant in 2004, MGA intervened the same year, asserting that its rights to the Bratz property were at stake in the litigation. The following April, Larian sued Mattel in federal court, accusing the company of unfair competition, intellectual property infringement, and 'serial copycatting'. The suit claimed Mattel's latest Barbie dolls mimicked the look, themes, and packaging of Bratz. It alleged that Mattel had threatened retailers and licensees with retribution if they did business with MGA. And finally, it complained that Mattel tried to lock up the supply of doll hair.

'I am just not going to be pushed around by these big bullies,' Larian has said. *Business Week* commented, 'All of which raises the question: Is Larian the little kid standing up to the bullies in the playground, or has he become the biggest brat in Toyland?' And Thomas P. Conley, president of the Toy Industry Association, has said, 'There's no question that he has had phenomenal success. But he has done it at terrific expense, in terms of people's relationships.'

*   *   *

With the success of Bratz, MGA claimed itself to be 'the fastest-growing entertainment company in the world'. It moved headquarters, but only a short distance to a nondescript office complex adjoining the airfield at Van Nuys. By 2005 it still had only 500 employees, a fraction of Mattell's 25,000. Larian himself comes across as totally unrepentant. 'My philosophy is that we are the Rodney Dangerfield of the toy business – we got no respect . . . We still don't have. A lot of people say, "Oh, he got lucky." I don't care what people say. I just keep on doing it . . . We won People's Choice which is a very important award. The industry did not vote for Bratz.' He laughs. 'But the people who are the main consumers voted for it. The toy industry is very political also. That's the problem with the toy industry frankly, a bunch of people who are sitting there scratching somebody else's back instead of coming up with innovation . . . It needs to get rid of the politicians, it needs to put creative people at the helm of the company, who love toys, who think like children, who are in touch with kids. When Ruth Handler was running Mattel, she loved toys, she and her husband, they loved toys. The biggest issue of the toy industry is that people are afraid to take a risk, they're afraid to be intuitive. It is controlled on the manufacturing side by two or three giant companies who have great resources but they are not willing to innovate and take a risk. I wanna keep this company private because I can do whatever I want, I don't have to answer to anybody and I'm having a lot of fun.[10] Once you become public, then

---

[10] In 2006 came a seeming change of mind as he publicly contemplated an initial public offering on the stock market. At the time of writing, though, no firm plans had materialized.

instead of saying, what is the best toy I'm gonna have in the next three months, your mind goes, oh my god what's gonna happen to the stock price, am I gonna make my numbers? People are driven by different things. I'm content with what I have. My life has not changed since this has become successful. Same house, same car, same school for the kids. I still go to soccer games with my kids, and I am driven to see the happiness in the kids' faces, and driven by the challenge. I'm not so much after the gold part, because I gotta tell you, I've been to many funerals, unfortunately, and every time I go I look very carefully – nobody's taking anything with them.'

He shows me a sign he says he has put up to remind him of his priorities. It reads: 'A hundred years from now it will not matter what my bank account was. The sort of house I lived in. Or the kind of car I drove. But the world may be different because I was important in the life of a child.'

Chapter Five

THE (VICIOUS) BUSINESS OF TOYS

'It's like gambling on the roulette table. You hit one bad item, make one wrong bet, it can wipe you out' – Charlie Woo, toy manufacturer and distributor and unofficial Mayor of the Los Angeles Toy District

We're taking our seats, a sharply barbered brigade of business suits beneath a huge screen filled with the frozen faces of ecstatic kids playing with toys. Before us on long tables, grey logo-embossed notebooks are squared off with military precision; pens wait to be cracked out of their cellophane. Most have already collected mounds of company handout packs, thick as sets of telephone directories, heavy enough to need wheels.

A few of us are locked into cellphone calls – 'I've just got back from Japan, must touch base.' Others are deep into the *Wall Street Journal*, the predominant paper. Most, though, talk, some half secretively in soft whispers ('I know a guy and it's costing him 500 Australian a unit . . .'), others loudly to faces they've just caught halfway across the room. It's obvious that many, maybe the majority, know each other. Mostly we're men, forties and up. The few women, outnumbered twenty to one, tend to be younger. Despite the odd guffaws and the hand-pumping, there's an underlying feeling of intensity. Or maybe it just seems that way to an outsider who knows what the room collectively represents. Billions of dollars of investment money, a great chunk of it in the hands of the guy on my right who just reached for the silver water jug filled with crushed ice, and poured me a drink.

It's eight o'clock on a Monday morning in the ballroom of the Grand Hyatt Hotel in midtown Manhattan. We've drunk our coffee, eaten our fruit and rolls and pastries, and now we are waiting for the nation's biggest toy men to come before us and pitch for money.

Behind most of the hot toys and games and the individuals who invent them is a hard-nosed, corporate-dominated business. It is run by men in suits who worry about the forward price of plastic, the value of the yuan, and whether the quarter's numbers are going to make it for Wall Street. How else, they ask, could toys get produced in such vast quantities, burst on the scene worldwide, or find aisle space in stores at prices people will pay? But what a business it is in its volatility, its dependence on the fickle, shifting whims of children each time a company gambles millions on a new toy. Not least, there is the light-years contrast between the industry's hard, often pitiless pragmatism and the cosy, lovable image of what it's selling. Toys may be cuddly, but the same cannot be said of the industry or some of those who produce them. With risks big, stakes high, wins huge, and failures massive, this is a tough, remorseless world. Sean McGowan, a veteran research analyst specializing in toys, and the man organizing today's conference, obviously loves the business, but has no illusions. 'It's gruelling, there's a lot of false smiling going on, and there's some bad people. There are some really slimy characters who have gone round in this business, unethical, and they cheat or they cut corners, working conditions, up and down the gambit. They steal each other's ideas regularly. It's almost a point of honour.'

Toys has all the features of the harsh modern corporate world in spades. Acquisitions and takeovers? In the hundreds. Layoffs? Constant. Marketing methods where results are the only criteria? Common. Deliver or be fired? Careers crash overnight. In many areas – like selling to kids with no restraint, or in closing plants and shifting production abroad – toys has led the way.

As the investment adviser next to me whispers, 'Whatever else it might be, the toy business is no game.'

Since the 1950s, toys has moved from a cottage industry to a vast worldwide business in which America and American products reign supreme. Once an arena for hundreds of competing manufacturers, the industry is now dominated by a few major companies. Although still sometimes called 'toy makers', they are really toy designing and marketing centres. Economic considerations have shifted large-scale manufacturing abroad, mainly to China. Two companies, Mattel and Hasbro, loom above all. Global enterprises, with their toys as well known in overseas cities as they are in Pittsburg or Santa Monica, the two companies control about a third of the US market; the eight companies below them divide under a fifth of the rest of the business between them. Key for those at the Grand Hyatt today is that most of these major companies – seven of the top ten – are public. As such, they need outside funds. To professional investment managers they are an opportunity to make money.

*　*　*

Two by two – CEOs with CFOs in tow – they take turns at the rostrum. They have different styles: Tom Kalinske, CEO of LeapFrog, makers of educational toys, and a major success story of recent years, now heading toward big problems, sways hypnotically as he tries to whip up enthusiasm. Patrick S. Feely, of Radica Games, producers of lines including Barbie electronic products and Twinkleberries dolls, uses the word 'fun' often without ever losing his perpetually concerned expression. Jody L. Taylor, CFO of RC2 Corporation, scarcely draws breath as she fast-talks. Mattel's Bob Eckert reads from notes, head down as though he has done it a thousand times before, which he probably has. You can see why *Fortune* said, 'Blandness becomes him.'

In the pitches the same words recur: 'strong balance sheet', 'core products', 'proven stability', 'targeted consumers', 'multiple channels of distribution', 'experienced and capable management team', 'repeat purchases'. Jody Taylor sells her company as a 'play' business; for many firms today, as traditional play-things battle electronics, 'toys' has become a four-letter word not to be uttered in Wall Street company. 'Play's bigger than toys,' she enthuses. 'Collectibles is play. And we play all our lives.' Investors remain mostly impassive throughout it all. Expressions stay inscrutable.

The toy business is like no other. Isaac Larian, the man behind Bratz, says, 'Fashion is the closest industry. But we are dealing with children, who are more fickle. Kids are like little aliens, little ants, they speak their own language. If you see ants, they communicate with each other. And these little aliens are telling each other, Pokemon is good today. And then one day, one big ant comes and says, No more Pokemon – and the message goes out and boom! That's the end of it. You have to learn that language.'

Jim Silver, publisher of toy-industry magazines, points out that with new moulds costing between $50,000 and $100,000, 'it costs a lot more to bring a toy to market than it does a T-shirt. The cost of tooling and sculpting, the cost of producing a toy, even just one piece, far exceeds that of producing apparel and most other industries, so there is greater risk and there's the catch-22: you want to produce a great toy but you also have a business to operate.' Charlie Woo, toy manufacturer and distributor and unofficial Mayor of the Los Angeles Toy District, says, 'It's like gambling on the roulette table. You hit one bad item, make one wrong bet, it can wipe you out.' Some liken it to oil where expensive exploration and drilling can turn up a gusher – or a dry hole.

Executives imported from other industries are often shocked when they arrive. Joe Eckroth, Mattel's chief information officer, recalled, 'When I came to Mattel from General Electric, everyone kept saying, "The toy industry is just different." And I would say, "You just *make* it different." ' Within his first year, he realized his mistake. Toy making is incredibly complex. It needs creativity to generate successful toys and practicality to handle huge turnover in the product line. Sales are highly seasonal, making forward planning vital. But so is the ability to adapt fast because of the dependency on fickle kids.

Although America now dominates the world toy market, neither the concentration of corporate power nor the supremacy was always so. The basic living and religious views of colonial America were not sympathetic to toys. But as the nation grew and prospered these factors changed. The rising dominance of railways and steamboats allowed wide distribution and encouraged mass production. The end of the Civil War provided an impetus as the newly created manufacturing industries, suddenly without business, turned to toys. By 1890, as America enjoyed vast wealth, toys boomed. By 1900 there were about 500 toy makers, three times the number shown in the 1880 census.

Even so, the majority of toys – lead, wood, steel and porcelain – still came from Europe, mostly from Germany. From a traditional folk art, their toy making had gradually been transformed into a substantial industry. In the mid nineteenth century German toy makers began to use metal on a large scale. The Lehmann firm had an astonishing clockwork Zeppelin that, propeller turning, flew around the room in circles, suspended from the ceiling.

Only a few American products could challenge these. In 1900, 22-year-old Joshua Lionel Cowen created a battery-powered train to attract attention to products in a store's display window. Lionel Trains began when he discovered customers were more keen on buying the 'advertisement' than the featured merchandise. Edwin Binney and C. Harold Smith produced the first Crayola Crayons, and Dr A. C. Gilbert, former Olympic gold-medallist pole-vaulter, invented the Erector set.

Overall, though, German imports were so cheap that the US could not compete. American toy makers founded the Toy Manufacturers Association of America, a tough campaigning body (since renamed the Toy Industry Association). They successfully lobbied for a 75 per cent tariff on all imports. Meanwhile, World War I and reparations crippled the German toy industry. The US industry continued to expand. The Depression wiped out many companies, but the man who was to father toy mass production, Louis Marx, prospered, buying out toy companies in trouble. Marx, born to German immigrant parents in Brooklyn, had started work in a New Jersey toy factory as a youth. After serving in World War I, he went into business with his brother, dealing between manufacturers and wholesalers. Toy sales were rising and Marx decided to concentrate on an idea that had been growing: low-cost mass production of toys which he would sell in volume. He bought out dies and began jobbing work, gradually building his business. He reintroduced the yo-yo, selling millions. A man with a dominating personality, he built three new plants in the thirties, two in Pennsylvania, one in Virginia. One produced nothing but toy trains, another toy cars.

America buzzed with toy making. Fred Kroll, who spent over sixty years in the toy business, recalled his early pre-World War II days: 'All the factories were in New York or Brooklyn or the suburbs. The wholesalers were on Broadway between 22nd Street and 17th Street or on the side streets east and west. Buyers would sit down at Toy Fair, place an order, probably get a 5 per cent early buying discount and extended terms, so factories kept going year long.'

The end of World War II saw a boom in toys as men returned home anxious to start families. Toy factories, converted for the war effort, returned to their original use. By the mid 1950s Marx was producing one in five of all toys sold in the US and had factories in ten different countries. *Time* magazine gave him the cover and named him 'The Toy King'. His company went out of business in 1979, largely a victim of a new age of toy marketing that he had failed to understand or accept.

With television as a selling tool and plastic as a material, the fifties and sixties were golden decades for the toy industry. It is impossible to overestimate the crucial role plastic played: with the end of World War II, it became plentiful and inexpensive. Initially, there was suspicion because it was associated with cheap (and often inflammable) goods from the Far East, but newer plastics held colour, were washable, hard-wearing, light, adaptable. And economical. A hundred metal toy soldiers cost $15. Now a boy could buy a hundred plastic ones and paint them himself for a cent apiece.[11]

Plastic is the heart of the toy industry. Seventy-one per cent of toys are made of it. Pliable, easy to mould, quick-hardening once moulded, non-rusting, and without sharp corners, it is the perfect material. Even though rising prices of oil, from which it is derived, have cut into margins, toy companies have one advantage over suppliers of other goods: because they are constantly introducing new products, it is easier for them to raise prices without appearing to do so.

In the eighties, the business underwent a major change. An industry that historically had thrived on the very number of its entrepreneurial players began to consolidate. Major companies gobbled up competitors one after another. An industry joke envisages only two companies surviving – Hasbro and Toys R Us. One year Toys R Us won't like any of Hasbro's toys – and so Christmas will be cancelled.

Of the top toy companies in existence in 1976, eleven were defunct by 1995 and thirteen more had been taken over by Mattel or Hasbro. The toy grave-yard is littered with companies that now exist only as names or subsidiaries: Monogram Models, Metaframe,

[11] There is a downside to plastic. Although it is a cheaper raw material than wood, the production tools cost more – so you need large quantities for it to make economic sense.

Turco, ARCO, Corolle (France), Corgi Toys (UK), Fisher-Price, Kransco, J.W. Spears, Tyco, Bluebird Toys, Tinkertoys, Playskool, Parker Bros, Tonka, Kenner, Milton Bradley, Larami Company, Cap Toys, OddzOn, Tiger Electronics, Galoob. In 1996 Mattel even tried to swallow up Hasbro with a $5.2 billion takeover offer – one that failed only after Hasbro pulled out all the stops, including utilizing Rhode Island political clout.

This means that today's toy industry is very different from how it was even a few years ago. It has polarized, a few large companies, many small, with medium businesses finding it hard to survive. The US is not unique: the European Union has 2,000 toy companies, but only 5 per cent of them with a turnover of over 40 million euros ($47 million). It is also an industry with prodigious problems. Many are those faced by industry in general – the increasing domination of big corporations, retail concentration with, especially, the impact of Wal-Mart, rising costs of materials (in the case of toys, plastic, paper, steel and zinc) and of transportation and labour. Many, though, are peculiar to it.

The toy industry is currently in a slump. During the 1990s traditional toy sales rose by about 5 per cent every year. In the new millennium sales started to fall – and kept falling. Kids have been deserting traditional toys younger and faster. Critics say this is partly because the toys themselves are so poor. Less contentiously, there is the fact that children are growing up in a world of hyper choice, with so many places to go, so many things to choose from. Many homes are full of toys: 'Children today are living in a world of tons of toys,' comments Richard Hastings, chief economist at Bernard Sands retail research. Additionally, it often seems that the toy is being slowly consumed by the electronics industry.

Norman Walker, CEO of K'Nex construction toys, Philadelphia, believes 2004 was the year of 'seismic change' when it became clear that the 'era of cheap consumer electronics (had changed) the rules of the game for ever . . . the ravages . . . (were) there for all to see and can no longer be ignored.'

Despite continuous attempts to spread the sale of toys across the whole year, it is still a highly seasonal business, dependent on a relatively short holiday period. Generally, two thirds of sales are made in the second half of the year: 50 per cent in the fourth quarter, 40 per cent in just the last two months. That seasonality has increased as large retailers have become better and tougher at controlling inventory levels. Now they only reorder when they have to, shifting more of the risk and the storage costs to the toy company itself.

Toys have always had a very real advantage over all other consumer products. They are traditionally economy-proof: parents cut back on themselves before their kids. In the UK in 2005, a year in which consumer spending generally was tight, a survey showed that £715 was still being spent on toys for the average child. However, ferocious retail competition often means that the best-selling toys are sold by stores at the lowest prices as come-ons, meaning ever-tighter margins for squeezed toy companies.

Demographics are not on the toy companies' side. Three quarters of toys go to children under twelve and the number has been falling – down to just over a fifth of the population in 2000, the lowest percentage for twenty years. Although the falling numbers are counteracted by children being born to older women (where family income is usually higher) and by more ready-to-spend grandparents, it is obvious that the more potential child customers there are, the better.

The double bind here has always been that hot toys are needed to set the market ablaze and make real money, but at the same time they are the very ones that carry the danger of huge losses, even self-destruction. First, you have to plough millions into the right product; if you overproduce to try to ensure you are ready for the buying deluge, you lose vast sums; if you underproduce you lose sales. Toy companies have to live with the fact that at times of swift sales, inventory can bring rich rewards. That same inventory can become worthless overnight. Even a winning product can be a first step to failure. When the big seller has no big follow-up, stores that stocked the company's products on the strength of the top seller will drop the lot. Coleco, which had the licence to mass-produce Cabbage Patch Dolls, had sales in 1985 of $600 million. The following year their estimate was $450 million, but sales were actually $230 million. Other sales did not make up. They struggled desperately to revive the market (and their finances) with gimmicks such as talking or burping dolls. It did not save them. They were forced to file for bankruptcy.

These days everyone is scrambling for their slice of the cake. That fact coupled with the singular nature of the toy industry is the reason, Sean McGowan believes, why the business is so brutal.

'There is virtually no growth so everyone is having to fight hard for their share of the market,' he claims. 'That may not be unusual in modern business, but in the toy industry there is a unique element. In most industries, the battle for the consumer results in winner and losers – with soft drinks the customer has to opt to drink a Coke or a Pepsi, not both. With toys, though, everyone can be winning – or losing – at the same time. There is no particular reason anyone has to buy these products, and there is no particular reason they can't buy all of them within reasonable financial limits. The level of interest kids have in toys has diminished because they have so many alternatives. Therefore every company, whether retailer, manufacturer, licensor, inventor, advertiser, is struggling to hold onto what share of the pie they have. And it drives people to kinds of behaviour that isn't necessary when the industry is growing rapidly.'

The result: 'They don't honour contracts. Often people's word doesn't mean anything – "I'll buy 50,000 units for delivery in August," they say. Come the middle of August and it's, "No I don't need it." "But we had a purchase order." It doesn't mean anything. You can even have it in writing. That's common.'

For years, toy companies lived with the risk realities as a fact of life. Risk, though, is anathema for big corporations and for Wall Street. They want big winners (because they are big earners) but without the associated exposure. Fads are good – provided they can be managed. Corporate toy land is convinced it can handle the dichotomy. In his presentation Eckert compares today's Mattel with consumer-goods companies like Procter & Gamble and Colgate-Palmolive. The big difference, of course, is that P & G don't have to reinvent most of their products every year. Dove is Dove this year and next year. Toys, for all the management techniques brought to it, remains a business constantly in need of the next thing. For Mattel, the truth remains that 70 per cent of sales are generated from new products. 'At the top level it may be like selling soap,' says one longtime toy man. 'What's different is that we're also trend-based, fashion-based. Whatever it is that's selling could be reversed tomorrow.'

Sean McGowan points out that a non-toy company

may be able to count on increased sales from its previous year's products. 'But a certain percentage of every toy company's sales are going to go away just because they go away. If you are lucky, 90 per cent of your sales will stick. So if you're Mattel's size, a $5 billion company, you're losing $500 million. If you want to grow mid-single digits, say 5 per cent, that's $250 million, so you have to come up with $750 million to grow 5 per cent. That's the size of the number three toy company. Every year you have to invent the number three toy company.'

The toy industry lives with the possibility of failure every day – 'Every major toy company is just a stone's throw away from disaster,' Jon Salisbury, a longtime observer says. Toys flare, then die. Companies vanish. Who now, even among toy men, remembers Henry Orenstein's Topper Toys? It once competed head to head with Mattel and boasted the world's largest toy plant, turning out Johnny Eagle rifle and pistol sets, the Johnny Service Body Shop, and a host of glamour dolls including Dawn Dolls, Orenstein's rival to Mattel's Barbie. Its early 1970s toy war with Mattel's involving Hot Wheels and its own Johnny Lightning cars, with both companies pouring in huge sums, was described by a reporter of the time as 'a rivalry like no other'.

Or the toys? When Hasbro launched Charmkits, a jewellery product, Steve Schwarz, then marketing director, remembers, 'We had this big room and 80 per cent of that line was Charmkits.' The product did not outlast the year. Bucky O'Hare and the Toad Wars was a line of toys released in the early 1990s, revolving around a green anthropomorphic hare that, with other mammals and one human, fought toads in an inter-galactic space war. Despite a tie-in TV show, it quickly died. Or take Bar Code Battler, a toy/game that involved swiping bar codes that then registered a score; Hyper Racer toy cars, vehicles that fitted into slots and competed against each other, and which had been huge successes in Japan; Butt Ugly Martians; and Ideal's Baby Jesus doll which rested in a straw-filled manger in a box made up like a Bible, and when the box lid was lifted a cut-out Christmas scene popped up . . .

Toy companies have devised many approaches to try to produce formulas for success. Licensing brings toys to the marketplace with pre-built recognition and sales impetus. Ann Kearns, vice-president of marketing at Sesame Workshop, explains the advantages for both parties: 'When you have a company like Fisher-Price, which is the master toy licensee for Sesame Street preschool toys, you get the added value of what Sesame Street brings to the table and what Fisher-Price means as a brand to the consumer.' Critics see licensing as a lazy way of sidestepping real inventiveness and of substituting product creativity with marketing. All have to agree it is prodigious – licensed products make up 25 to 30 per cent of industry sales. Licensing first developed at the beginning of the twentieth century from comic-strip characters. First was Buster Brown who featured on toys and games and others followed – companies like Pepsi and Ford whose logos appeared on other products, and movie characters. Mickey Mouse was first sold for $300 to appear on a school notebook.

The rewards from licensing can be phenomenal. In 2002 Nickelodeon had $2.5 billion in sales of its toys through arrangements with companies like Mattel and Jakks Pacific. SpongeBob SquarePants alone produced $750 million in retail revenue. Nickelodeon's licensing income paled, though, beside that of AOL-Time

Warner ($6.6 billion) and Disney ($13 billion).

A large part of the strength of the leading two companies, Mattel and Hasbro, is that their size and resources allow them to dominate licensing deals with 'star properties'. In 2004 Hasbro spent 7.4 per cent of its operating expenses on royalties, compared with 5.2 per cent on research and development. Mattel has Harry Potter, Batman, Dora the Explorer, and SpongeBob SquarePants. Hasbro, among others, has the property credited with starting modern licensing, the ultra-special Star Wars. Seth Siegel, co-chairman of Beanstalk Group, a licensing company, says, 'These two are the only companies that have very significant franchise brands that they either own or control. It's getting harder and harder for [other] toy companies to be serious competitors.' Marvel Entertainment emerged from bankruptcy in 1998, and turned itself around by shedding capital-intensive toy-making plants to concentrate on selling licences to its 4,700 characters. Toy and game makers who bought into the 2002 *Spiderman* movie, either as makers or retailers, gambled and won big. It grossed $822 million and sold two million video games. Today Hasbro's Star Wars franchise is one of its strongest assets, though it struggled for years with the consequences of overpaying for the licence for the first Star Wars sequel – $600 million and a 20 per cent royalty. (The Mattel deal for Harry Potter was a mere $20 million and a 15 per cent royalty.) Still, licensing can bring utter and totally unpredictable flops. Dr Seuss's *How the Grinch Stole Christmas* was the top-grossing movie of the year 2000 – but it did not click with toy buyers, and retailers were stuck with slow-moving Grinch merchandise. After the failure of *The Incredible Hulk*, toy figures remained unsold everywhere. Skeleton Warriors, TV-linked action figures from Playmates Toys, were forecast to be massive successes. The trouble was that on television the villains were much cooler than the heroes, and the animation was edgy and scary for potential young buyers.

Even hot toys usually hit a wall after a time. That is one of the reasons today's toy companies look less at launching single items than at developing long-term lines. Like most consumer marketers, toy companies are extending existing lines that are popular and pre-sold rather than taking risks with new ones. It is not that different from Kellogg's Raisin Bran begetting Kellogg's Raisin Bran Crunch. Some date the real start of lines back to 1980 with the arrival of Strawberry Shortcake. Critics – like toy designer Erik Erickson – believe that was the moment that the 'real' toy industry self-destructed, switching the energy and ingenuity that had gone into exciting single toys into a search for what best suited marketing needs.

Before then, said Erickson, 'you could make a stand-alone toy, one that was so sensational for itself that it would support advertising and people would get excited about it. But after Strawberry Shortcake, you had to create toys that were licensed lines.'

It began with one of American Greetings most successful cards, which featured a little girl with strawberries on her bonnet. There are many versions of how the idea of the card becoming a toy developed. Bernie Loomis, a legendary toy business figure, then heading Kenner Products, had been considering ways of taking some of the uncertainty out of the business. He had concluded that expandable lines of toys, rather than individual products, was the answer. Just like Barbie, it was a concept that could be extended indefinitely – the first buy was just for openers. Kenner started manufacturing Strawberry Shortcake, the first scented doll to hit the market. The set that appeared comprised Strawberry Shortcake, Huckleberry Pie, Blueberry Muffin, and Apple Dumplin' with her hard-shelled friend Tea Time Turtle. Over 25 million dolls and 35 million accessories were sold during the height of its popularity. Products also included other toys, books, records, and clothes. Over its first five years, retail sales brought in $1 billion.

American Greetings and its licensing agent DIC Entertainment reintroduced the brand in 2003. More than 350 licensees worldwide came on board, including Playmates Toys, with a range of scented dolls and play-sets. This time licensing included infants and ranged from home furnishing to clothes to electronics.

Toy companies have gone back to what they call their 'core brands', ones that have been around for some time with their own history and familiarity, and turned these into lines and licensed properties. Hasbro's chairman Alan Hassenfeld says, 'We spent more time on Star Wars and on X, Y and Z. We weren't taking care of our children, so they were withering.' He volunteers an example: Play-Doh, that wonderful non-toxic reusable modelling compound first intro-duced in the mid 1950s. 'How do you expand Play-Doh?' he asks. 'You bring a group of people together and you basically say, OK what is the Play-Doh story?' Play-Doh, it seems, is no longer just a creative plaything. It began in Doh-Doh Island. 'And who lives on Doh-Doh Island?' he continues. 'It's inhabited by Doh-Dohs and now you have the chance to create books, maybe entertainment, because you've opened up a universe. You basically haven't been linear. You've just opened up that imagination.' What is actually opened in hard terms is a chance to pro-duce and sell scores more product on the back of

Play-Doh – a staggering sixty-seven products by Christmas 2005. They included the Play Doh-Doh Island, a farm, a pet parlour, an ice-cream truck, a fridge, a magic hat, a tractor, farm animals – and McDonald's fries, and a George Foreman grill. It's a long way from Play-Doh's 1956 beginning as an off-white compound in a one-and-a-half-pound can.

This is a world where size does indeed make a difference. A humungous company is rewarded with economies of scale, brand recognition, the greater ability to cut costs, the resources to buy licences and to promote heavily. Not least there is the clout to get shelf space: leading retailers like dealing with leading producers. 'Stores are much happier with a Hasbro or a Mattel because they know they're going to supply and if there's a problem, they're going to fix it,' says one small company toy man.

In its quest for sales growth, the mighty can make the world its marketplace. The potential is enormous: the US per capita spending on toys may be high – three times that of Europe, ten times that of Asia – but there are only about 60 million American kids compared with 300 million prospective Chinese consumers and 400 million Indian.

Partly because of the vast global entertainment machine, kids all over the world often want the same properties, so it has become common marketing practice to launch new hot toys everywhere at the same time. There are certainly problems, whether of pricing in Latin America or of distribution in Eastern Europe, or more competition from knock-offs. But there are the rewards – Hasbro in 2003 drew nearly 40 per cent of its revenue from abroad.

Pricing competition in non-American countries is usually less fierce, meaning mark-ups can be so much higher than in the US. In January 2005, the toy magazine *Playthings* published 'representative prices' being charged in a number of European countries for identical toys. Barbie Princess and the Pauper horse and carriage that was selling for $28.73 in the US was over $61 in the Netherlands, nearly $64 in Sweden, and up in the fifties most everywhere else. Twister, less than $10 in the US, was nearly three times as much in other countries listed. Domestically, Lego's pirate ship retailed at $38.31 compared with over $70 in Italy, nearly $80 in Sweden, and $65 in Belgium. A basket of toys that cost $507.50 in the US went for over $800 in Belgium and Germany, and over $900 in the Netherlands, Italy, Spain and Sweden. Major US toy companies can also use overseas countries to dump products that have failed at home. An executive of one company, to illustrate how merciless a business it was, detailed a major toy failure that had just occurred. He then caught himself, paused, and requested that what he had said should be forgotten – 'We're launching it in the UK next year.'[12]

Today's larger companies and the men who run them operate and view the world very differently from their counterparts of the past. Sheldon Hirsch, an industry veteran, says: 'What you have now – Hasbro, Mattel – are very bureaucratic. They're companies that have layers of command, and you're very vulnerable then because nobody can make a decision. One thing about toy companies, they're very entrepreneurial, these are guys with ideas, these are guys who take risks. They are entertainers. The smart guys – even at some of the big companies – had a circle of three or four key advisers who would make all decisions, and

[12] UK toy companies often protest the country is used as a US dumping ground for toys that failed at home.

they wouldn't leave the table until they'd done so. At most of the companies now the purpose of having a meeting is not to make a decision, it is to defer the decision. They're the first to find something – and the last to come out with it.'

'The best thing about the toy industry,' says Sean McGowan, 'is the worst thing also. The best thing is you get to start over every year. The worst thing is you have to.'

It is hungry newcomers who are ready to gamble and able to move fast that can best take advantage. Andrew Berton, president of Excel Development Group, Minneapolis, says, 'Because major toy companies eschew new concepts likely to generate less than $20 million in their first year of sales, there are gaps in the marketplace for entrepreneurs and smaller toy companies.' Alan Hassenfeld adds, 'I believe it's easier to enter this business than many people believe as long as you're going to work hard and you get great ideas. If you're expecting it to be easy, it's not.'

Sam Harwell started Big Time Toys out of his basement in Nashville in 1995 with Sock'em Boppers, oversized cushioned boxing gloves, an old toy that he was able to buy at a knockdown price. With clever marketing, he sold three million sets in two years. When the toy peaked, he came up with his own idea – Super Swimwear, which includes shark and killer-whale fins. After being turned down by Wal-Mart three times, he flew to the company's headquarters unannounced and gave a face-to-face sales pitch. He was successful. The product was given space at all the major retailers, and in 2001 ranked in the top ten toys by dollar sales. Everything that can be contracted out is: advertising, graphic design, warehousing and manufacturing (in China).

In the UK Martin Grossman ran a small company in

Glasgow, Scotland, selling a few me-too products. Then, on a visit to Hong Kong, he saw an item called Alien Eggs. The offbeat toy – pods containing a yucky multicoloured gel and inside that a tiny alien – grabbed his attention. He brought it to the UK, engaged in some clever PR – and it became one of the hottest-selling toys in the industry. In competition with toys from all the big-name companies, it earned the 'Craze of the Year' award from the UK toy retailers.

Sometimes it would seem impossible that a major new plaything can emerge – there are already so many toys. K'Nex, though, managed to beat the odds. Born in 1992, it is an ingenious construction toy consisting basically of rods that fit into circular connecting pieces called 'snowflakes'. Over the years, items like wheels, pulleys, gearing systems and motors have been added, making possible complex constructions like a 3-ft-high musical Ferris wheel. Today K'Nex, a privately held company located in Hatfield, Pennsylvania, is a multi-million dollar worldwide business, and the number one construction-toy company in the non-brick cate-gory. Ironically, some of its overseas distribution is handled by Hasbro, one of the companies that turned down the product in the first place.

K'Nex got its start at a wedding. Joel Glickman, whose family owned a plastic components company, absent-mindedly put a drinking straw over a fork prong. The following day he started thinking of toy possibilities and months later, after some innovative product engineering, Joel had devised a practicable way of fitting pieces together. Mattel and Hasbro were both offered the new toy – their turndown letters are now framed in the K'Nex foyer. Glickman finally arranged a meeting with a buyer from Toys R Us. As Joel's brother Robert, co-founder of the company, recalled, 'The man looked at it for about twenty seconds and said, "How much does it cost and where can I get one?"'

Nothing better illustrates the extraordinary and capricious nature of the toy industry than the fact that even as K'Nex was growing and expanding across continents, another company – the maker of one of the world's most famous and loved toys – was struggling to survive.

Changing tastes, economic realities and futile attempts to ride the fashion roller coaster had brought Lego close to economic disaster. Despite its continuing problems, it remains an astounding product. It is estimated that more than 400 million children and adults play with Lego bricks every year. In a 2003 UK survey they emerged as the most popular toy in history, ahead of the teddy bear, Barbie and Action Man. Fifteen million bricks and components are produced annually: 2,400 different parts in ninety colours and thirty materials. Moulds are made to a precision tolerance as fine as .0002 mm; all are fully compatible whether made in 1958 or this year. Lego claims there are 915 million ways to combine six bricks. I have not – as yet – verified this.

The story begins with a carpenter named Ole Kirk Christiansen who built homes and furniture for Danish farmers. Wooden toys were a sideline until, in 1932, the Depression still prevailing, he gambled that no matter how bad the economy, parents would buy for their children – a truth which has held good for the industry ever since. The Danish words *leg godt* mean 'play well', and fortuitously, as Christiansen later learned, Lego itself means 'I put together' in Latin. His company motto declares 'Only the best is good enough' and his Lego System of Play has an evangelical ring: 'Unlimited play potential; for girls and boys; imagination, creativity, development; the more elements, the greater the value; quality in every detail.' The company is now owned by a grandson. The rural town of Billund, 300 kilometres from Copenhagen, grew up around the Lego plant and in 2005 still employed one in four of the residents. Over the years firms like Mattel and Hasbro are said to have lusted after it, but, 'No way it can be acquired,' one financial director insisted. 'You'd have to declare war on Denmark to get it.'

In 1947 Lego became the first company in Denmark to invest in a plastic injection-moulding machine, and the first plastic forerunner of today's brick was introduced two years later. The 1950s brought the technology to make them click together and the famous brick with tubes underneath emerged under the son of the founder in 1958.[13]

Other products followed – the train, the Technic system with gears, beams and gearboxes, Duplo's larger bricks for younger children. The first Legoland Park appeared in 1968. The 1970s brought Lego figures. In the 1990s, partnership with MIT led to Mindstorms

[13] The bricks were inspired by a London child psychologist, Hilary Harry Fisher Page, who invented and patented pre-World War II plastic blocks that lock together with small knobs. He went on to found Kiddicraft. Some detail of the toy's history emerged in a copyright case in Hong Kong between Lego and the American manufacturer Tyco. The inspiration appears to have followed the son of Lego's founder receiving sample bricks two years before the company produced its own version, with key adaptations. These plastic bricks, with studs, were very similar to the later Lego. (A major difference is the treatment of windows and doors, which slide into grooves at the end of the bricks.) Page committed suicide before the Lego bricks entered the British market. Lego bought all rights to the Kiddicraft blocks in 1981. (See the *Mail on Sunday,* 26 July 1987.)

Lego with integrated robot technology, enabling children to create and program intelligent models. In 1998 Lego began to produce sets based on Star Wars, Harry Potter, Bob the Builder and Winnie the Pooh. In 2002 Bionicle emerged, a mixture of construction toys and action figures.

Lego was a name on everyone's lips. It was voted plastic product of all time and best toy of the twentieth century. Still, its problems were escalating. As it flirted with licensed and fashion products like other toy companies, it began to experience the same tribulations. Licences brought success for periods of time, but sales volumes depended on the showing of the related movie. Some licensed products even cannibalized their own items: Harry Potter sold big but a non-licence linked medieval castle-themed product waned. Lego went from a stable, predictable steady business to boom or bust.

At the same time its dominating position as a construction toy was being whittled away by imitators, direct copies or even fresher, cheaper building concepts. It started to lose out to Mega Bloks, Canada's largest toy company, which added Lego-sized bricks to its Jumbo range, and a string of lawsuits resulted. Although the last major patents covering Lego's building blocks expired in 1988, the firm, zealously guarding what it sees as its rights, has fought on complex trademark and copyright law. Lego has won against Mega Bloks in China, but lost in France and Italy. Between the early 1990s and early 2005, Mega Bloks was involved in about a dozen lawsuits, mainly filed by Lego. Best-Lock (Europe) which makes blocks compatible with Lego, was also involved in eight lawsuits with them in Germany alone. 'They [Lego] are a company that enjoyed many years of monopoly in this market category and now they want to stifle anything competing against them in the construction-toy aisle,' says Brahm Segal, vice-president and lawyer for Mega Bloks Montreal. His company successfully applied to have the European Community trademark for Lego's bricks delisted in the construction-toy category. In 2005 the Supreme Court in Canada overturned a legal decision made nine years earlier and Mega Bloks declared they had finally won the trademark dispute.

One obvious reason for Lego's problems was pricing. Toys R Us was selling a Lego Bulk Tub of 140 pieces for $19.99 against a Mega Bloks bag of 100 pieces at only $9.99. Lego uses its own mix of resins producing better-quality plastic, while Mega Bloks utilizes commodity-grade resins and makes at least half its bricks in China. But Lego executives had a problem: to move to similar low-cost manufacture, perhaps using cheaper resins, would involve the prohibitive initial cost of changing tens of thousands of moulds at an estimated $100,000 each.

Five years later Lego faced a desperate financial crisis. In 1999 a new Legoland theme park had opened in California alongside massive expansion into other goods such as Lego clothes, watches and computer games. A US executive announced, 'Our goal is to be the number 1 brand with families with young children by 2005.' In 2004, the company lost a record 1.9 billion kroner ($311 million). Owner Kristansen[14] admitted, 'We tried to follow trends, to have toys that were in fashion, that are "in" one year and "out" the next. But it didn't work.' The CEO's job was given to non-family member Jorge Vig Knudstorp. A major reversal took the company away from wide licensing and diversification to concentrate on its core business,

[14] The spelling of his name differs from that of his grandfather because it was misspelled on a birth certificate.

its famous coloured plastic building blocks. The following year it sold its Legoland theme parks to New York-based private equity firm Blackstone for $457.2 million. It also closed a high-cost factory in Switzerland and five European distribution centres, moving those operations to the Czech Republic. It had suddenly become clear that everything, including following its competitors into China, was possible.

Lego may be the most dramatic illustration of the unpredictable and mercurial nature of the toy business, but it has ridden high for almost a century and there is plenty of mileage in it yet. New companies today follow the same pattern – only much, much faster – and often without the extended life expectancy that comes from familiarity.

The LeapPad is an innovative learning system using a custom-designed chip, software and a built-in speaker, which makes paper produce sound as kids of four-plus interact with it. Made by US toymaker LeapFrog, founded in 1995, it sold nearly 9 million in its first three years and in December 2000 became the first educational toy for at least fifteen years to become the top-selling toy in America. Michael Milken, financier of junk-bond fame, became a backer and when LeapFrog went public it proved to be the best-performing initial public offering of 2002.

Its age range has been extended to cover infant and up – its 'learn and groove' activity station, for example, is a sit-inside play centre aimed at children as young as three months. As one store blurb says, 'Five stimulating activity stations bring the fun and learning full circle, surrounding your baby with lights, sounds, music, and manipulatives. This rocking, spinning, sit-inside play center introduces your baby to a wide variety of music styles while teaching ABCs, counting, colors, and language-stimulating nursery rhymes.' And yet growth came to a halt in 2004. Rising costs and overall slowdown in toy sales produced an $8 million loss. Between 2003 and 2005, shares fell from a high of nearly $47 to less than $11. Workers were laid off, executives left or were fired. The founder, Michael Wood, left.

One problem was that the big three retailers, who account for 70 per cent of LeapFrog sales, wanted the company to hold more inventory. Another was that by 2005, those fickle kids were finding LeapPad not so cool any more; they had moved on to using a real computer.

This is the disturbing truth that lies at the core of the industry's present dilemma: children are actually losing the ability to play as the sources of their happiness become increasingly commercial. The form and structure of society has shifted. Instead of being regarded as vulnerable and in need of nurture, children have become an exploitable resource. Assailed by market forces that even adults find overwhelming, immature children are indulged. They demand – and promptly receive – instant gratification.

It is not just LeapPad's potential customers who have been flocking to the real thing. Some even ask whether the days of toys are numbered, except as niche products sold by a shrinking pool of speciality shops. If it happens, claim some critics, much of the fault will lie with the toy makers. A disgruntled, born-again ex-marketer from one of the major companies complained, 'Lots of the toys and games developed at the beginning of mass marketing are still the best things about the industry. Since then it has become the game of trying to put the least amount of plastic in a toy so you can keep the price low, of trying to get first in line when Hollywood comes out with a blockbuster, of squeezing the last half-cent out of something.'

Toy marketing has shot itself in the foot with its emphasis on the new hot, fad toy to replace the last new hot, fad toy: craftsmanship and longevity mean nothing; kids get bored with their toys before they break them, sometimes even before they have played with them. In any event, the play value is low. In fact, many toys are no longer created for play. They are designed to sell, to be possessed, to be a badge of status.[15] The more toys, the happier the child. A survey in the UK in 2005 showed 80 per cent of under-twelves were given more than ten toys a year, but 60 per cent of those toys were soon thrown out even though there was nothing wrong with them.

Some commentators are totally pessimistic, seeing a seismic change in kids' tastes. They argue that the attempts by toy companies to remain cool by adding technology to toys and by producing child versions of products such as cellphones and video players are doomed long term: kids will prefer the real thing which, in the nature of electronics, will be increasingly affordable.

The changing nature of both the marketplace and play-things has prompted many toy companies to decide against that description of themselves. Even the International Toy Center, the emotional heart of the industry for almost eighty years, contemplated dropping the t-word from its title.

Jim Silver, longtime publisher of toy-trade journals,

[15] According to Ian Henley, a UK toy buyer, most of the real crazes happen with toys kids can carry in their pockets to school: 'And the best thing that can happen is for the schools to start wanting to ban them.'

says, 'I no longer consider it the toy business. I consider it the family entertainment business.' Fred Paprin of the Wildflower Group, a licensing agency, concurs. '[Toy makers] are realizing "we're not just in the toy business, we're in the children's entertainment business."' These comments are born not of choice but necessity: with sales of traditional toys down, companies have perforce moved into such categories as direct-to-video movies, music and consumer electronics. LeapFrog and Vtech already position themselves as educational companies. Hasbro, Mattel and MGA say they have evolved into 'lifestyle companies', leveraging their brands beyond toys. By 2005 only 65 per cent of MGA's sales came from toys, the rest from furniture, sporting goods and electronics. Their aim is to continue to reduce that 65 per cent further.

'The toy business is shrinking,' admits Lisa Shapiro, in charge of licensing for MGA's Bratz. 'We're all losing kids to clothing, computers and DVDs. So we want to take Bratz out of the toy aisle and into lifestyle. We want girls to live the Bratz life – wear the mascara, use the hair product, send the greeting card.' Founder and CEO Isaac Larian insists MGA is a 'consumer entertainment products company. We exist in lots of categories. We don't want to limit ourselves to just being a toy company.'

SpinMaster, a Canadian company internationally recognized for its ingenious toys, including air-pressure-powered toy planes and bubble-catching and stacking machines, has already dropped 'toys' from its corporate name and developed a complete line of children's furnishings. It told the trade it should be considered 'a company focused on lifestyle and children's entertainment'.

Perhaps more strikingly, Gund, which for more than a century has been creating world-renowned teddy bears and other soft toys, now insists it is a 'gift company' and 'not in the toy industry'. 'We've got a 52-week-a-year business,' says Jim Madonna, Gund's president. 'We're not fourth-quarter driven.' This from a company that was one of the first to design and produce teddy bears in the early 1900s. It was Gund that introduced the concept of industry licensing with well-known cartoon characters such as Felix the Cat, Mickey Mouse, Donald Duck, Popeye and others. It was also the first company to produce musical toys that were affordably priced for the average American family.

Despite the changes, the problems, and the corporateness, the toy industry likes to see itself as retaining a particular magic. Tom Conley, president of the Toy Industry Association, enthuses: 'It really takes a special kind of person to devote their life to making products that children and people that are children at heart enjoy, and yet deal in this oppressive atmosphere of government regulation, profit squeeze, raw material shortages and labor shortages.'

Even cynical investors regard the industry as extraordinary. Wall Street is as prone to the business's hype as anyone else. The buzz around Toy Fair generally means stocks are up in late winter and spring. Summer is not toy-buying or PR time, so stocks tend to be down, as they often are in December too – the month that is reality time. But it goes beyond this. Sean McGowan says, 'There is something about toys that gets grown men and women to act as they wouldn't act in other categories. Investors will want to talk about toy stocks when they really have no business doing so. They're tiny companies for the most part, they really don't even have the time – but they want to talk about them. I've seen grown men who make millions of dollars a year standing in line jostling to get free toys at investor conferences that I've hosted. I've seen executives at toy retailers walking out with bags of free toys. There's something about connecting with toys, whether it reminds them of their own youth or gives them a chance to be a hero with their own kid.

'This industry in terms of market capitalization, it's not that big, it's not that important. And yet it gets investors' attention. They want to look at it and say, "That's fun, that's more fun than oil, that's more fun than paper, that's more fun than automobiles." When I tell people I work in the stock market, they have no idea what an analyst does. When I'm asked what I do, I say I follow toy companies. Everybody knows something about toys so you have an instant connection to everybody. And they all want to know what's the hot one, so that's a topic.' As for the business itself, being in it, he admits, 'is sometimes the least fun' but the people 'at some level, they feel they're doing good public works, they're keeping kids happy.'

The industry sees one sign for optimism in the growing adult market for toys – purchases are made by adults not for children, but for themselves. Just as we see children getting older younger, so adults are staying younger for longer. This is known as the Harley-Davidson effect – men in their forties and fifties desperate to reclaim lost youth. Toys also appeal to many adults who grew up during times when there was less access to material goods, and are eager now to enjoy them.

One company that has benefited is among the great names of toy history. The English inventor Frank Hornby was responsible for Meccano construction toys and Dinky cars, as well as the eponymous Hornby trains. In recent years these have enjoyed renewed success in their home country, as well as the US. Frank Martin, the company's chief executive, says: 'About 70 per cent of our product is sold in the form of individual locomotives, wagons and accessories and we're pretty sure most of that is sold to adults. There's clear evidence of adults now, particularly if kids are off their hands and they've got space in the house and more disposable income, saying OK, I want a hobby in the home – stock-car racing, model railways. We have to respond to that by giving them a product that is clearly acceptable as an adult purchase and doesn't trivialize the interest. So the dimensional accuracy and the decoration and so on has to be absolutely spot on – they're very discerning.'

In America, adult collectors account for an estimated three-quarters of sales of toy trains. Steven Spielberg is famously a lifelong aficionado of Lionel trains, the largest US maker of miniature locomotives. Rock star Neil Young holds a 20 per cent stake in Lionel and has a 'train barn' at his Californian ranch, housing his model-railway collection.

Alan Hassenfeld says: 'I do believe toys, if we use our heads properly, will be bought by fifty- and sixty-year-olds. Toys will be sold from zero to 120.' Japan, for so many years the world leader in electronics, may just be showing the way again. There, robotic baby dolls have been introduced, designed to give comfort to the lonely elderly. One is programmed with 1,200 phrases, goes to sleep when patted and will wake in the morning. If the owner is too busy to follow the regime the doll will enquire, 'Aren't you pushing yourself too hard?'

Chapter Six

WAR OF THE AISLES: THE RETAIL BATTLEGROUND

'Today's buyer (at the big retailers) isn't educated in the toy business; they wouldn't know a good toy if it fell in their lap' – Jim Silver, publisher of toy industry magazines

It's Sunday morning and Main Street in Concord, Massachusetts, is quiet in the winter sun. The American flag flutters gently, high on its pole. On side streets, sleek lawns are empty in front of elegant white houses. The Visitor Center has a sign that it is closed for the season, but a lone tourist wanders the graves of the steeply sloped Old Hill Burying Ground, from the top of which you can see most of this historic town and the rich rolling fields that cushion it.

It is not yet opening time for the stores that line either side of Main Street – a candy shop, a clothes store, old-fashioned hardware, crafts, and Patriot Travel. But already there is a kid with his nose pressed against the windows of one of them. They are that sort of window. They start in Main Street, go round the corner into Walden Street. Five of them, framed by white trim against red brick. Not big, but packed, each one a feast of colour, of promise, of fun, of dreams.

In no particular order, there are Madame Alexander dolls with authentic costumes and perfect faces, a Folkmanis dragon puppet, an owl perched on a play house, its clock set at six thirty. A huge furry donkey stands near an equally large lion, resplendent with gold braid mane. There is an Apache attack helicopter, a pro-action hockey game, a giant crane kit from Germany, a two-foot-long rocket (with a sign promising it will fly to 500 feet).

Deeper inside the store, and hard to see due to the brightness outside, there are secret-marker kits, metal soldiers, pirate ships, model cowboys and Indians, coloured crayons, wind-up fish, scooters, a giant snowman, and Victorian doll's houses.

A Lego Star Wars display covers an entire wall. A red-caped teddy bear rides a high wire stretched across the ceiling. An elevated train stands ready to speed around the store once it opens.

This is a toyshop the way it ought to be, straight out of Norman Rockwell America, but as current as any childhood wish.

The storefront sign has raised gold letters against a green background reading simply 'The Toy Shop'.

Not displayed is the information that it is probably the oldest toyshop in the United States, that in its life it has had only three owners. Some would claim its survival, let alone its continued success, is a sort of miracle, that the Toy Shop of Concord is a wonderful anachronism among all the discounters and big-box companies – a glimmer of light in a pile 'em high, sell 'em cheap plastic world.

Concord may be the living dream. The fundamentals of toy selling in twenty-first-century USA are very different. America still has maybe 1,500 small speciality toyshops like Concord's. But the number is falling, and for those that remain the struggle grows increasingly hard. The number of people who shop in them remains modest, the number of toys they shift minuscule compared to the overall market.

Harsh reality lies within a thirty-minute drive of the Toy Shop – three Wal-Marts, three Targets, three Toys R Us. These chains together control about 60 per cent of the US toy market.[16] Without them, no large-scale toy maker can hope to survive. Collectively they rule the industry, influencing the toys, the prices, even determining the packaging. Of the three, the greatest is Wal-Mart. It is the feared juggernaut, making everyone else sweat and most toy companies jump through hoops. It has smashed many, sent others reeling, rewritten the face of toy selling as it has of so many other areas. Its dominance is so great that it sells more each year by mid March than its nearest rival, Target, sells in a whole year.

The superlatives about Wal-Mart – the world's largest retailer with more reach and power than any other in history, 100 million customers a week, if the company were an independent nation it would be China's eighth largest trading partner – are part of the currency. Familiar too are the claims of its supporters – its cost-cutting saves US consumers a staggering $100 million a year. Its opponents accuse it of every-thing from destroying neighbourhoods to exploiting workers.

So great is the company's impact that the *Wall Street*

---

[16] Elsewhere specialist independent toyshops face similar battles against the huge combines. In the UK, about 500 specialist shops (down from about 1,500 in twenty years) compete against Argos, Woolworths, Toys R Us, and – increasingly – Tesco and Wal-Mart-owned Asda.

Journal stated it could probably produce an edition just for Bentonville, Arkansas, Wal-Mart's headquarters.

With its skill, ability and single-mindedness about buying and selling cheap, it has outperformed competitors in many areas, toys only one of the latest – and one with particular attractions.

It took over as the nation's largest toy retailer in 1998, and seven years later held an estimated 30 per cent of the market, about twice as much as each rival, Target and Toys R Us. Its power is huge. 'Wal-Mart is increasingly playing a role of kingmaker in the toy business,' says John Taylor, analyst, Arcadia Investments Corp.

Wal-Mart has a great advantage over toy stores, including Toys R Us. It has a more constant traffic of customers – twenty-two to twenty-six visits a year by the average family, compared with four to five at Toys R Us, according to retail analyst Donald Trott. Furthermore, it can expand or contract its toy-selling area as it wishes. A peculiarity about dedicated toyshops, it has been pointed out, is that they rent premises for twelve months a year, but only use them fully perhaps three to five months a year at special buying periods, notably Christmas. The rest of the time they're stuck with space costing money but earning little.

That's just the start, though, for Wal-Mart. When they do decide to push toys hard, they have other special advantages. The company is famous – some would say notorious – for squeezing the lowest price out of suppliers. Executives will sit down with a supplier and his annual report and say, 'We see you increased your gross profit margin by 100 basis points, why don't we share it?' If toy companies want Wal-Mart, they jump – the numbers involved are so huge.

Companies line up to woo Wal-Mart's buyers.

Hundreds of suppliers have opened offices near Wal-Mart's headquarters – they stretch out over a twenty-mile radius like a series of foreign legations around a mighty monarch, albeit in this case a drab brick building with faded carpets. Disney has been there since 1999; Bratz creators MGA are more recent inhabitants; toy makers SpinMaster moved in – and doubled their sales to the store in a year.

But then comes the next impact. Toys are only a small part of Wal-Mart's business, but a very high-profile one. Toys, priced cheap, are excellent traffic-boosters, drawing in customers. And Wal-Mart can offer the cheapest prices. Rivals claim they sell hot toys at even less than they pay for them, making up the money on high-margin products. Because what Wal-Mart does pay its suppliers remains closely guarded, the store may just be selling at cost: one anonymous toy executive admitted, 'I have a price sheet for Wal-Mart and a price sheet for everyone else.' With global sales of over $250 billion and toy sales in US stores around $5 billion, it has been pointed out that Wal-Mart could give away toys free and hardly dent its bottom line.

But the fact is no other store can compete with them. Toys not only draw buyers, but the much-publicized lowest prices convey a sense of good value to everything else in the store, whatever the actuality. For toy companies, it is a double-edged sword: they need Wal-Mart for volume; margins can be small. As analyst Dennis McAlpine says, 'If you're a toy manufacturer, it's better to have Wal-Mart (as a customer) than not have it. But even as you love 'em, you hate 'em. Wal-Mart is always tough on suppliers.'

In most industries, the higher the demand, the higher the price. 'Do you see florists putting prices of flowers down for Mothering Sunday?' asks Keith

Elmer, head of a UK retail toy-buying consortium. But it is a perversion of the toy industry that, because toys can be used to pull in custom, the hotter the toy, the lower the price. The reason is that it is hard to overestimate the impact on business of a really hot toy, like Tickle Me Elmo. It can turn around sales. Consumers will chase it – and even if they can't get it, they will almost certainly spend more on other toys: one retail consultant estimates that a really big Wow product can increase toy sales overall by up to 40 per cent.

Toy price wars are nothing new, but the one waged in the United States in 2003 is worth revisiting because it was the most brutal and industry-changing battle ever seen. It introduced a scorched-earth policy that devastated the vulnerable and left the entire retail world looking very different.

Wal-Mart moved first, starting unusually early with cuts that reverberated throughout the industry. Mattel's Hot Wheels T-Wrecks Playset, originally priced at $49.88, was slashed to $29.74. Target followed. Other toyshops found themselves faced with selling at a loss – or losing sales altogether. KB Toys, buying in Hokey Pokey Elmo at $24, saw Wal-Mart selling the same toy at more than $4.50 less. KB Toys did the best it could, selling at $24.99, at a price the chain declared was 'giving away toys'.

The impact across the rest of toy retailing was massive and drastic. During 2003 and 2004, the toy industry lost over 700 storefronts dedicated to selling toys. This included about 600 KB Toy stores, fifteen FAO Schwarz, and eighty-nine Zany Brainy stores – in addition to the incalculable number of small private toyshops that died. Many companies that survived live on precariously: FAO, owners of FAO Schwarz, filed for bankruptcy twice and liquidated the majority of its stores; Wizards of the Coast closed all its eighty-five stores to focus on designing games.

Perhaps most ironically, the chain that was left reeling and facing an uncertain future was yesterday's Big Bully of the business. Toys R Us, the 'Category Killer' that had itself in its time killed off so many toy stores, was now getting a taste of its own medicine. The significance reverberated far beyond toy retailing. Aram Rubinson, Bank of America Securities analyst, commented, 'To see the pioneer of category killers get killed by the mass market is a major step in the evolution of retailing.'

The rise, fall and still uncertain survival of Toys R Us covers the years of the modern toy industry.

Charles Lazarus, twenty-five and back from World War II, opened his first children's furniture store on the ground floor of his father's bicycle-repair shop in Washington DC. He added toys because he saw them as repeat business, unveiling his 'toy supermarket', no frills, cart-push warehouses in 1952. It really was a different shopping age: malls and discount stores were not yet recognizable on the retail landscape.

Lazarus built up a four-store chain, and then sold out to Interstate Stores in 1966, continuing to run the toy operation for them. That company went bankrupt, re-emerging in 1978 under their old name Toys R Us.[17] With Lazarus in control, the company went public.

Its power in toy land became undisputed. By 1987 Lazarus was the US's highest-paid executive, drawing $69 million in earnings, largely because of stock gains. In 1990 he was selling a quarter of all toys sold in America. But even that figure underestimated the

---

[17] From the start Lazarus spelt the R backwards as a marketing ploy.

omnipotence: in some cities, it was over half. A toy-industry commentators noted, 'The predominance of Toys R Us is unprecedented, and everyone assumes it is permanent.'

From the start, Lazarus offered toy manufacturers the tantalizing picture of year-round toy sales and the ability to produce twelve months a year. But for that he could extract a price – and he did. He insisted on deliveries instantly – and payment much later, when the toys were sold. He admitted, 'Without this dating, I never would have been able to afford the inventory.' He also insisted on a range of other benefits that raised him above any rivals: among them advance delivery of hot toys and allowances for ordered toys that then failed to sell as well as expected. In one instance, recorded in a Mattel memo, TRU received well over $1 million in free goods in compensation for 'special discounts' on slow-moving items. For suppliers not willing to comply, there were a host of retaliations, from denying the best shelf space (at the end of an aisle or in the front of the store) through to cancelling orders.[18]

His senior buyer Sy Ziv, who had been a wholesale and factory rep, reigned as the foremost determiner of America's toys. A larger-than-life figure, Ziv's antics were renowned. One much-repeated story was of Mattel showing him its new Slime product. Assured it was non-staining, he slung it over the carpet and ground it in with his heel, adding a cup of coffee for good measure. It is proof of his – and Toys R Us's – power that Mattel executives are said to have laughed, albeit nervously.

The company grew into 1,500 superstores through-

[18] It is a feature of the toy industry that orders are regarded as cancellable up until the moment they are shipped.

out the United States and worldwide with a turnover reaching $11 billion. By the end of the nineties, though, its supremacy had evaporated. John Eyler, a new CEO recruited from FAO Schwarz, shut stores, remodelled shops, spent millions to improve customer services, boosted exclusives and the store's own brands. In just two years he poured out $500 million in capital improvements.

In the 1990s Toys R Us had ruined several competitors, notably its two biggest rivals Kiddie City and Child World. Now came retribution. In the fierce 2003 holiday-toy price wars, Toys R Us was forced to sell the best-selling Hokey Pokey Elmo at $19.99 to be within reach of Wal-Mart (who was cheaper still). Eyler believes everyone could have sold out of all their stock at $29.99. But, he said, 'Our choice was short-term profit versus long-term market share; we chose to protect market share.' As it was, even this did not succeed: in 2005, after twenty-five years as a public company, TRU was taken over by two private equity firms and a real estate developer. It became a privately held corporation, and new store closures and more questions over long-term viability commenced.[19]

There are many who think Toys R Us lost its crown because it simply ceased to be very good – it fell behind in technology, failed to do enough to drive traffic through its stores: a former executive who toured stores with me lamented the day the company stopped selling diapers. 'We were the biggest sellers of them in the country. We didn't make much on them, if anything. But they kept people coming in.' Sheldon Hirsch agrees: 'They made a very big tactical mistake.

[19] John Eyler proved better at selling the company than he had running it, achieving $6.6 billion – and $65 million as his own retirement pay-off.

They also sold baby formula, probably at or below cost, as a draw. They brought in a new executive to head merchandising, the first thing she does is say, "I don't wanna have products in here that have no margin, so get rid of it." And guess what? Mom had no reason to go there.' And there lay another irony. The one thing that might have saved Toys R Us was something it had tried before, ending in failure. Price-fixing.

By the mid eighties Toys R Us had become the largest retailer of toys, but in the early nineties a new threat emerged. Warehouse clubs had begun selling toys – and at lower prices. Toys R Us found its market share being eroded.

It decided to use its clout. One by one toy companies were taken aside and agreements were forced upon them: they would withhold toys from the clubs, selling them only less desirable and more expensive special packs. The toy companies were unhappy – they wanted all the outlets they could get – but they feared reprisals. Mattel, before the enforced orchestrated agreement with TRU, accepted an order from one club, the Pace Club, for its Air Pro Hockey product. Although Mattel later tried to steer Pace to a 'special version', it found itself forced to supply the original item after protests. Toys R Us hit back. It reduced its price on the product by nearly 20 per cent and then withheld over $540,000 it owed Mattel, until the toy maker agreed to split the cost of its markdown.

The Federal Trade Commission ruled that Toys R Us had violated anticompetition laws, a decision later upheld by the US Court of Appeal. Separately, forty-three states filed actions against the chain and toy makers concerned. As a result, Toys R Us agreed to pay $40.5 million in cash and toys, Mattel, $8.2 million in cash and toys, and Little Tikes Company $1.2 million in cash and toys. Hasbro, another defendant, also agreed to pay $5.9 million in cash and toys. As part of the settlements here, the defendants admitted no wrongdoing. The toys were distributed to children in all fifty states, Washington DC, and Puerto Rico by the US Marine Corp's 'Toys for Tots' programme.

In the industry, retailers have always been known as 'the Trade', a term often used derogatorily. As a rule, there is rarely trust between sellers and buyers. On the one hand, they need each other; on the other, they screw the hardest possible deals. And, of course, it follows that the larger the power of any company, the tougher the terms it can enforce. Not surprisingly, in the face of Wal-Mart's might and relentless pursuit of margins, toy companies have been desperate to see Toys R Us survive. Rick Jackson, a sales manager at McFarlane Toys, shared his worries with fellow toy men on a website run by toy-industry insider Philip Bloom. Conceding that Wal-Mart and Target provided huge volume sales, he was sceptical about how big a percentage of toy-company lines that represented. 'The industry sat by in 1991 and watched as Lionel Kiddie City closed its door, thinking we still have TRU and Child World and Kay Bee.[20] Then in 1992, Child World also ran into trouble and was gone by 1993, but no one really cared – we still had TRU and Kay Bee.' Kay Bee had problems and closed stores. 'Should TRU leave the business, just where are all those items, all those manufacturers going to be placed . . . We need TRU to survive.'

No toy company would dare be seen discriminating against Wal-Mart, but many have given Toys R Us toys

[20] Now KB Toys.

exclusively – Wild Planet Toys' interactive Aquapets enjoyed a three-month advance run in its stores before being released onto the rest of the market. 'The success of Toys R Us is important to the health of the toy industry,' said Wild Planet's founder and CEO Danny Grossman. In 2004, when it looked like Toys R Us could vanish, several companies not only released exclusives to them, but even paid for the advertising. They included Mattel, Hasbro, LeapFrog, and Lego.

More surreptitiously, many toy companies shipped fewer hot toys to Wal-Mart. Insiders murmur that when Wal-Mart sells out of a sought-after toy, companies will say they have no more in stock to supply them: 'None of us would admit it, though.'

Such mutual dependency, far from alleviating the love–hate, nervy relationship between toy marketers and sellers, actually intensifies it.

With margins small or even non-existent on hot toys, retailers strive to compensate with higher mark-ups on items that customers are not clamouring after. Hence private-label lines, bought in either from third-party suppliers or contracted straight from factories in the Far East. The brand/own-brand balance varies from time to time, but a 2003 survey by the researchers Funosophy Inc. showed big stores giving first or second place to their own lines. In Wal-Mart, their own vehicles got more shelf space than Mattel's.

Margins shoot up on such toys. A private-label toy selling at $15.99 ($4 less than the brand equivalent) probably costs $6.50 less to buy in, increasing the profit by almost another $2.

The problem for toy companies is when private-label toys start to look remarkably like the similar offerings from major brands, barely distinguishable from illegitimate knock-offs. It means the chains get the advantage of research and of shelf recognition without having to pay for any development or advertising. Toys R Us games are often indistinguishable from Hasbro's. Wal-Mart Kid Connection has products very similar to LeapFrog in colour and shape; its own Barbie-compatible accessories come packed in that famous Barbie pink colour; its construction blocks are interchangeable with Lego.

'All the retailers do is copy toys that are already out there,' says Jim Silver. 'They might save consumers ten cents but they're killing innovation.' The UK has the same problem. Jon Salisbury, a well-known toy-industry observer, calls the chain Early Learning Centre 'a master of the legitimate knock-off . . . A request from the ELC buyers has usually meant that a lookalike product was just around the corner.' He adds, 'Privately they might be steaming, but manufacturers know this is the way of the world and can't exactly go public with their disgruntlement . . . you want to have the chance of trading with them in future.'

The need to become less dependent on the giant retailers is one reason toy makers desperately seek more and more alternative outlets.

'We plan to sell product to every nook and cranny in the world,' says Hasbro's Wayne Charness. A slight exaggeration, but it is startling to note just which aisles toys have now infiltrated. They are in drugstores, supermarkets, video stores, bookshops, convenience stores, even sporting-goods shops. Customers can find toys at Auto Zone, Bed Bath and Beyond, 7-Eleven, Radio Shack, Claire's, Staples and Starbucks. Hasbro produced a special Mr Potato Head Santa set for grocery chain Publix, RC2 made a John Deere toy tractor for Home Depot. Mattel put Car-Go Fun Games into Chevron gas stations. Disney had a Mickey Mouse doll as a special offer at Filene's department stores. GapKids gets Wild Planet 'spy equipment', Circuit City has Hasbro's colour-screen version of its VideoNow personal video recorder, and Limited Too has a plush interactive Neopets toy. Lego rolled out a special low-price version of its famous bricks – X-Pod – to sell near the checkouts in drugstores and supermarkets. For toy companies, such specifically targeted items prop up sales over the year, reduce dependency, and although prices are low, margins are good. The outlets do well too: it's all extra, the toys help lure customers who spend on other goods, and the toy sales can be substantial: Radio Shack had its most successful product launch ever in 2002 with a toy, a micro radio-controlled car called ZipZaps.

Nearly a third of all the toys distributed in the United States never see the inside of a store. Instead, they are dished out by fast-food restaurant chains. McDonald's 31,000 restaurants in more than a hundred countries have made McDonald's the biggest distributor of toys in the world with its Happy Meals combination.

The Happy Meal – hamburger, cheeseburger or chicken nuggets plus fries, a small drink and a toy – create frequent visits and early brand loyalty. On the promotion's twenty-fifth anniversary in 2004, McDonald's described it as 'the most successful children's menu item in restaurant history'.

McDonald's was not the first food company to use toys in marketing: Cracker Jack Popcorn and Peanuts promoted itself with the promise 'A Prize in every Box' when toys were inserted into each package in 1912. By 2004, Cracker Jack, then owned by Frito Lay, had given out more than 17 billion toys. The Happy Meal, nonetheless, broke new ground. It had its birth in 1977 when Dick Brams, the chain's regional advertising manager in St Louis, asked local advertising agencies in Kansas City to develop a children's meal concept. In the marketing world Bob Bernstein, an advertising executive who had been working with the chain's franchisees for ten years, is credited with coming up with the exact idea after watching his nine-year-old son stare at the cereal box each morning as he ate. 'I got to thinking,' he said later, 'kids want something to do while they're eating.' The idea was tested for two years and then went national. Each meal featured a regular hamburger or cheeseburger, fries, McDonaldland Cookies sampler (no longer included), a soft drink, and McDonaldland graphics, puzzles, games and other activities.[21]

In the early years, the toy was an original, including McDonald's figures like Hamburglar. Today toys are tied in with movies, such as *Monsters, Inc.* or *Toy Story*, or are patterned after major brands.

By the late 1980s, fast-food restaurants had become vastly reliant on the toy giveaways as their major weapon in a business in which there were too many chains and when many baby boomers were starting to turn away from junk food. Several marketing departments latched onto the importance of concentrating on kids – one study carried out for Wendy's, for example, showed 83 per cent of parents were influenced by their children in deciding where to eat, and that toys were a great persuader. (As a result of that research, Wendy's quadrupled its spending on toys.)

The success of McDonald's 1997 Beanie Babies promotion, during which Happy Meals sales doubled, became renowned in the business. *Nation's Restaurant News* reported in June 1999, 'Customers have responded

[21] Within McDonald's, Brams is now honoured as the 'Father of the Happy Meal'.

to recent premium offers with fanatic devotion, often returning to restaurants numerous times to snap up complete sets of toys or even taking to the Internet to barter among themselves.' By the end of the 1990s, some fast-food insiders joked that some chains were now toy stores serving food on the side. By 2003, Happy Meals accounted for $3.5 billion revenue a year, more than a fifth of the chain's US business. 'One has to wonder how the fast-food industry could live without its kid meals,' commented one observer.

More money is spent on the toys aimed at girls than those aimed at boys – for the simple reason that girls are harder to attract to fast-food chains. Some research shows that girls lose interest in eating at McDonald's earlier than boys: one survey by Children's Market Services Inc. showed that while 45 per cent of six-to-eight-year-old girls said McDonald's was their favourite restaurant. The percentage had fallen to 22 by age nine to eleven (boys' favour fell much less).

At McDonald's girls have received Bratz packs, tiny Barbies, and miniature-edition Madame Alexander dolls. Boys get He-Man figures, Matchbox cars, Hot Wheels, and Buzz Lightyear.

The promotions are backed by huge advertising and marketing budgets. Eight Finding Nemo characters were supported with TV ads, a website, movie tickets, and chances to win trips to Walt Disney World in Florida. For its SpongeBob SquarePants promotion, Burger King linked with Nickelodeon as an on-screen sponsor of an episode of the cartoon.

Pretty obviously, extra sales also result from the parents who take the kids. A Burger King Rugrats promotion, offering twelve toys and four wristwatches, produced double-digit sales gains *overall*, according to the company.

Using toys and games to sell junk food at a time of

growing obesity has not, unnaturally, attracted criticism. Chains have tried to fend it off, usually by small token gestures – in England low-fat milk was added to the Happy Meal mix. In the UK the Food Standards Agency has even organized meetings to canvass opinion to put to government ministers on whether toy giveaways with fast food should be banned.

And still there is the Toy Shop in Concord, and maybe another 1,500 other small speciality shops. Over all of them looms the massive uncertainty of survival. Their numbers have fallen from about 4,000 in the nineties. For every $100 spent on toys, they account for less than $3.50.

They know the chastening story of FAO Schwarz, an enchanted name for generations of parents and kids. It billed itself as the world's 'finest toy store'. Frederick August Otto Schwarz, a native of Maryland, opened his first store in Baltimore in 1862, and relocated to lower Broadway eight years later. By 1931 he had moved uptown to his flagship on Fifth; the store has been in its present site since 1986.

A cherished institution, it has been an unassailable living monument for over 130 years. But by 2003, it trembled on the brink of extinction. A number of factors were involved. A year earlier Schwarz was taken over by another toy retailer, Right Start Inc., already owners of the toy chain Zany Brainy, which had itself bought out of bankruptcy another toy chain Noodle Kidoodle. The new 2002 group – FAO Inc. – managed to combine three money-losers. In addition there was the tourism fall after 9/11, and the toy-discount wars, and it came as no surprise when in 2003 the company declared bankruptcy. When it emerged, now owned by an investment bank, just two stores remained: New York and Las Vegas. The company retreated from the foray of trying to compete with the likes of Toys R Us, and returned to its upscale, exclusive, high-end position offering toys not commonly available, particularly from the mass marketers. David Niggli, the COO, said, 'People said to us, "Is there going to be enough product to fill the store? Are there enough unique products out there?" There are.'[22]

The store's new strategy had four cornerstones: more interactive toys – kids could design and produce their own Hot Wheels car or they could 'adopt' a newborn doll from the nursery. Lots of attractions to add fizz to the store, like a wandering cast of costumed characters. A 'rec room' full of arcade-style games, with an ice-cream parlour. And those exclusives, including a $50,000 child-size Ferrari.

Reduced to basics, its tactic was the same as anyone attempting to compete with the juggernaut Wal-Mart and other huge discounters – to offer something consumers couldn't get at the giants.

The encouragement that there can be life after Wal-Mart is in those stores that have survived and prospered, such as American Girl and Build A Bear.

It is yet another irony of the toy industry that American Girl, a line of historically themed dolls introduced in 1986, a kind of anti-Barbie, should today be one of the earnings successes of Mattel, the pink doll's owners. Pleasant Rowland introduced the dolls in 1986. The most popular line remains eight

[22] Its close equivalent in the UK, the 250-year-old Hamleys, again a tourism icon, also concentrates on providing a theatre-like atmosphere and unique products. But it too has struggled. In 2003 it was taken over by the Icelandic investment group Baugur, but by the financial year 2004–5 its annual losses had increased to £3.6 million.

ethnically diverse characters from different periods of history – such as Addy Walker, who escapes from slavery with her mother in 1864, Kit Kiltredge, living through the Depression, Felicity, a 'spritely girl' of English descent growing up in Virginia in 1774. The brilliance of the idea, not least from a marketing view, is that each has its own storybook, accessories and furniture. More recently, a line of contemporary dolls emerged whose hair, eyes and skin colour can be customized to mirror the girls who own them.

Mattel bought the Pleasant Company for $700 million in 1998. The first of the stores opened in Chicago that same year, the second in New York opposite the Rockefeller Center in 2003 and the third in Los Angeles three years later. Visiting is an experience, something like going to an indoor, ride-less theme park. I lined up, a lone male, with mothers and daughters on New York's opening day, the excitement of the tween girls palpable. These are not just shops, they are destinations. I'm told that advance reservations for the café where girls can take their newly bought dolls to tea had reached 30,000 pre-opening. No rush to grab a box and make for checkout here: average stays are two hours. Basic dolls cost over $80 but that's just the starter – each has books, accessories and related furniture. Then there is the dolls' hospital, dolls' hairdressing salon, the café (with pink flowers on each table and waiters in pink aprons) and live theatre where singers and dancers tell the stories of American Girls (at $30 a seat). Customers often spend hundreds of dollars.

American Girl stores can never be numerous – a major part of their appeal is their cachet, their individuality. Build A Bear has more stores, its largest in Fifth Avenue at 46th Street proclaiming itself the largest teddy-bear store in the world. Again, the appeal here is selling a personal experience. First opened in 1996, the idea for the enterprise came to Maxine Clark, former president of a division of May Department Stores, after taking a friend's daughter on an abortive expedition to buy a Beanie Baby. Customers choose an animal (it's not just bears) without stuffing, take it to a station where it is stuffed 'to the right amount of huggability' and (crucial touch) a heart placed inside. A bar code that is inserted registers it as a one-off owned by a named person. Soundchips can be chosen to giggle, bark and speak messages such as 'I love you'. The buyer can then choose from a variety of outfits, shoes, and accessories, including sunglasses and jewellery. To complete the personalization, a birth certificate records the name and birth date.

This may all be hard to beat for sheer idiosyncrasy. Within ten years there were nearly 200 Build A Bear stores throughout the US and Canada, and fifteen internationally. Nevertheless, like American Girl, because they revolve around a proprietary product, their growth is limited: they can never aspire to super-store status. They offer hope, though, for a toy-selling industry not totally controlled by discounters. Part of their secret is that they are less of a seasonal destination and that they do not have to compete in the one area they could not win – price.

Matters are not so clear-cut for the remaining small speciality toy shops. They too need to provide something not available at the discounters. Store owners are well rehearsed in what that is: service, expertise, caring – and distinctive 'real' toys.

Kathleen McHugh, executive director of the American Specialty Toy Retailers Association, says, 'It's clear now that you can either go to a big-box store and take what they have or find quality, unique toy products at a local store. There's nothing in between now.'

Many stress the 'educational value' of toys. Often they make a virtue of what they *don't* sell, like weapons or certain kinds of action figures. In that respect, many small toyshop owners see themselves almost as a retail market's conscience.

Some offer child-friendly settings. Aunty Hilary's Toys and Books in Tucson was laid out entirely from a child's perspective after input from an architect and from children's designs. It has been described as 'like entering a child's drawing' and features private nooks where a child can snuggle up with a toy or a book. Such shops often adapt to the area. Debi Grymes, owner of The Little House in Baton Rouge, La., notes that 'Southern women love their children looking good,' the reasoning behind a back room where little girls can dress up and throw tea parties, wear white gloves, fancy hats and feather boas.

All this plus smiles, special orders and gift-wrapping may be important, but offering something unusual and original is generally considered vital.

To many in the toy industry, toy fairs are an anachronism. Not so to small toy-store owners, who scour the aisles in the hope of discovering a hot new toy that customers will not be able to get at Target, Wal-Mart or Toys R Us. 'What am I looking for?' asks one. 'New, new, new stuff. I will be scouting the nooks and crannies looking for the guy who is splitting a booth because he's so new he can't afford his own.'

Some will tour showrooms in Hong Kong, buying toys direct in what in the business is known as FOB (free on board or freight on board). FOB can apply to generic or branded toys – companies like Mattel allow some of their non-advertised goods to be sold this way. The buyer has to ship them home himself. In this way, not only can offbeat novelty toys be provided, but margins can be huge, often exceeding 100 per cent.[23]

Wearing their retail-conscience hats, many toyshop owners may play down the hot, novelty element. However, when speciality stores almost died during the 1980s, one such product saved anything up to 2,000 of them – albeit temporarily.

H. Ty Warner is perhaps the greatest living example of what a hot toy can mean financially. Today he has a place among the billionaires on *Forbes* 400; in 1986 he was using his savings and a small inheritance to start Ty Inc., importing cuddly plush cats from Italy.

Warner had already spent eighteen years selling plush animals for Dakin, a San Francisco-based company. Reckoning that people buy from salesmen they notice, he made calls in a Rolls-Royce convertible wearing a fur coat and top hat. With his own company, he graduated to having plush animals made to order in Korea. Then, in 1993, came his masterwork, Beanie Babies.

The first nine under-stuffed plush beanbag toys – a dog, platypus, moose, bear, dolphin, frog, lobster, pig and whale – were not an instant success. Warner had decided his new toy would be small enough to fit a child's hand, inexpensive so children could afford it themselves, and that it would be collectible – the characters, such as Cheeks the baboon, all had names and birth dates. Distribution should be restricted to small outlets, so he retained control, with individual stores restricted in the number of any one item. His real shrewdness emerged when he

[23] In the UK the Toy Retailers Association advises store owners to strive for 40 per cent margin, but warns that TV-hyped product will be 20 per cent or less.

set about creating shortages to build word-of-mouth demand.

Toy makers are often accused of using this strategy deliberately as a marketing tool. As the business academic M. Eric Johnson says, they are 'keenly aware that shortage creates buzz and buzz creates a hot toy'. Mostly they deny it, claiming that when shortages occur it is simply a result of not risking over-production of an item that could fail and cost millions. As a Hasbro annual report comments, 'It is general industry practice that orders are subject to amendment or cancellation by customers prior to shipment.' Thus, a change in taste, a more exciting competing product, an economic downturn, can all mean that the toy maker is stuck with near-worthless inventory. For that reason, stores have an incentive to overorder, toy makers to underproduce.

Warner's shortages were totally deliberate, though – a rolling operation in which specific lines were dropped and replaced with others. The message was: if you don't buy now, it will be too late.[24]

The result was a sales and collecting frenzy. Customers ransacked stores, which in itself further fed the mania. Queues formed whenever there were rumours of new shipments. People believed certain Babies were rare and consequently valuable. Dick Tenschen, a Fort Myers store owner, recalled 'people coming in and spending hundreds and hundreds of dollars'. In 1998 Ty Inc. earned $700 million profit, the only time figures for the very privately owned company were disclosed. The money that poured in came

[24] Others have practised similar ploys. Yu Gi Oh produced 'limited editions' trading cards, each lasting eight weeks and featuring about 100 characters. With nine trading cards in each $5 pack, it cost at least $60 to collect 100 characters.

not only from Beanie Babies. Ty Inc. had other products, and store owners had to stock these also if they wanted to receive their allocation of Beanie Babies. Compliance was compelled by visits from what they termed the 'Beanie Police'.

Speciality shops that had been on the brink of folding found themselves taking in tens of thousands of dollars in unexpected profit: at many stores the tiny plush figures made up a fifth of their business. One owner recalled, 'Our best year, we sold 20,000 at five dollars apiece. I call that found money, 'cause you didn't see it coming on the horizon at all.' He decided it could not last, and put the money back into the business. Many used it to keep going. With the end of the craze came the end for several of them.[25]

Keeping his toy away from mass retailers was crucial to Warner's marketing plan. Other manufacturers have traditionally sold through speciality stores, usually because of cost, quality and volume. Many come from small and high-end makers, several are imported European brands, wood features often. Much hinges on the probability that the majority of the customers at speciality stores are parents and grandparents, not directly the kids themselves.

Some toys, starting small, begin life in speciality stores – and are subsequently dropped by them when the mass retailers come on board. At Where'd You Get That? in Williamstown, Massachusetts, Ken Gietz describes his co-owner wife Michele as a 'trade-show

[25] Many Beanie Babies buyers were convinced their collections would soar in value. David Marks, a Westport, Conn., toy-store owner still sees such customers. When they ask him what to do with their collections, he tells them: 'They make great insulation if you stick them in the walls.' (*Seattle Times*, Tuesday 31 August 2004.)

warrior' who picks up new trends and new toys. 'When the big-box retailers take over selling the toy, we stop selling it.' Over at Mystical Toys, Mystic, co-owner Barbara Sinnett takes the same line: 'We deal only in unique,' she says. Pamela Powers, owner of Magic Mouse Toys, Seattle, says of the toys she stocks – like Steiff teddy bears and Breyer horse toys – 'We don't sell Big Macs. We sell nice steak dinners.'

But you cannot eat steak all the time. Even speciality toy makers need sales – and the big retailers promise volume.

Around 2003, toys traditionally offered solely to speciality began to creep over into mass outlets: Thomas the Tank Engine, Erector metal sets, Rokenbok construction toys. Brio, Sweden's 125-year-old most prestigious toy company, renowned for wooden toys with cheerful colours and simple designs and board games, hit problems, shed jobs, began to farm out production, and can now be found in stores like Costco.

Not least of the problem with crossover toys, of course, is that customers can compare prices charged by the discounters and their local small store. Because of the buying power of the giants, it is no contest. At The Learning Tree, Kansas, owner Jonny Girson says of products that could draw him into the price wars, 'I have a decision to make. Either I buy it and try to sell it for what I can, or I choose not to sell it at all and get something else. We have 35,000 items in this store, so it's very easy to get rid of a couple of thousand.' Tree Top Toys, McLean, Virginia, sold a collection of plastic farm pieces called Chunky Farm for five years at $32 a time. Then a nearby Wal-Mart put it on sale at $14, just $2 more than it had cost them to buy in. Tree Top Toys dropped the toy. 'I can't compete with that,' said the buyer, Susan Hancuff-Sellers.

Toy makers themselves can find they are caught in a

devil's trap. Hands on Toys, a small company in Wilmington, Massachusetts, launched Toobers and Zots, a foam construction kit, into the speciality market in the nineties. Wal-Mart's Sam's Club offered to stock the line, but were refused. Sam's Club then introduced its own very similar kits. Acting protectively, Hands on Toys licensed its toy to Hasbro, who then sold it to Target and Wal-Mart. Hundreds of individual speciality shops cancelled orders in response.

In many respects, Target may represent an even bigger problem for speciality shops than other discounters and big-box stores. Target is more upmarket, offers keen prices – and has gone for toys traditionally found in speciality shops, like Thomas the Tank Engine. It has also created new lines with National Geographic and Discovery Channel, specifically designed to appeal to that shopper. Its Internet site boasts of the chain's 'unique toy boutique in-store and online' and 'our surprising selection of high-quality toys from well-respected brands' and promotes names like Schleich and Breyer, which are more usually found in small stores.

And yet today a large number of independent stores continue to survive, even thrive. There are still bullish views: Joe Diaz, president of Learning Express, a toy specialist chain: 'We . . . think there will be a return to the values of the neighborhood toy store, with unique high-quality toys, great staff and meaningful connections to the community.'

The independent stores do have things going for them. Two years after the brutal price wars of 2003, some observers thought they detected a shift away from price as the greatest criterion.

There is a backlash against mass market toys among parents and grandparents who prefer the more traditional ones found in speciality stores. In that respect, the demographics favour those stores – over 21 per cent of the population is over fifty-five, more than the population of the states of New York, California, Massachusetts, Washington and the District of Columbia combined.

A broad selection, knowledgeable staff and a tradition of excellence are the qualities the Concord Toy Shop offers customers.

A half-swing door and an Employees Only sign is all that separates the office from the rest of the store. From his swivel chair, David Hesel can turn his head away from his computer terminal and take in rows of toys. A glass case displays German Steiff bears, with their pointed snouts and the famous button in their ears, and a mohair teddy only 5 inches long that costs $100. Beyond them is a boutique devoted to vanilla-scented, soft-bodied French Corolle dolls. There is a dress-up corner featuring a fantasy dress with gold lace and ribbons from Fairytale Fashions.

Hesel is only the store's third owner in over sixty years. A soft-spoken man with a courteous manner and an acute mind, he wears an open-necked grey shirt over a grey T-shirt, a neat greying moustache. The screensaver on his computer alternates pictures of his wife Beverley and his daughters, and all the staff here seem to be women. He sips coffee from a paper cup and confesses that when he gets together with a fellow speciality toyshop owner acquaintance at the annual Nuremberg Toy Fair, they speculate over whether when the time comes to retire they will still have toy businesses to sell. It is not that business is bad; just that Hesel and his friend, like everyone else in toy retail, are mindful of the pressures of changing times. And the answer they come up with? He pauses to show it's a question he has considered frequently. 'Yes,' he says at last. 'We think there will be.'

The store carries about 6,000 products. Some are core, like ABC bricks and games such as Monopoly, but each year Hesel looks to replace about a fifth of his total stock – 'you always have to be showing your customers fresh items.'

Some come via manufacturers' reps, some from visits to toy and gift fairs, notably New York and Nuremberg. 'There are fewer barriers to entry in the specialty market for a manufacturer: you just get an eight by ten booth. We'll say, "Cute product, we'll buy it," and they're in business.' The skill lies in not only deciding on the products, but on the quantities. 'In January Brio, for example, will come in and say, "If you buy ten thousand dollars' worth now, you'll pay for it in October." So I will sit here and say to myself, well, I'm never going to buy on last year's business, I'm always going to hedge, probably 75 per cent of last year's business. You buy a safe amount. I don't mind exposing myself to a two- or three-thousand-dollar risk, a five-thousand-dollar risk. But if I do five $5,000-dollar risks that don't pay for me, then I have a $25,000 exposure and I don't want that. They don't take back. Because we pay our bills on time, because we don't screw around with vendors, if I had a problem, I would go to a vendor and say I need inventory relief. But I believe you can only do that once in a while.'

The toys he currently stocks range from a marble at ten cents to a $1,700 porcelain doll by Regina Sandreuter, a limited-edition-doll maker he met at the Nuremberg toy fair. She used to make dolls out of wood until her hands became too sore after years of carving. Hesel is a patient man: he waited four years to get the first order of three wooden dolls. Priced at $2,000 each, they sold in a week.

The most expensive items he has stocked are magnificent wooden horses made by Stevenson Brothers in the UK – they are works of art rather than toys. Hesel sells these to rich locals, while Stevenson Brothers find Arab princes are very partial to them. He sold three horses at $6,000 each, but has held back the past few years: 'I get a little nervous in this economy about taking that risk.'

They are the exceptional items, though. He carries brands familiar to most shoppers at speciality toy stores: Brio, Lego, Breyer, Gotz dolls, Ravensburger games and handmade puzzles, Playmobil's enormous range including fire engines and stagecoaches. Something else his business shares with many speciality toy shops is what it does not sell. Hesel is conscious that customers have a vision of the shop and its tradition, and expect it to conform: 'It's always kinda like, does it belong here?' The founder, Louise Pratt, a relative of Louisa May Alcott, would not carry wagons – because a child might turn around and bump into something. Today's Toy Shop is not that strict, but it will not sell guns. 'Hasbro had a really cool thing, like a gun, you pump and it shoots out these very soft balls. I thought, I'd love to have this toy myself, but we didn't buy it because it was the shooting process. Then next year they had one that shot three balls out at a time. I thought, this is even better. But you have to draw the line: you can't define it all the time – you know it's not correct for us.'

Barbie shares a similar fate: 'If my regular toy customers come in and say, "Do you carry Barbie?" we say, "No, you have to go to Toys R Us." They say, "We don't want to go to Toys R Us." But they will. I mean, my kids wanted Barbie and I had to go to Toys R Us or KB Toys.'

Toyshop ownership attracts dreamers who see it as a gentle self-fulfilling lifestyle, rather than as a business. Hesel says, 'This is not uncommon. People say, "I love kids. I was a teacher, I didn't want to teach any more, so I opened a toy store." All the wrong reasons. I was talking to a friend about my frustration with the specialty toy industry and I said, they don't get it. He said, "No, no, no, *you* don't get it, that's the problem. You think people wanna run professional stores – that's not particularly their goal." They talk about it being a dream, an extended hobby. And there's nothing wrong with that. This is my hobby, I love what I do, but it's also got to take a lot of other things.' There are, he says in a disbelieving tone, toyshop owners who do not use computerized accounting.

It is a phenomenon not confined to America. In the UK Keith Elmer, managing director of Youngsters, a buying group for small toy retailers, tells a similar story: 'We're constantly seeing people who've just got £10,000 on their redundancy and think they can go and run a toyshop. Why? "We know about toys – we've got children," they say. We put off 90 per cent. We say, don't bother, you need more than £10,000 for a start. Toys is just a supply and demand thing, but it's incredibly fashionable and incredibly risky. You need a lot of stock, you need to have wide choice. You have to find the range you want to run with out of a dozen ranges that could all do the job for you. It's finding the right one. A couple of years ago one of the manufacturers told me there were thirty-five different mechanical dolls – burping, farting, crying, kissing – being advertised on TV that Christmas. You can't stock all thirty-five. How do you know which one is going to be the must-have one? If there's a new range and the shopkeeper buys twenty-four pieces and gets left with six in January he won't make any money – probably not till he's sold the last two or three. So that's tough for him. If he'd only bought a dozen and sold a dozen, he counts that as a success. Being brave and bullish about business is very risky because if you get it wrong it can go wrong big-time. In January that manufacturer might delete that line completely and it's sold off to the clearance houses at a third of the price. So we tell that 90 per cent, you might just as well sign that £10,000 cheque across to us now, because you're going to lose it. We're being cruel to be kind.'

Hesel believes, though, that while being professional is vital, it is not everything. 'One difference between specialty and big-box stores is that I've always felt that the buyer at Wal-Mart or Toys R Us is driven by sales and margins, by salary bonus and compensation, and therefore they're not buying based on anything else. Not that we're not driven by sales and margins, that's all very important to us, but we try to balance those out with what we should be responsible for as parents and as members of the community, and what belongs here.'

He knows better than most that the number of speciality toy stores has been shrinking: 'I think rightfully so, I actually think that's OK. I came to this business with a master's in finance so I said, hey, this is a business, this is not a game, I mean, you can have fun but I support my wife with this, I don't have a secondary source of income.'

There have been tough times, he admits. 'We signed away our house four times as security. I recall saying to my wife, "You know we lose everything if we don't make this thing work." It's not to say we didn't have the confidence to make it work.'

Hesel is positive that speciality shops run professionally and efficiently have a strong advantage over the discounters and big-box stores. They have at their call toys that won't make it to the giants; they can shape themselves to fit into their local environment; in return for service, they can win customers for years. 'Take Home Depot – this is a true example – if you want screws and you say to a salesperson, "Excuse me, I'm looking for help," they run away from you, they don't show you where screws are, it's not their area. That's very true of Toys R Us. We get customers one at a time in the specialty toy market and it's very hard but once you win them over as a new parent, you have them. That's an annuity, effectively, for ten or twelve years.'

As to price, Hesel is a believer that speciality shops just have to take heed of those at the discounters. 'I can match price on the very narrow selection that Wal-Mart has. If I had to I would do it. The customer then says, "I'm not being screwed by the Toy Shop."' He holds up a small box. 'We buy this item from a distributor, and we make two cents on it – it retails for three dollars, it costs us $2.98. But it's a highly identifiable mass market item, you have to have it in your toy store. In another vein, Monopoly, Risk, Scrabble – all those classic board games, whatever Toy R Us sells them for, that's where I want to be within fifty cents. I have to keep an eye all the time on what they're doing because that's the last thing I want my customer to do. I sell Monopoly for $17. It costs me like $15.20 because I buy through a distributor, so it should be thirty dollars. But it's not selling for that in KB, Wal-Mart, Kmart. So my customer goes to KB, Wal-Mart or Kmart and sees it at $17 and I'm at $30, I think their response to me is, you're screwing me all across the board, not only on Monopoly but on Lego and Playmobil. You have to be very careful on those price-impression items.'

* * *

It is almost Christmas. This week the Toy Shop's staff is at its maximum of twenty, and the Seasonal Display, a permanent fixture always geared to the current occasion, is brimming with Santas and reindeers, Christmas and Hanukkah activity books and stocking-fillers. A mouse Christmas-tree topper holding a gold star is priced at $175. A blow-up snowman with a top hat points his orange nose, snowflakes swirl in globes. In the dolls section, a girl lifts one into a carriage – they are always left out so potential buyers can play. A small boy heads for the Lego, purposely set halfway to the back of the store so that kids will have to pass spellbindingly tempting toys: Viking helmets, banjos, doctor outfits, revolving mice and clowns beating drums from Selecta Sprielzug.

Inside the office, the telephone keeps ringing. The manager, Danielle (who also buys in merchandise) answers the endless calls. 'They're 70 dollars, we always have them in stock . . .' 'Sure, we have puppet sets . . .' 'We're down to five, d'you want me to keep one for you?'

Hesel breaks off to confide, 'We do enough business that I still work pretty hard but not as hard as I used to. I look in the mirror and say, this is your life, and it's not nearly as stressed as my customers' lives, so I have to do something to satisfy their scheduling problems.' That's why he remains open seven days a week, even in January, although it goes against the grain. He displays old-fashioned values when he admits, 'If I had a choice I wouldn't open on Sundays. It should be a day of reverence, even just a day to spend with your family.' He shrugs, smiles. 'But in society today, Sunday's a shopping day.' And adds ruefully, 'If I want to shop at Christmas, I have to do it at night.'

He takes a bite of pastry, watching the electric train purring purposefully around its elevated track. 'This toy store has given me the ability to have a lifestyle where I am more in control than a lot of people who work for companies.'

A child giggles, the red-caped teddy bear balances on its high wire. 'You know,' says David Hesel, 'I don't feel I'm really going to work in the morning.'

Chapter Seven

GRABBING THEM YOUNG: TOY MARKETERS LEAD THE WAY

'A five-year-old kid is not a sophisticated buying machine; if a five-year-old sees a toy he or she wants the odds are pretty good that he or she is going to get that toy' – Robert Eckert, CEO, Mattel

'Kids suffer from what I call "windshield wiper": "I want this, I want that, I want this, I want that." They want everything, they're consumption machines' – Sheldon Hirsch, veteran toy adman

On a good day the car ride from Hasbro's Pawtucket, Rhode Island headquarters to New York City takes around three and a quarter hours. Time enough for four advertising and marketing men to brainstorm, especially if their creativity is still in overdrive.

Advertising agency men Joe Bacal, Tom Griffin and Paul Kurnit and Hasbro chief marketing executive Stephen Schwarz had already spent hours bouncing around ideas. Preoccupying everyone, from CEO Stephen Hassenfeld down, was what to do with a toy they had just bought. Its Japanese creators had spent a year trying to sell it in the United States with little success. Kids weren't intrigued or excited. The toy just was not moving. In the jargon, it was nailed to the shelves, it looked like a stiff.

Stephen Hassenfeld, grandson of Hasbro's founder and the man regarded by many as the genius and architect of the modern toy business,[26] was convinced the idea – cars and planes that transformed into robots – could be a winner. Hassenfeld had instinctively made the decision to license the idea. Now came the moment of truth – how to make it work.

What happened during that car ride and in the following months helped propel a massive shift in toy marketing that would change for ever how toys were sold, the degree to which kids are considered fair game and exploited, even the toys themselves and the nature of play. Today, marketing rules the toy industry. Toys have become part of kid culture, coveted for myriad reasons divorced from play. Toys and the entertainment industry have become two sides of the same coin: children's television programmes and some movies exist only because of product tie-in and are structured to maximize sales of those products. All that matters in toy marketing is Does it work? Rules, such as they are, exist to be sidestepped or overcome. For most toy companies, it is only about profit. The role of children is a clear one – they are cash cows to be milked. This brainstorming session was the turning point when total marketing of toys to kids began, the bare-knuckle moment. What inevitably followed was the embrace of persuasion expertise and the meltdown of morality, a willingness to bend rules if they got in the way, and the ascendancy of hyped fantasy over product.

[26] His induction into the TIA Hall of Fame read: 'His business acumen, compassion and kindness forever changed Hasbro, the toy industry and all those whose lives he touched.'

The groundwork for all of this was laid during that car ride two decades ago.

Toy advertising at the time was pretty much straight sell, not least because of tight guidelines laid down by the National Association of Broadcasters to which networks and stations adhered. The use of animation, for example, was strictly limited in order to protect child viewers from confusion over what was real and what was fantasy sell.

Tom Griffin and Joe Bacal had founded a new agency, Griffin Bacal, and had set out to change all that. Although fantasy sell was banned when advertising toys, it was allowed for other products: 'With cereals, as long as you worked in the balanced breakfast, you could do whatever you wanted.'

One after another decisions emerged. The transforming toys were no longer going to be three-dimensional puzzles; they would be characters in a story. All the men knew that good fighting evil is a major psychological element in boys' play so there would be good guys and bad guys, each with a leader. The cars would be the good guys, the planes the bad guys. Paul contributed the psychological underpinning: cars are earthbound and kind of innocent, planes are more stealthy, more demonic, more powerful – now you see them, now you don't.

The talk scarcely paused. Tom, who was driving, was the reflective one, Joe, the more animated and openly excited – he had a reputation for calling agency staff at any hour of the night if a great idea struck him. Often, like a married couple, the two men finished each other's sentences. Steve fast talked, decisive.

If the cars were the good guys, it followed their leader would probably also be a vehicle, so he would be a truck. A gun was always bad so that would be the leader of the bad guys.

Names came next. The good figures would be the Autobots, auto from car, bots from robots. Their leader would be Optimus Prime, who turned from a truck into a robot and missile launcher. The bad guys, the Decepticons, from deceptive and the negative suffix con, would be led by Megatron, who morphed from a large gun into a robot with a gun.

Joe came up with the new name for the toy – Transformers. The others were uncertain, worried that it suggested electric trains. Joe was insistent: transformer signified to a kid that the toy could be anything he wanted it to be. In retrospect, all involved agree the word itself was key – cool but conveying a meaning.

A back story was thrashed out. Transformers had all come from Cybertron, a distant planet, where civil war raged between giant alien robots, under siege and desperately in need of fuel supplies. The brilliant core of the idea was that the fundamental form of Transformers was the robot. (It later enabled the marketing line 'Robots in Disguise', a phrase that virtually every boy in America and in a host of other countries would learn.) Both the Autobots and the Decepticons needed to be able to blend in on earth, hence their camouflage as cars and planes.

No longer was this a stand-alone three-dimensional puzzle toy. As Transformers, it had broken away from its role of toy as object. Now it was defined characters in a preplotted scenario. The play pattern was spelled out. So, too was the inducement to keep buying Transformer merchandise. Playtime with Transformers needed lots of characters and props. Its subsequent colossal success would be another nail in the coffin of the old toy company idea that it was simply great product alone that drove great sales.

The only problem remaining was: with toys as fantasy, how do you sell them on television, with its rigid rules against making toys appear to be animate objects?

Griffin Bacal again had the answer, one it had earlier applied to another Hasbro toy. G.I. Joe was first unveiled at the 1964 Toy Fair, quickly soared to massive money-making stardom, but by the early seventies was struggling. Its days were numbered in the face of the onslaught of toys from the new awesome phenomenon, Star Wars. These toys had a whole movie to promote them; poor G.I. Joe could not even use animation fantasy in its commercials. It was no contest, until Bacal and Griffin came up with an idea that would drive a coach and horses right through the NAB guidelines.

Their breakthrough stemmed from the fact that there were no guidelines for commercials for comic books, for the simple reason that comic books did not advertise on television. 'We went to the head of Marvel Comics,' recalls Schwarz. 'We said, "Have we got a deal for you. We're going to license you G.I. Joe comic books and we're going to spend about $5 million advertising them for you. All we want in return is royalties." He looked at us as though we were crazy.'

What Griffin Bacal had realized was that television commercials for G.I. Joe comic books would, in fact, be selling the toy of the same name. And the commercials could include all the animation Hasbro wished because they were not directly for the toys. If there were objections, Hasbro and Griffin Bacal could argue that animation was the appropriate medium for a comic book which, by its very nature, was animated. The ploy was an enormous success. Weeks after the advertisement bombardment, the revamped G.I. Joe toy range was launched. The kids had got the message and rushed to buy it. 'Everything just fell into place,' says Schwarz.

To launch Transformers, Hasbro now used the same ruse. As a bonus, the comic book not only legitimized the commercials, but acted as a sales tool in itself. Larry Hama, who wrote them for twelve years starting in 1982, recalled, 'I was always told what new characters and vehicles to push. I had to figure out a way to make it all work into the storyline.'

There was one more ingredient.

Back in 1969 Hasbro's rival Mattel had tried to position its Hot Wheels toy as the centrepiece of a children's programme. The Federal Communications Commission had cracked down, saying, 'We find this pattern disturbing . . . [it] subordinates programming in the interests of the public to programming in the interests of its saleability.' But now, under a Reagan administration, it was a different world. The go-ahead was given for toy-led programmes. Transformers was free to become a 'programme-length commercial'. It was not alone. Within three years there were more than sixty such programmes where control lay with the toy companies, and where the name of the game was unloading more product. One company, Lorimar-Telepictures, even had a system whereby they offered broadcasting stations a percentage of toy profits in return for screening their *Thundercats* show. Critics called the programmes 'deceptive and cynical' and claimed they were displacing other types of broadcast entertainment for children. Even *Advertising Age*, the industry magazine, called them 'A TV License to Steal from Kids'. But another dividing line had been crossed. The old idea of basing toys on characters in books or movies or programmes had been turned upside down. Now the toy came first. The borders between programme and product became forever blurred. This move would lead the way for other forms of stealth advertising that have taken over much of television, the movies and the Internet today.

There was another major effect. Because the back story and the programmes dictated play, the nature of play itself changed – TV took control of the play environment. The old adage that a child should dictate what the toy does was discarded. Today it is not only shows and toys that are linked. The chain is an extended one – the toys are also tied to food and movies, to games and clothes.

So, much – if not most – TV for kids is now a shop window for merchandise. But at the time what was significant to those in the industry was this: Transformers sold $100 million worth of product in its first year, making it the most successful toy introduction there had ever been.

The scale of marketing to kids today is unprecedented: children have become the holy grail for marketing men. The amount spent on children's advertising in America rose from $100 million in 1980 to over $2 billion by 2004. Vast though it is, that is only a small part of the total spent on marketing, estimated at $12 billion plus the same year. Even in such a world, toy companies stand out as big spenders. Advertising costs typically chew up about 15 to 20 cents of every dollar of revenue a toy manufacturer earns, much more for new products. The promotion budget often exceeds all the other costs of developing a toy and getting it onto the shelves. In 2003 the top four companies spent over $5 billion to promote and market their products. Such spending is essential: the industry depends on fast turnover, quick returns, big hits, and on constantly reinventing those few items that do have staying power. That means creating desires for immediate fulfilment, capitalizing on the guilt many parents feel for not spending enough time with their kids. It may cost big bucks, but fortunately, thanks to China (see next chapter), actually making the toys is pretty cheap. And, perversely, it is children's very vulnerability that makes them so attractive a target – they are easier to hit than adults. A number of advertising men do have qualms. One told the UK advertising trade magazine *Campaign*, 'I've never been able to work on a toy account without feeling pangs of guilt.' Another executive volunteered, 'The rate at which mass marketers encourage children to consume frightens me. I find it obscene.'

Early advertising to kids was constrained not just because children were considered in need of special safeguards, but because it was not considered worthwhile. It was adults who did the buying. When children appeared in advertisements, they were there purely to interest the parent.

In the fifties marketers began to change their minds about kids having no significant consumer power. The baby boomers were growing up and beginning to spend. They knew what they wanted and their parents were listening. Television now provided the perfect way to reach them, where formerly print and radio had had severe limitations. Cereal manufacturers led the way, becoming experts at characters, animation and jingles, all things kids loved.

Television proved even more important for the toy industry. Seeing a toy on television brought it to life in a way print never had. Toys had been *doing* things for years – Thomas Edison invented a talking doll around 1890. However, complicated products had been hard to sell – they needed a demonstration. Now TV allowed that. Products could now be shown in movement – figures could walk or talk, cars could race and crash. In fact, suddenly the toys that *could* do things were the ones that pitched best. Ad agencies, experts on what would *look* good on TV, began to have an impact on design. Stephen Hassenfeld was quick to realize that the appearance and performance of a product on TV was much more important than how it looked on the shelf in the toy store. G.I. Joe's vehicles became yellow because marketing ordained that was the best colour for commercials, a trait that endures today.

Hasbro was the first toy company to advertise on TV with its new Mr Potato Head toy, but, apart from paving the way, its advertising scarcely broke new ground. The real breakthrough was left to Mattel in October 1955. The struggling network ABC made a deal with Disney to bring the Mickey Mouse Club and Disneyland into children's afternoon television programming, a step that marked children's TV becoming an industry in its own right. The Mickey Mouse Club, with its mix of dramatic offerings and animated cartoons, focused on targeting kids as a peer-culture group.

To finalize the deal, though, ABC needed twenty advertisers willing to buy at least $500,000 of time for the first series. Mattel's Elliot and Ruth Handler were excited by the idea, but there was one big problem: the cost of ABC's year-long contract was their company's entire net worth. They went for it and the impact was tremendous. Kids loved the show, those without television sets at home visited friends. The result for Mattel was a major sales success.

Mattel had proved two things that would have enormous and growing impact. The first was that spending money on advertising to kids was worthwhile. Before the Mickey Mouse Club, the total spent annually on children's television advertising was only about $1 million. The giant of the old-time toy industry, Louis Marx and Company, spent only $312 on publicity in 1955 despite sales of $50 million. Mattel, with sales of merely $6 million, now spent $500,000. It was no coincidence that Marx would perish, Mattel would boom. The second thing that Mattel had demonstrated was that kids no longer needed to be reached through their parents – with TV, they could be targeted directly.

Despite their newfound power, toy companies remained restrained in those early years. For many marketers, though, there was growing frustration that the vast financial clout of kids was not being tapped as effectively as they knew it could be.

Then came the 1980s. With toys like Transformers or Mattel's He Men, the only practical barrier to how many a kid could be persuaded to buy was how far he could push the parent who put up the money.

In the two decades since Transformers was born, the tie between toys and entertainment and total marketing has grown ever more solid. Of toys and toy-related programmes, Regis Brown, the LA-based senior vice-president of international TV and video for the Just Group, a UK media company, said, 'In the past they were two different worlds. Now it's really just one business.'

Toy-led programming, though still not without its critics, has become part of mainstream marketing. It now embraces toys from Barbie and Bratz, to Hot Wheels, Play-Doh, Beyblades, Bob the Builder, and Thomas the Tank Engine. Lego's Bionicle started with an animated storyline on the Internet. Then came toys, comic books and books, and the video. Michael McNally, senior brand relations manager, said, 'We reverse-engineered the process, turning a toy into an entertainment property, and the films are critical to deepening the brand story for young boys.' Within four years, Lego was reportedly earning $175 million from the merchandise sales.

Analysts call this process of starting with toys and moving into TV programmes or movies 'going upstream'. Apart from the toys sold, other returns can be well worthwhile. In three years Mattel sold over $100 million worth of Barbie videos for an outlay of only $10–20 million each. Each video in turn also brought in about $150 million in merchandise sales.

At the same time, toys have become increasingly vital to programmes and movies where merchandise comes second. Routinely, many only survive or ever get made if they already have toy and other merchandising deals in place. It's not simply whether a programme will attract a large child audience, but whether it is an audience likely to buy the spin-offs. 'There's a huge difference between what kids will watch and what they'll buy,' Joy Tashjian, head of a marketing group, told a trade magazine. Al Kahn, CEO of 4Kids Entertainment, a company responsible for much toy-related children's TV, agrees. 'Who cares if the non-target audience is watching the show.' Toy licences have a lot to offer programme and film makers. The big toy brands are global, and major ones have been around for a long time. They bring not only familiarity but positive emotional messages, say marketers. And they have huge advertising promotion behind them.

Transformers had more than sixty products linked to each TV series. Not just toys, but everything from greetings cards and juice drinks to backpacks and sneakers. A live-action remake of the early Transformers cartoon opens summer 2007. Steven Spielberg is executive producer.

The film/toy tie-in industry is a phenomenon for which we can thank Star Wars. When the first Star Wars movie opened in 1977, such tie-ins were little more than a twinkle in the eye of director George Lucas. By the time the final episode in the series, *Star Wars: Episode III – Revenge of the Sith*, screened in 2005, there were licence deals with about 400 companies, covering many thousands of products. Even before that final episode, retail sales of Star Wars-related products, including toys, totalled over $9 billion, nearly three times the worldwide box office. Little wonder that Lucas claims, 'if I wasn't a film maker I'd be a toy maker.'

Because much, if not most, of children's TV depends on licensing tie-in, it follows that what kids watch is increasingly determined by how well it will make them consume its products. 4Kids Entertainment is a global provider of children's entertainment and merchandise licensing, specializing in importing and Americanizing action-packed, often violent Japanese cartoons. It took over the Fox network's Saturday morning TV programming in 2004, paying $101 million to lease the prime preteen slot of 8 a.m.–noon for four years. The company recoups the cost by selling advertising, home-video income and merchandise licensing. Its hottest offerings have been Pokemon and Yu-Gi-Oh. Al Kahn is open about what he seeks in programmes. 'We look for properties . . . that will sell product, that are attractive to ages that will support product – typically 3- to 12-year-olds.' The Pokemon cartoon, in fact, not only has its range of spin-offs, but centres around the idea that the best way to be cool is to own more of the 150 or so Pokemon models than anyone else.

Ian Downes, of Fox Kids Europe's Licensing Division,

UK, boasts of providing 'a great promotional platform for new shows, bringing . . . focused promotion and an integrated approach between television, online and consumer products'. He gave *Totally Spies* as a 'good example of a well-packaged and thought-through series that is tailor-made for toys, with characters that are always using accessories and gadgets. Indeed this series was developed with consumer research to try to aid styling and visual imagery in the series.' Toy-sale influence can grind small. Animators working on a new UK television show for showing in 2006 created a duck with a long yellow neck, certain this would appeal to kids; executives at ITV, Britain's biggest commercial TV network, vetoed the look – the neck was too long to be made into the planned soft toy due to go on sale later that year. It was shortened.

Many toy-related TV series are made attractive to foreign broadcasting stations by their cheapness. In Australia, reported Young Media in 2002, they are 'either subsidized or screened with the promise of associated toy advertising'.

As toy companies increasingly try to reposition themselves as entertainment companies, and their toys as entertainment or lifestyle properties, the books, TV series and movies are not purely to sell more toys, but rather to enhance and reinforce the brand. 'When it's a proven toy brand and you add any kind of entertainment to it, it puts it back into top of mind,' said Ben Ferguson, president of Bendon, which markets toy-linked books including My Little Pony, Candy Land, Barbie and Cabbage Patch Kids. *Business Week* commented, 'The irony of toys turning into film stars is rich. At a time when critics decry far more subtle product placement in children's TV programming, parents and grandparents are scooping up movies where the brand isn't just sprinkled into the programming, it *is* the programming.'[27]

One very important plus for the toymakers is that videos and DVDs are watched over and over again – according to Disney research, a preschool child will view his or her favourite seventeen times on average. What that means, of course, is a constant reminder of the toys there for the wanting.

It is not only in commercial television that the distinction between content and commerce is being deliberately smudged. The impact of toys on non-commercial broadcasting has been more subtle, but nonetheless real. Defenders claim that without toy marketing, children's entertainment would be hard to find.[28]

Today, even the best programmes exist thanks to commercial tie-ins; unless kids buy the merchandise, the show is dead. 'If we didn't have products available that represent these shows,' said Al Kahn, of 4Kids Entertainment, 'no shows for kids would ever be available, including *Sesame Street*.' *Sesame Street*, in fact, depends on revenue from merchandise like Tickle Me Elmo to pay about half of its budget, $15 million in 2003. It recognizes the potential conflicts. 'We are not entirely driven by commercial branding,' Anne Gorfinkle, the vice-president of project development, told *KidScreen magazine*. 'We want our properties to

[27] Product placement – or 'brand casting' as many marketers like to call it – is prohibited by law in children's programming, although is widespread in programmes children watch, such as *American Idol*. It is also booming in video games.
[28] The era of children's TV programmes existing without the support of merchandise virtually ended with the death of Fred Rogers in 2003 – *Mr Rogers' Neighborhood* was able to be self-supportive partly because costs were low.

be commercially successful, but we are also focused on building properties around programs like literacy and fitness.'

Teletubbies – once universally pervasive – was the first television programme ever broadcast in the US for an audience down to one-year-olds. Seen by critics as the nadir in merchandising to the very young, it arrived at Public Broadcasting System (PBS) in 1998, an import from the BBC, another organization constantly in need of money despite its compulsory licensing-fee system. Two BBC properties, *Teletubbies* and *Tweenies*, generated £169 million in a four-year period, according to a report on the children's TV business by *Screen Digest*. Teletubbies gift packs have been distributed in hospitals to newborns, and have engaged in promotions with Burger King and McDonald's. In the UK, fresh marketing campaigns in 2007 to push the product range to a new generation of infants marked the tenth anniversary of the BBC's *Teletubbies* debut.

Its creator Anne Wood came up with another PBS programme, *Boohbah*, featuring soft, giggly, sherbet-coloured blobs of energy that live in a magical shimmering ball of white light. Again, these were backed with a vast range of merchandise. Both programmes have been attacked. Dr Stacey O. Irwin, who teaches a course on children and television at Towson University in Maryland, takes issue with the age of viewers, raising serious health concerns. 'The website for *Boohbah* says it is for children three to six, but I think the content is a bit young for that age group. I think they probably do not want to admit that children two and under are viewing it because the American Academy of Pediatrics strongly states that there should be no television for that age group.'

PBS consistently denies that merchandising has

anything to do with decisions to run programmes. However, it has constantly refused to divulge how much money individual shows raise through merchandising and licensing. Meanwhile, some gripe that PBS's underwriting announcements have come to look suspiciously like ads: *Sesame Street* might be preceded by thinly veiled promotions for Beaches Family Resorts, Pampers diapers and McDonald's. A new 24-hour digital Comcast cable channel called PBS KIDS Sprout, packed with reruns of some PBS staples, along with outright ads for Huggies and Pull-Ups diapers, began in 2005. Its founding partners were HIT Entertainment, PBS, and Sesame Workshop. A Comcast spokesman said that commercials on the channel would be targeted at parents and caregivers, not children. Critics, though, attacked PBS for allowing its name to be used in the title of a commercial channel. Gary Ruskin, executive director of Commercial Alert, a group focused on preventing the commercial exploitation of children, commented, 'The public broadcasting system is supposed to be a sanctuary from the more obnoxious aspects of our culture. Kids are already getting hammered by lots of ads. Why hammer them with more?' Peggy Charren, a children's television activist and board member at the New England public broadcaster, WGBH, protested: 'It took so long to educate the public that PBS is different, that if you put your child in front of a PBS program, it's a safe haven. In one minute, they have violated everything about that agreement.'

In April 2006, Sesame Workshop and Zero to Three, a national non-profit organization, were unashamedly open about the target age of a new series of DVDs, *Sesame Beginnings* – six months and up. Zero to Three defended the project by pointing out that, according to a Henry J. Kaiser Family Foundation study, 68 per cent of children under six, including six-month-olds, were already watching TV for an average two hours a day. 'The reality is that the current generation of parents, millions and millions of them, view media as a positive tool. They put their babies in front of it despite advice to the contrary. We wanted to meet parents in that reality.'

The preschool market is a lucrative one for merchandising. In 2003 it emerged that a BBC children's show that was being used as a launch pad for a new range of product from Lego was devised and part-funded by the toy company. The programme, *Little Robots*, did not carry any Lego branding, and the BBC insisted it had full editorial control. Critics, however, pointed out that the programmes gave great marketing advantage to the toy range based on the show.

In 2005 when the BBC revived its series *Dr Who*, it hoped to cash in on its £10 million gamble with a range of toys and other merchandise, including a radio-controlled Dalek. In its first year, it was expected that the range of licensed products would have a turnover of £5–6 million at retail. A full-page advertisement for the series *Bob the Builder* carried the headline 'Don't miss my new series on BBC2 and CBeebies' (the BBC's dedicated preschool channel). The twist was that the ad was directed not at potential viewers, but at toy-store owners in a trade magazine. Jocelyn Stevenson, senior vice-president for HIT Entertainment, the company responsible for the show and others, explained, 'It's my job to come up with the gentle, lovely, wonderful preschool programming so that the company can then go out and do all the marketing and branding, then sell the toys and the DVDs and so on and so on.'

Exposure to characters – and thus product – can be intense. When the BBC reintroduced its fifties character Muffin the Mule in autumn 2005, it came complete with character licensing (with promises of enough advance retailer interest to achieve international brand success) – and an unprecedented three-times-a-day airing.

Time was when ads, like the toys themselves, were produced more or less instinctively. But successful commercials have to attack simultaneously on two fronts – targeting deep-seated timeless needs and desires, and maximizing the impact of the current cultural influences. As companies grew bigger and volumes larger, the airwaves more cluttered with messages, and the gap between the toy maker and the child wider, research became the norm. Children are 'targets'; the research is meant to show how best to capture them. Norman Grossfeld, president of 4Kids Entertainment, admits, 'We're not only looking for ratings, but how to get into kids' psyches on a day-to-day basis.' To achieve this some might think dubious end, research takes many forms. Toy companies and advertising agencies send out executives and researchers to study children and what they absorb. They utilize psychologists, observe kids at home and play, follow them around stores, watch them through one-way mirrors, pore over their diaries, even study their bedrooms. Many US companies use 'cool hunters', who scour the streets to find out what is hot and what is not. Hasbro sent its executives to roam the SoHo district of New York to gauge what was selling at the cutting edge, from stores to music. Insights were gained, it was claimed, into the strength of the retro revival, Asian styling influences, and the merge of hi-tech and sensory experiences.

Attempting to make pitches infiltrate all aspects of child life, the marketers have devised other 'non-advertising' methods. Marketing strategies have always followed the development of new technologies. The Internet has taken on an increasingly important role, not least because it moves direct communication with kids another vital step forward.

The marketing bombardment may be as basic as flooding the Internet with seemingly independent material that is then picked up and repeated by youth websites. Unlike TV marketing content, this material can also be turned into a two-way dialogue or made to appear 'special' for the target child. Websites encourage frequent returns and longer stays, allowing constant brand reinforcement. The US promoters of *Yu-Gi-Oh*, the TV show with a mass of linked merchandise including trading cards and action figures, peppered the Net with material. Brian Hershey, of SSA Public Relations, explained the idea was 'to let kids think they were discovering *Yu-Gi-Oh* themselves while surfing the Net'. Merchandise the following year generated a staggering $1.6 billion.

The Internet has also added new dimensions to collecting information. Lightspeed Research, a subsidiary of WPP, the world's largest advertising agency, formed an alliance with Worldpop to gain access to 250,000 kids online, offering them incentives to take part in its surveys. Such information-gathering methods can sometimes be highly questionable. Two large list companies, American Student List and Student Marketing Group, settled with the FTC in 2003 over charges that they collected personal information from students as young as ten – through surveys administered at their schools – by claiming they would use the information only to connect students with higher education. They then sold the information to marketers. The current Student Marketing Group Inc. website offered detail on tweens

– 'These students are just beginning to understand the meaning of purchase power! You can select junior high school students by class year, head of household, zip code or SCF, and other segments are selectable.'

Sophisticated software and other technologies allow firms to search message boards, discussion sites and blogs for words, phrases and even emotions expressed in order to gauge consumer views. Blogs particularly are seen as a 'huge unsolicited focus group' according to one marketing manager, Sue MacDonald of Intelliseek, Ohio. In one day alone, her company analysed 475,000 individual blogger posts to gauge what they had to say about products or individual companies.

Toy companies have been highly successful in attracting kids to their sites. In 2003 the top five Internet destinations for two- to eleven-year-olds were Diva Starz (Mattel), Toon Town Online, Polly Peck (Mattel), Barbie and Disney Channel.com. These websites have been skilful in creating entire online environments that build associations with products, establish brand loyalty, and collect information. Marketing is blended with content in such a way that advertising, entertainment and information overlap. For its My Scene Barbie range, Mattel showed 'cliffhanger' TV commercials that sent viewers to the Internet to find the rest of the story. In the first month the 'webisodes' were available, Mattel said there were 1 million visits.

Virtual environments are constructed to make kids feel they are entering an actual place – they employ words like clubhouse and world. Once the sites have a child's name on file, it's used to welcome them back on subsequent visits. Cartoon characters seem to personally relate – and reinforce memory of the brand. At Crayola's site kids can send electronic cards, colour pictures – and shop or learn where to buy.

Advergaming is a way of involving and keeping kids and linking their play with a desire to buy. Steve Mellow, of the research agency RDS, says of attracting kids to a site, 'If they like games, create a games site where your brand is woven into the games and becomes part of the experience.' Games give companies ten minutes or more to get their pitch across – and they may be played over and over again. 'If a kid likes a game, they'll play it fifteen times,' said Tom Spengler of Initiative, a media services company.

In a significant departure from its normal heavy TV launches, Mattel marketed its new BattleX toy line in 2005 largely on the basis of an online game and a series of animations produced and hosted by the online game producer Shockwave. This private San Francisco-based company's website contains over 1,500 game, film, animation, and entertainment software titles, and bills itself as the best place to play free online games. Sponsors, in addition to Mattel, include McDonald's, Nintendo, Microsoft, Sony, and Warner Bros.

NeoPets, the online virtual-pet community, offers what the industry calls 'immersive advertising packages' for advertisers including Hasbro, Mattel and Disney, that make branded games and activities an integral part of the website. NeoPets offers kids points for taking part in advertiser-sponsored activities, like watching film or playing games. The points can be used at the NeoPoints Food Shop to feed virtual pets, a key part of the experience for an estimated 11 million kids, who spend on an average three and a half hours a month on the site. NeoPets tracks site activity, providing data to customers.

Under the Children's Online Privacy Protection Rule, there are laws that require, for example, website operators to obtain verifiable permission from a parent or guardian before they collect personal information from children under thirteen. Violations emerge – Ohio Art, manufacturers of Etch-A-Sketch, used registration in its birthday club to collect names, ages, addresses and birthdays. Independently, in a case reported in 2000, Simson Garfinkel found that a program called DSSAgent had been installed secretly on his computer when his daughter loaded a CD-ROM into his laptop. The program, he discovered, was written by a company owned by Mattel Interactive. According to Debbie Galdin, a spokeswoman for Mattel Interactive, DSSAgent is part of a service that Mattel calls 'Broadcast'. Galdin said, 'Broadcast is designed to provide additional content for our more up-to-date products. The program does not send personal information to Mattel and does nothing to identify a particular user.' Garfinkel's response was, 'Maybe Mattel knows something about rapidly advancing phonics theories that I don't, but I can't imagine what kind of "up-to-date" content the company wants to rush out to all the five-year-olds using "learn to read" software. Actually, the only sort of up-to-date information I'd bet Mattel is really interested in offering would come in the form of advertisements for its own just-released products.' Mattel later decided to remove the software from its CD-ROMs.

Advergaming – and the Internet generally – lends itself easily to viral marketing, another way of attracting kids without appearing to be involved. Children are encouraged to persuade friends to play advergames they have 'discovered', thus drawing them into the marketing web. A survey by the Internet research company Jupiter showed 38 per cent of US teenagers shared information they found on the Web with their friends *several times every week*. The UK trade magazine *Marketing* commented, 'The significance of this figure for viral marketing is clear.' In another survey, eight per cent of kids forwarded marketing messages to three others, producing a snowball or cascading effect.

Viral marketing is wider than the Internet. It has many names – buzz marketing, orchestrated word of mouth, consumer-generated marketing. . . Opponents, who fight to curb and control its use among children, often prefer to call it stealth marketing. Whatever the name used, it is the technique of spreading messages by word of mouth, from person to person, often surreptitiously. At its heart is the question, who is the best salesman – an ad or a friend? The answer is obvious, says Paul Kurnit, ex Griffin Bacal president and now founder and president of KidShop, a youth marketing company. 'It's someone you trust, a friend. It is more powerful than anything you might see on television. More and more advertisers are trying to bottle that.'

Advertisers across the spectrum, not just toy companies, use viral marketing. Many have brought astonishing ingenuity to the technique – witness the 'tourists' wandering Times Square in 2002 asking passers by to photograph them with a new camera phone from Sony Erickson. It is especially well suited to kids and toys, though. Marketers can place brand information not only in games, but by planting messages in Internet chat rooms or embedding them in entertainment videos. Passers on of viral messages often do not realize they are marketing-inspired.

Some approaches are even more worrying, intruding into areas parents could scarcely have envisaged. Hasbro, Mattel, and Disney have all been clients of Girls Intelligence Agency, the Los Angeles market research firm behind infamous 'slumber parties'. The agency recruits eight- to thirteen-year-olds as 'secret agents' by giving them free product. These girls then report back on what their friends think of the product, and spread it into the environment. ('GIA tracks the infiltration of your product into the field.') To woo recruits, GIA enthuses: 'You and your 10 best buds hangin out all night with the hottest, yet-to-be-seen-in-stores, stuff for chicas like you.' It bills itself to potential clients as 'A viral marketing service produced quarterly to help create enthusiasm for your brand/product.' It offers 500 slumber parties nationwide, with an estimated 600,000 word-of-mouth participant girls. The message at the time was a disturbing one: 'GIA gets you into girls' bedrooms.'

GIA are not alone. Viral marketers have taken to the streets. Hasbro researchers toured playgrounds, skate parks and video arcades in Chicago to track down eight- to thirteen-year-olds deemed cool and likely to be copied by their peers – a group marketers designated 'alpha pups'. Field workers found 1,600 such kids by interviewing them, their teachers and coaches and by getting parents to answer a five-page questionnaire. Successful recruits were then offered $30 to learn how to use Hasbro's new Pox hand-held video-game units, devices that play an alien-virus-battling game with other Pox units in range. After a day-long training session, the recruits were each given ten units to hand out to friends, and sent out to infect 900 of Chicago's 1,400 schools. Critics called the tactic, 'cool kids and shifty tricks'.

By the year 2001, American children were seeing about 40,000 commercials a year, double the number in the 1970s. Professor James McNeal, a guru of marketing to children, notes that 'At six months – the same age they're imitating simple sounds like "mama" – babies are forming mental images of corporate logos and mascots.' By the age of ten, according to one Boston College sociologist, they have memorized 300–400 brands. Half the commercials seen were toy advertisements. This figure underestimates the amount of advertising that sells toys, however. Many commercials for other products – ranging from movies to children's furniture – are indirectly selling linked toys at the same time.

To enable marketers to devise the most powerful selling methods, kids are gathered and observed by hidden watchers as they confront toys or commercials. They are followed around and videoed in their homes or as they shop. They are given diaries to note what they watch, listen to, what clothes they and their friends admire; disposable cameras to snap favourite images; small dictating machines to record their thoughts. These devices tell advertisers all about their lifestyle. The results help determine every product stage, from initiation to the marketing campaign.

Many toy companies have in-house observation rooms complete with one-way mirrors. Batches of two-to five-year-olds are brought to what Hasbro calls their 'funlab'. Here, in two sessions a day, four days a week, children play under watchful toy men's eyes. Sometimes a competitor's toy may be pitched against Hasbro's own to see which is preferred. There are focus groups with older children to check their response to commercials, whether they have got the 'right' message. Over at Fisher-Price, there is a full-time staff of seven people, several with advanced degrees in developmental psychology. Every year 3–4,000 children are filmed by video cameras, and take part in focus groups or one-on-one sessions.

Details such as colours are researched. Joe Bacal

recalls, 'When the idea first came up of My Little Pony, there was a division at Hasbro between the people who wanted to have fantasy colors for the ponies and those who said it should be like real colors and so they tested it. The fantasy colors just blew the real colors away.' Applause, a plush company in California, researches working prototypes to decide which features should proceed to the next stage. Mel Harner, senior vice-president of marketing, says, 'Changes in features, colors, fabrics or construction can be incorporated in response.'

As kids are targeted younger, so are those drawn into research. Kathryn Malvisi, who identifies children for focus groups in London, UK, says she has been asked to recruit three-year-olds – 'Though heaven alone knows what they get out of them at that age.' Kids are recruited through advertising, personal contact, door-to-door enquiries or by approaching parents in the street or in malls.

The business of researching kids has mushroomed. Twenty years ago, there were about a dozen companies involved, says Deborah Roedder John, a University of Minnesota professor who specializes in child marketing. 'Now, there are many firms out there I've never heard of.'

As children become more savvy about advertising, researchers have to become more sophisticated to ensure they understand what their subjects *really* think. Researchers say that kids now routinely use marketing jargon when answering questions – words like 'the target market', 'input', 'niche'.

Sheldon Hirsch, head of Summit, the second largest toy media buyer in the US, has developed techniques to counter kid shrewdness: 'I sit behind the glass, and we set out a reel of commercials, three, four, five of them and the one we're testing is somewhere in the middle. And these kids immediately know which one is brand new. They know they're being tested, and in a test you want to do well, you tell me what I want to hear. The ultimate test is that after they tell us how much they loved what we showed them we take them to a room and give them 25 dollars and say, "You can't take the 25 dollars out of the room, here's the table of product that you can buy, so let's see what you wanna buy: you wanna buy this Teenage Mutant Ninja Turtle? You wanna buy this Power Ranger? Or you wanna buy this new toy, it's called The Bottle?" And if they've told you all this wonderful stuff about The Bottle and if they put their money on The Bottle you know they're legit. But if they buy the Turtle or the Power Ranger, they're bullshitting, they suckered you. The test is a failure.'

Toy commercials are made by a specialist group of directors, much in demand, but not highly ranked in the pecking order of the wider advertising business. Kevin Dole, a toy commercials director, says: 'Ad agencies go to great lengths to hide from other clients that they do toys. Often a large agency will have a false satellite agency in the same building, but with employees and accounts under a different agency name so they don't have to list some toy company on their regular ad roster.'

The reasons are pragmatic and largely financial. Toy advertising is not one of the hot areas, like cars or booze. Because advertisements are for individual toys, not lengthy campaigns, the budget for each commercial is much less than for an adult product – even though the total company budget may be the same.[29] A very expensive toy commercial would be

[29] Most toy commercials are now made in Canada where costs are lower.

$300,000, while that for a soft drink can cost more than a million. Says Kevin Dole, 'Partly it's the nature of the product. Classic games are about the only toy that remains constant over the years. Everything else is essentially a disposable item: manufacturers want them to be disposable, they want you to buy a new toy for your kid every six months – one month preferably.' Creativity has to be curtailed; not least, the product itself must be shown and its real (or fantasized) features pitched hard. 'You can sell truckloads of beer – irrespective of the taste – to grown men by just showing some gorgeous models in tight wet T-shirts,' says Dole. 'You may not even show the beer at all. You cannot do that with kids. You must show the actual product, you must show it clearly, you must show it colourfully, you must show the actual features. Otherwise the kid just won't be interested.'

It is easy to admire the skills and techniques that go into toy commercials, even while feeling qualms about their aims and the ages of the targets. Such is the clamour of ads directed at kids that they have to strive hard to stand out, especially around Christmas, when there are usually four competing 30-second toy spots every single break. There are particular technical problems of toy advertising – very tiny pieces of plastic and wood have to be made to look dramatic. A Hot Wheel car, for example, is two inches long, a Lego figure an inch and a quarter tall. Kevin Dole explains that a standard cinema lens, wide-angle to make the figure look 'heroic', is too large to allow the toy to fill the movie frame. 'With a standard cinema lens, the only way you could make him full size on the screen would be to use a longer lens. But when you do that he doesn't look impressive, he looks flat.' Consequently, directors use small lenses originally devised for getting into tight spaces for special effects shots.

Edward Rupp, co-founder of Funky Pumpkin, a decidedly cool New York agency, points out, 'If you watch a commercial from twenty-five years ago, an action figure back then might have ended up looking six inches tall. If you get a wide-angle lens – they didn't have that then – an action figure will look 4 feet tall on the same TV.'

There are givens in toy ads, not all of them always totally true but rules that are disregarded at the advertiser's peril. Ads need to be fun and positive, and should always end on an up. Music is hugely important, but it has to be right: 'We underestimate what kids are really listening to,' says Funky Pumpkin's Helen Polise. 'You think it's more a pop kind of sound, but they're ahead of that, listening to stuff it's hard to keep track of.' If a toy is not specific to one gender, it is safer to cast a boy because, according to much research, girls will listen to boys, but boys won't necessarily listen to girls. Because youngsters always aspire to what the older ones do, directors cast older rather than younger. 'That's basic biology,' says Dole. 'Children who are four can't wait until they're big enough, strong enough, fast enough to do the things kids of six can do. Six-year-olds want to be eight, eight-year-olds want to be ten, ten-year-olds want to drive a car.' Bob Moehl has a reservation: 'There comes some magical point when the kid says, "There's bullshit here." He'll look at some older kid playing with the toy in a commercial and say, "He wouldn't play with that, he's too old." '

For girls and for boys, there are different approaches. Girls prefer light, airy music, female voices, pastel colours, and soft images. If the toy is a doll, the secret is to create a wanting relationship between the screen toy and the girl at home. Kevin Dole explains, 'In doll commercials, no matter what they're doing, at the beginning of the shot the doll seems to be looking directly at camera. The whole idea is to feed the growth of the psychological relationship between the child watching at home and the doll – you want that doll to play with, the doll is your friend.'

Boys go for adventurous music, loud voices, strong images and colours. Because combat sells action figures, violence is common in ads for boys' toys. Leo Zahn, a California commercials director, defines the secret of selling toys to boys: 'Boys' spots are usually aggressive, battle-oriented. There is constant attack and destruction.' Boys' ads often have rapid cuts, making for fast pacing, echoing 'the stereotype of masculinity as action-oriented'.[30]

All commercials have become faster-paced, but this is especially so of ads to juveniles. In a decade, the average shot length has fallen from about two and a half seconds to one and a quarter – in other words, twice as many shots in every commercial.

Colours too are often frantic. Funky Pumpkin's Edward Rupp says: 'You want a living room as Funky Pumpkin do it? Right now it would be four walls in three tones of green. You may not live in that living room but the kids can relate to it – it's a hyper-reality living room. It's what they see in *SpongeBob*, *Cat in the Hat*, *Edward Scissorhands*. It's almost like living cartoons.' Helen Polise cuts in, 'Kids are so aware of colour, it's a stimulus.'

Hyped-up motion implies that passive toys are actually capable of independent activity. Commercials director Alan Munro, who has directed numerous toy commercials, says he asks himself, 'What can we do to

[30] One of the most brilliant pieces of marketing in toy history was the decision to call boys' dolls action figures.

imply that the toy is doing a lot more than it really is?' His answer: if necessary make the child go berserk. Dolls – or action figures – are kept in constant motion to suggest they are live.

In deciding which emotions to attack and how best to do so, toy companies and their ad agencies have a wealth of expert help. Observers claim an upswing of mentions of psychologists in advertising journals. Sixty-one mental-health professionals and scholars from institutions including Harvard Medical School and Cornell University issued a public letter to the American Psychological Association to declare un-ethical the practice of child psychologists giving their expert advice on how to target kids.[31] Many ads play on insecurities and the need to fit in with peers. Sean Brierley, author of *The Advertising Handbook*, says, 'It's the fear of social failure. You have to have the latest. You don't want to feel like an outcast.' In the 1960s Mattel introduced product promotions based on a principle formulated by Cy Schneider, children's marketing guru, that brands popular with children take on a meaning beyond personal preferences. With toys, this special meaning is that 'There is a peer pressure within the child's world to use the right one – a pressure that doesn't exist to the same degree with adults.' Nancy Shalek, president of the Shalek agency, said, 'Advertising at its best is making people feel that without the product you're a loser. Kids are very sensitive to that. If you tell them to buy something, they are resistant. But if you tell them that they'll be a

[31] In 2004 the Association called for regulations to restrict advertising aimed at children of eight and under, citing research that showed youngsters accept a commercial's claims without question.

dork if they don't, you've got their attention. You open up emotional vulnerabilities, and it's very easy to do with kids.'

Showing a lot of joyful kids together sends out a clear message: get this toy and you'll have more friends. Allan M. Due, of Ipsos-ASI, Norwalk, Connecticut, the world's largest provider of advertising pre-testing services comments, 'Self-image and security are extremely important to children. They want to belong. Commercials need to reinforce how kids see themselves or how they want to be seen.'

Psychologists advise that one trait that can be exploited is the feeling children have of not being in control of their lives. The Leo Burnett advertising agency spelled it out in a document: 'Although they are now able to throw and catch, wash and dress, and talk in complex sentences, they still live in an adult world and depend on adults and older siblings for protection and security. However, by the age of seven they begin to resent this, they do not want to be thought of as babyish and they don't like feeling unimportant. Both ads and brands are quickly dismissed when children think that a younger age group is starting to adopt them. They fantasize about taking more control; this could be achieved by getting the better of, or appearing more clever than, adults. Empowerment – getting over a feeling of child mastery – is a classic dynamic of kid marketing, tapping into these psychological needs.'

Transformers endure partly because the toy achieves this to perfection. 'Put it in a kid's hand,' says one insider, 'and they transform it automatically. Give it to an adult and they ask for instructions.' John Geraci, vice-president of youth research at Harris Interactive, says, 'Culturally, we've empowered kids. I don't think that's something that companies have created.

Companies have seen it and done what they can to capitalize on it.'

Pester power, or the nag factor, is much used by all advertisers. A senior marketing manager at H.J. Heinz Co. was quoted in the *Chicago Sun–Times*: 'All of our advertising is targeted to kids. You want that nag factor so that 7-year-old Sarah is nagging Mom in the grocery store to buy Funky Purple (ketchup). We're not sure Mom would reach out for it on her own.' But advertisers regard it as especially effective with playthings. Dr Ernest Dichter was the great pioneer of motivational research, the manipulation of deep psychological cravings as persuasion techniques. In a report to Mattel on how to sell Barbie to mothers (who hated the doll), he wrote, 'The child exerts a certain amount of pressure, the effectiveness of which depends on his (or her) ability to argue sensibly with an adult. The toy advertiser can help the child by providing him (or her) with arguments which will satisfy mother.' Cheryl Idell, as chief strategic officer for Western Initiative Media Worldwide, a major market research firm, did a study called 'The Nag Factor' that gave her legendary status in the child marketing world. It debated the difference in effectiveness between 'importance' and mere persistence. Idell later explained 'it basically distinguished between "Gee, I want the pink Barbie because she's pretty," and "Gee, I really want the Barbie Dreamhouse so Barbie and Ken can have a family." We found more products were bought when kids whined with importance rather than persistence. You have to put copy into the ad that gives kids all the reasons they should want this, in language they can express to parents.'

With one-parent families, divorces, parents working longer hours than ever, the nag factor can be used to reinforce the guilt many adults feel. Bratz's Isaac

Larian says, 'You've . . . got the guilt trip from parents working so hard. If your daughter nags you for a doll, you'll buy her one, two, maybe three.' As Nicholas Tucker, a British child psychologist, says, 'Parents have always bribed children. You know you can't buy love, but you can try to get rid of your guilt by showering children with expensive things.' One US specialist in focus groups reports that 80 per cent of children complain that parents do not read to them. Those parents will spend a great deal of money on them. 'What they will not do is give too much of their own time.' The idea of promoting family games nights was dreamed up because sales of some of Hasbro's classic games were falling. 'We found out through our own research that parents felt a little guilty about not spending as much time with their kids as they probably felt that they should because of work,' recalls Joe Bacal.

There is a switch on the playing on guilt that also taps into parents' competitiveness and their (understandable) desire to do the very best for their children despite pressures of time. Electronic learning toys have been one of the few bright spots for toy companies when sales have been stagnant or falling. Toys that promise to teach skills such as colour, letter, and shape recognition, or the basics of subjects including reading and maths, all play on the pressure to 'do right' by a child by giving them the best start in life.

Whether these toys have any real educational worth or whether they are just entertainment or another form of passive babysitting is at best debatable. Many would regard them as a con. Certainly, they are no substitute for parent input – the one factor all child experts agree is crucial. Professor Kathy Hirsch-Pasek, expert on infant language development at Temple University, Philadelphia, comments on one educational toy that claimed it could teach a six-month-old to be social: 'The only thing I know that will teach a child to be social is another human being.' Still, the products began flooding onto the market in the second half of the 1990s. Before then, the starting age for any educational media product was generally regarded as three. With the advent of companies like Baby Einstein and Brainy Baby, the aim was directed at infants. Neurosmith's Sunshine Symphony is targeted at birth upwards, with the claim that it 'develops attention and focus using classical music to stimulate your little one's senses and teaches cause and effect'.

The companies involved, not surprisingly, are quick to claim that the new products fill a need and produce real benefits. Brainy Baby claims its products 'serve as a stepping stone in helping children six months to five years develop cognitive skills, spatial reasoning, object recognition, and an overall foundation of learning'. Disney-owned Baby Einstein's website contains a number of parent testimonials: 'My 9-month-old has loved the videos and DVDs since he was 2 months old. Not only have they bought me precious minutes (and hours) of time to do things like "take a shower", but also I have actually seen his recognition skills develop.'

The learning category has grown to embrace video-game consoles, hand-held game systems, computers, and a range of other toys such as telephones, mirrors and electronic musical instruments that now come with the 'educational' or 'learning' tags attached. Sales increased by 19 per cent from $421 million in 2003 to $510 million in 2004, and the market for 'educational' videos aimed at babies alone reached an estimated $100 million in 2005.

This is despite the fact that objective advice seems clear: the American Academy of Pediatrics says babies under two should not watch videos, television or computer screens at all – it might displace human interaction and impede brain growth and development. And a Kaiser Family Foundation Report in 2005 made it clear there is almost no research to support the idea that new media products are educational – there appeared to be no theoretical basis for saying that children under two can learn from media. A cynic might argue that the real reasons so many companies have moved into the field are, first, that technology has made such products economically possible to produce, and, secondly, that the price that can be charged for them is about three times the average price for toys generally.

Not surprisingly, many see advertising directed at kids as an unequal contest – skilled, money-laden adult experts against naive unformed children, still developing the skills needed to cope with the often harsh grown-up world. The American Academy of Pediatrics was unequivocal in its view: 'Many studies have shown that children under eight cannot tell the difference between a program and a commercial. We consider that advertising aimed at children is deceptive.' In 2004 the American Psychological Association called for sharp federal restrictions on commercials aimed at this age group, younger than eight. In the UK research by the Chartered Institute of Marketing showed that over half of the general public would support restrictions on advertising aimed at children, and 20 per cent would like it banned completely. Even marketing insiders have doubts. In a survey by Harris Interactive, 61 per cent of people involved said advertising was being directed at too young an age. More than half (58 per cent) said there was too much advertising to kids.

Alarmed by possible clampdowns, the Toy Industry Association engaged a consulting firm to track efforts to limit youth advertising in nearly twenty countries. In Europe, an 'informal' industry-lobbying group called The Children's Programme was formed 'to ensure that responsible advertising to children will continue to be produced and exported'. Children's advertising lobbyists argue that it is a weak influence compared with other pressures, and that it has positive sides: it creates jobs, keeps down the cost of toys – in Sweden, they claim, toys cost up to 40 per cent more than in the rest of the European Union because of the advertising ban there. Furthermore, without it there would be devastating effects on children's television programming. And in any event, living in a consumer society, children have to learn to live with marketing – only that way will they learn the realities of the commercial world. Besides, they tell you, kids are much more sophisticated now, well able to take care of themselves.

They further argue that children's advertising is already self-regulating. In the US, marketing to children is broadly viewed as a First Amendment right. The Children's Advertising Review Unit – CARU – is financed by the children's advertising industry, and has described its purpose as ensuring that advertising to children is 'truthful, accurate and appropriate'. Its guidelines say ads should not mislead children or exploit their imagination, nor should they urge children to ask parents and others to buy a product. Critics say that CARU's brief is too narrow and that its small staff (six in 2005) and budget ($650,000) have no chance against the vast marketing machine. It is understaffed and impotent, and has lagged behind newer forms of advertising. Additionally, the Federal Communications Commission requires networks to clearly delineate between programme content and commercials, and bans ads with character endorsements being shown during or adjacent to shows with those characters. There are time limits on the amount of advertising (as at 2005, 10.5 minutes during one-hour programmes at weekends, 12 minutes in the week) though there are many cases of these being exceeded. Programme-length commercials are not prohibited 'for fear of jeopardizing positive shows like *Sesame Street*, despite the fact that it has inspired countless lines of toys'.

In Europe there is a different approach – by 2004 Sweden, Norway, Belgium and Poland had all enacted bans on advertising of varying degrees to children. Sweden banned all advertising during children's prime time in 1991. In Italy in 2003, Parliament approved a new media law banning the use of children under fourteen in TV advertising. 'What are we supposed to do?' asked Federica Ariagno, creative director of McCann-Erickson, Milan. 'Use little dolls or teenagers dressed up as children.'[32] The European Union in February 2005 banned pester-power ads aimed at children – any that include 'a direct exhortation to children to buy or to persuade their parents or other adults to buy advertised products for them'.

There is a further worrying feature of toy – and other children's product – advertising: how much younger the targets have become. Bob Moehl volunteers, 'I guess when I started, they thought the youngest child

---

[32] Advertisers are skilled at circumventing rules – they overcame the ban by filming commercials outside the country, in adjoining, tiny, sovereign San Marino, Europe's third smallest state. The ministery who introduced the law had to admit it had clearly proved unworkable.

you could advertise to and get a result was five, now they think it's somewhere between two and three.' Many would say he is already out of date – targets have grown even younger than that. With the toy-buying window reduced, toy men struggle to extend their market. Just a decade ago, marketing to tots was regarded as unethical; now 0–3 is a hot demographic. Mike Searles, as president of Kids R Us, made the memorable comment: 'If you own this child at an early age, you can own this child for years to come. Companies are saying, Hey, I want to own the kid younger and younger.'

Marketers now grab babies as soon as they are born. Children can be locked into brands early – if you don't capture them fast, someone else surely will. It is not in the spirit of philanthropy that Teletubbies gift packs were distributed to newborns in hospitals.

Even within the industry, there are some dissenting voices, some qualms. Mario Messina, a New York-based toy advertising man, insists he will only direct preschool advertising, which is aimed at parents, not children. Rational or not, products now aim at infants as young as one month old. Selling a toy as 'educational' takes it right down to the crib. Neurosmith's Babbler, a brightly coloured pillow-sized cuddly toy complete with multicoloured lights, teaches newborns sounds in French, Japanese and Spanish when touched. You can buy computer mice for babies as young as nine months. Keith Elmer, managing director of a UK retail toy-buying consortium, says: 'People say we will have some prenatal toys sooner or later. As soon as they're born you must grab them – you have got them (as toy buyers) for so little time.'

Although the American Academy of Pediatrics discourages 'screen time' for the under-twos, children smaller than that do of course watch television. And thanks to licensing, there is a mass of enticing product for them. Blues Clues fruit chews, Rescue Heroes action figures or pyjamas, Buzz Lightyear cereal and racing cars, Bob the Builder toys and clothing. It's the starting point of the marketer's dream 'cradle to grave' selling.

Toys, candy and cereals were the pioneers in tough marketing to kids. Today products chasing children range through clothes, fast food, computers, cosmetics, even cars and credit cards. By eighteen months, in no small measure thanks to toys, there is strong brand awareness. And a strong awareness of one particular brand, it has been estimated, is worth about $100,000 extra sales over a person's lifetime.

Toy men still love to proclaim Product is King. Sadly, it's no longer true. For the vast majority of toys, marketing is sovereign. The toys come a poor second; so does the child.

First television, then the Internet, enabled toy companies to bypass parents and make their pitches directly to children. It was a heady new power, initially used with caution. But, as times for the toy men grew progressively tougher, restraints were removed.

Marketing uses every trick and device that can be mustered. The line between selling and entertainment – on TV, in movies, in games, on the Web – is blurred to the point of near-invisibility. Experts, including psychologists, help tap into emotions from insecurities to guilt. Toy sellers creep disguised into kids' Internet chat rooms.

Defending themselves, the marketers argue that kids are sophisticated, they can look after themselves today. But in truth, it is an unequal contest: practised, adept, money-laden adult experts against naive un-formed children, still developing the skills needed to cope with a grown-up world. Robert Eckert, CEO of Mattel, said memorably, 'A five-year-old kid is not a sophisticated buying machine; if a five-year-old sees a toy he or she wants the odds are pretty good that he or she is going to get that toy.'

The major aim of today's mass market toy industry is to ensure that that unsophisticated kid – whether five or older or much younger – does want that toy, does demand it, does get it. If, in the process, kids are reduced to profit points, play itself is changed, child-hood shattered, so be it.

Without our being aware of it, the selling of toys has subtly morphed into the nursery slopes of consumerism, the training ground where the innocent are indoctrinated.

Chapter Eight

SANTA'S SWEATSHOP

The Chinese have a special word for death from overwork – *guolaosi*. 'Factory deaths due to overwork across various industrial sectors are becoming a common phenomenon in China and often the reason is the indirect pressure of foreign multinationals' – *Ethical Corporation Magazine*, November 2004

This is where it happens. This is what makes today's toy industry possible. This is where toys are produced for a few cents each by vast numbers of young migrants toiling in sweatshop conditions. This is what makes it possible for the modern toy business to be able to spend such huge sums on marketing. This is the hidden face of the toy industry, without which it could not exist . . .

The Pearl River Delta, China. The workshop of the world. Behind high fences, sprawling factory compounds stretch mile after dusty, depressing mile along the congested roads cut like scars across the landscape. Guarded gates control entry and exit. Adjoining many of the blocks are identical concrete boxes – the washing at the chicken-wire-covered windows, adding flashes of colour, is the only indication that these are the dormitories.

Between shifts the workers, mostly young women, their faces set in exhaustion, shuffle from building to building. Shifts can last fifteen hours a day or more, seven days a week – unlawful, but far from uncommon in the peak toy-making season. Inside the fetid dormitories, their only living space, and often packed illegally with as many as twenty-two to a room, they collapse into curtained-off bunks.

At lunch breaks, thousands of them in uniform, ID cards dangling on ribbons, pour past the guards and onto the streets. Some hold hands. Most of them seem so young they could be on their way to or from school – if only they did not look so weary from working most of their waking hours.

We are under a day's flying time from New York, much less from Los Angeles. But the toy aisles of Wal-Mart and Toys R Us, and happy American kids in the television toy commercials, could be a hundred years and a million miles away. In picture books, Santa's beaming elves may still be making the toys for America's children. But this is the reality, twenty-first century. For elves, read migrants – millions of them who have travelled in by bus from rural areas up to three days' journey away, plastic-covered belongings in hand, part of the biggest movement of people in human history. It is of such enormity that it is almost impossible to comprehend. Try to imagine the movement of the combined populations of America's ten biggest cities – and then multiply it seven times. That is the number of migrant workers now officially estimated to exist in China. They come mainly from underdeveloped, poor areas. In Sichuan, a major agricultural province, nearly 15 million people – 30 per cent of the whole population – went away to work in the year 2004. Since the migration began, over 50 million have passed through the factories of this one province, Guangdong. Hours may be long with forced overtime, wages below even the low legal minimum, and conditions often dangerous with unsafe equipment and chemicals. But the alternative back home is often worse.

The dominance of China in toy production is staggering. There are about 8,000 toy factories, employing 3 million workers, spread over six main production areas, of which the Pearl River Delta is the largest by far. Virtually all the familiar American toy names, from G.I. Joe to Etch-a-Sketch, are made there.

These workers make 80 per cent of all America's toys. Without this place with its swirling red dust, its toxic rivers, its thick, choking smog that hovers everywhere, stinging eyes and throats,[33] its anything-goes gold rush feel, the modern toy industry simply would not exist.

The Pearl River Delta in southern China, just north of Hong Kong, occupies an area about twice the size of Rhode Island. It is home to over 100,000 plants, with more mushrooming every week. Not just toys are produced here. There are clothes, watches, shoes, cellphones, light fittings . . . About 300 of the world's 500 largest companies have a presence. The area's low-cost manufacturing is perhaps the biggest single reason why Wal-Mart can keep its prices so aggressively cheap. Forty per cent of all China's exports originate from here. In what is still nominally a Communist country, this is a heartland of unrestrained, often brutal, capitalism.

[33] Pollution averages two to three times the level permitted in the United States.

* * *

To tour Guangdong province today is a breathtaking as well as a frequently depressing experience. It is a major railway hub, with more than fifty ports, a new network of major roads, several airports including a new international one, and advanced telecommunications.

When I first came to China in the 1980s, this whole area was farmland and small rural villages. The Chinese Communist Party leader who changed all that, Deng Xiaoping, now beams down from huge billboards. Under him, the Pearl River Delta became an open economic zone, most of its counties and towns declared open to foreign investors and allowed special economic policies.

Across the border in British Colonial Hong Kong, the Government had been encouraging manufacturing ever since the establishment of China as a Communist People's Republic. The colony rapidly developed labour-intensive industries and became a major exporter of clothes, watches, transistor radios – and toys. By the mid 1970s, though, labour shortages and consequent higher wage rates were beginning to bite. China's Open Door policy came at precisely the right moment: Hong Kong started to shift its production a few miles north onto the mainland.

With its tax advantages, low-cost land, cheap and relatively well-educated labour, a system where workers literally lived on the job and marched to work, the boom took off. Guangdong, and especially that part of it that is the Delta, became the mainland's economic powerhouse.

The Delta's cities exploded. The population of Shenzhen, a small fishing village bounded by rice paddies, soared to over 12 million people, 10.7 million of them migrants. Dongguan, a sleepy town, attracted over 14,000 foreign-backed companies, thousands of factories and a Wal-Mart store at which the workers who produce the goods cannot afford to shop.

Not all of the Delta is ugly and depressing – it is a place of contrasts, sharply defining the enormous gap between the millions of migrant workers and the new beneficiaries of China's frantic boom. Along with the sprawl, the massage parlours, the beggars, there are salubrious housing estates, skyscrapers, expensive golf courses and glitzy hotels for the procession of visiting foreign executives. But it is the miles upon miles of dreary factories – you can drive past them for hour after hour – that create the wealth and linger in the visitor's mind.

Toy making, a comparatively low-skill, high-labour industry, came early to the Far East. It is a business that follows the supply of cheap workers. After World War II it thrived in Taiwan and Japan – the latter country loved it not only because it gave work to huge numbers of its unemployed, but also because it conveyed a suitably non-violent image to the rest of the world.

Moving production to countries like China has advantages for toy companies far beyond cheap and plentiful labour. It saves investment in plant and equipment; it brings the ability to increase manufacturing capacity fast without having an idle plant lying around at quiet periods; it enables the companies to push a key part of the risk of a high-risk business over to the suppliers. In China specifically, there is another somewhat perverse attraction: the entrenched, Communist regime ensures a setting of order and stability. China's tight control on the exchange value of its currency and on labour organizing subsidizes manufacturing costs there. Because the boom has been wide-ranging, all the right infrastructure, such as transportation facilities, is there – customs men at

Shenzhen alone handle 300 containers of imported raw materials for toys and another forty containers of ready-made toys for export every day. Also present are the supporting industries and services, such as the manufacture of plastic moulds and parts and components from the textile, electrical and metal industries. Factories of all sizes may make different products for several competing companies and brands. (With the notable exception of Mattel, foreign toy companies generally have no direct investment in the plants they use, and even in Mattel's case the investment is only minor.) The vast majority of the factories have one thing in common – they simply churn out the product. Design and raw materials are all provided. Because they only process, their share of the total toy cake is infinitesimal. Of the $9.99 retail price of a Chinese-made Barbie doll, according to an investigation in 2000, only 35 cents went to the producers in China for providing the factory, the electricity – and the labour. Another $1.65 went to management and transportation in Hong Kong, and for the raw materials. The bulk, $8, went for transportation, marketing, retailing, wholesale and in profits for Mattel.

The Hong Kong Christian Industrial Committee is a much respected body set up in 1967. Through its contact with Hong Kong owners of mainland toy factories, it obtained the direct labour costs for fifty toys on sale in America as a proportion of retail prices. The figures make instructive reading. In the case of one $16.99 doll, the direct labour cost is 56 cents, a $44.99 electric toy a mere 81 cents, a $34.99 play-set, 25 cents, an $11.99 action figure, 66 cents. In none of the fifty cases was the cost of the worker more than 6 per cent; in one case the toy company paid as little as 0.4 per cent.

*   *   *

If it is almost impossible to comprehend the scale of the migrant movement, it is even more difficult for a Westerner to imagine the daily life of a migrant toy worker. Exact conditions obviously vary, from the acceptable to the unimaginably awful, but it is possible, from a host of reports and of interviews conducted clandestinely well away from toy factory premises, to construct a composite of the life and working conditions of one of the mass of migrant workers in the country's toy factories.

Li Mei is worn out, so she looks older than her eighteen years. Her hair is in a smooth black ponytail, but her skin is bad from too little daylight and she has many healing and still-open cuts on her hands. Her neck, chest and forearms are heavily mottled with the raised red patches of allergy caused by toxic chemicals, which she scratches as she speaks. She coughs a lot, has chronic aches and pains, frequent headaches and sometimes, blurred vision. All these ailments appeared during the last two years: Li Mei works in a toy factory.

She is a rural migrant from Xiaoeshan, a remote mountain hamlet in the rural province of western Sichuan. Li Mei was thrilled to be one of the dagongmei, *the working girls, to quit the hamlet where there are no roads, one telephone and only limited electricity. She was also frightened because she knew that Dongguan has a reputation as a sweatshop. Many young people returned home from the factories with disfigurements and strange illnesses. And then there was the fate of Li Chunmei, who was born in their village. She had been a runner in the Bainan Toy Factory in Songgang near Shenzhen, rushing stuffed animals swiftly from one worker to the next for each step in production. They said in the village that she* ran all the time, sixteen hours a day, seven days a week, for two solid months without a day off. She was paid the equivalent of 12 cents an hour. She collapsed one night, bleeding from nose and mouth on the bathroom floor, and was found hours later. She died before the ambulance arrived: she was just nineteen. Her parents were told it was 'unknown death' and received a small sum in compensation. But the villagers said it was the new disease, guolaosi. Overwork death.

That was in 2002. Li Mei was certain nothing like this would happen to her: she was strong, accustomed to physically demanding tasks such as drawing water and cutting wood. Her parents had borrowed heavily, several hundred yuan, to buy the various personal documents she needed. First, an identity card and the unmarried-status certificate. (Married women required a birth-control certificate.) There was a permit to work elsewhere – and, not long ago, a border certificate was also necessary to enter the Shenzhen economic zone. There was also the bus ticket and money to keep her until she found a job. Then she would help her father and mother and their old parents, and save for her dowry. In four or five years she would come home and buy a house and get married. She thought about this for the three days and three nights on the bus ride south with her cousin, who was returning to her job after the Chinese New Year holiday.

Dongguan has a huge central square, a fascinating place to hang out in the evening, but vast areas are lined with sprawling, fenced-in industrial complexes. Inside Li Mei could see people hunched over machines under fluorescent lights. Young men and women strolled in groups, factory ID tags pinned to their uniforms, time cards tucked in shirt pockets. Motorcycles and bicycles wove through the throng. Li Mei could hear music and off-key karaoke songs. She wanted to sit in a café and have a soft drink but they could not afford it.

At her cousin's factory, the girls found there was no job for Li Mei but fortunately they managed to arrange another a few streets away. She was told she could start next morning. Li Mei paid the woman in the office a deposit of 50 rmb ($6.02 US borrowed from her cousin, an illegal but standard practice). There was no mention of a contract, which was a relief: her father had taken her out of school at third grade, to work with the animals, before she had even learned to write her name. Her cousin had signed a contract with her toy factory, but was not given a copy, which contained her legal rights and obligations. The woman reeled off a lot of things Li Mei couldn't understand about earnings, piece-rate systems, incentives and attendance bonuses. She was told that overtime was mandatory, a word she didn't understand, and that she would be fined if she missed it. There was a long list of items to be deducted before she received her pay. The largest was 90 rmb (over $10 US) for temporary residency and work permits, necessary because the Government controls population movement with these. Another 10 rmb ($1.23 US) was for her factory ID card. There were other deductions for benefits and insurance, for training, for family planning (which made her cover her mouth and laugh uncertainly). It would cost 35 rmb a month to live in the dormitory. Meal coupons would be 120 rmb a month for two meals daily. (She found out much later this meant she would pay back half her earnings to the plant.) The woman informed Li Mei that she would get her first month's salary seventy days after beginning work. Li Mei's cousin had explained that this prevented leaving: if the worker went in less than six months, the factory kept her wages as well as her deposit – and possibly her ID card also, without which her life could only become more *or less impossible. Her cousin hurried away: the dormitory at her factory was locked down at nine o'clock. Li Mei was left to confront factory life on her own.*

What makes newly-made toys so cheap, of course, is mainly how little workers earn for producing them.

For over a decade, there has been agitation to improve the conditions of toy factory workers. It began with two fires. The first, on Monday 10 May 1993, became the world's worst-ever factory fire. It swept through the Kadar Industrial Toy Company outside Bangkok, Thailand, killing 188 workers and injuring 500. The factory was making many famous American toys – Bart Simpson and Cabbage Patch Dolls among them – for leading companies including Fisher-Price, Hasbro, Tyco and Kenner. An inquiry found that defective three-in-one building design where the workshop, the warehouse, and the dormitories are built above each other, coupled with inadequate and blocked fire exits, prevented quick escape. Flammable material was stacked randomly. The building's main exit was locked and there were no fire alarms or extinguishers. In doomed attempts to escape, women leapt from windows.

Just six months later came the second fire at another toy plant, the Zhili Handicraft Factory, this time in Shenzhen in the Pearl River Delta. Most of the toys being made there were destined for the Italian company Chicco, whose preschool toys are widely sold in America. Most of the migrant workers involved were young women aged sixteen to twenty-five. Eighty-seven died, forty-seven were severely injured. At the factory, windows were barred, and only one exit door was unlocked.

These fires provoked calls for action. In 1994 Hong

Kong non-government organizations established the Hong Kong Coalition for the Safe Production of Toys.

In 1996, a year after NBC reported that Indonesian factory girls as young as thirteen were making clothes for Barbie dolls, Mattel became the first company to take public action. A company spokesman made clear one reason for its initiative: 'No one wants to invest in a company they believe is acting irresponsibly.' It issued a directive to its suppliers to abide by decent standards. The action did not stop *The Nation* pointing out that in 1995, Mattel's CEO earned in salary and stock options more than the combined annual salaries of all the workers producing for Mattel in China. In 1997, the company went further, announcing that all plants producing for Mattel would have to comply with a code of conduct regarding hours, wages, conditions, and the minimum age of workers. To oversee it, Mattel established what is now called the International Center for Corporate Responsibility, a nonprofit body of observers funded by the company but administered through the Zicklin School of Business at Baruch College, part of the City University of New York. The following year, the International Council of Toys Industries adopted a code for conditions in toy-making factories.

Looking back, it is hard not to be cynical about the wholeheartedness of the industry's efforts. Toy industry executives with whom I discussed China showed more interest in the problems of preventing product being knock-off (admittedly a frequent occurrence) or the dizzying prospect of selling their toys to the embryonic Chinese market. Many preferred to dismiss the wealth of information about bad conditions as the ranting of unions, NGOs and the media. Toy company executives complained to me that the industry was being criticized because it was 'an easy target', the implication being that it was unfair. After one detailed report by the New York-based National Labor Committee in 2002, the Toy Industry Association issued a statement: 'We are disturbed by the report on alleged conditions in Chinese factories. The conditions described in the report, if true, would be appalling. Fortunately, they are not.' Tom Conley, a subsequent president of the Association, made what read like a tiny, grudging concession in an interview with the industry magazine *TD Monthly* three years later. 'Quite frankly, their [the Chinese] labor standards are stricter than our labor standards. But recently there have been a lot of local exceptions to those labor standards.' He also made it clear who he felt lay behind publicizing abuses: 'We know that the U.S. labor movement has invested sizeable amounts of money to point out repeated abuses in China for the purpose of stopping the exodus of jobs out of the United States. Maybe in some industries, it makes sense: in the toy industry it makes no sense because those jobs have been gone for 20 years.'

Tom Conley may be right about the labour movement's motives for helping publicize abuses; it still doesn't alter the abuses themselves. Moreover, although his point about China's labour standards being tougher than those of the US is correct in theory, in practice, the gap between the law and reality is vast. *The China Business Review*, the official magazine of the US–China Business Council, says, 'Labor rights violations are so widespread in China that violations can be presumed to exist in every factory until proven otherwise.'

China has labour laws setting out everything from minimum wages (which vary city by city), to the working week (40 hours), to maximum overtime (36 hours a month), and the minimum working age (16). In practice the laws are routinely violated. A Swedish study found that five out of nine suppliers it investigated in depth contravened the law by not having any minimum-wage guarantee. At one of the plants, the workers said that their weekly wages during the low season could be well under half the legal minimum. The money they received was simply not sufficient for them to sustain themselves outside the plants, which was why the majority lived in the factory dormitories.

The result, claim many, is a nineteenth-century world. In an interview with a newspaper published by China's Department of Labour and Social Security, Han Zhili, who runs a citizens' rights centre, does not mince his words: 'Our labour relations are going back in time, back to the early days of the industrial revolution in . . . Europe.'

By law, the maximum time per week any Chinese worker should be on the assembly line works out at 53 hours. Robin Munro, research director of the *China Labour Bulletin*, a Hong Kong-based journal supporting independent unions and workers' rights, asks, 'How many factories in southern China do you know that work 53 hours a week? None. Eighty hours is very common.' Zhang Ye, China country director of the Asia Foundation in Beijing, says the average working day for migrants in 2003 was 11–12 hours, typically seven days a week. In August 2006, the Chinese press carried the story of a female migrant worker who died from brain-stem bleeding after reportedly working non-stop for 21 hours in a toy factory in Zengzheng county in Guangzhou. Yang Xixiang had left her home village in Chongqing to find work to support her husband's hepatitis B treatment. On this occasion, the toy factory finally agreed to pay her family 52,000 yuan in compensation after fellow workers went on strike in protest. One co-worker said they routinely started work at 8 a.m. and finished at 2 a.m. or 3 a.m. the next day. As to pay, even the state-controlled ACFTU estimated there were 94 million migrant workers whose bosses had kept back over 100 billion yuan in wages.

Because of China's laws on residence, migrant workers do not qualify for many basic services: the National Economic Research Institute in Beijing found 17 per cent of migrants in a survey could not even afford to see a doctor.

Li Mei's factory is one of three buildings in a compound with high fences and a sliding metal gate where two guards check everyone going in and out. Beside it stands a long warehouse and then the tall dormitory block. Li Mei was taken up many stone stairs so narrow it was difficult for two people to pass. Her dormitory was on the eighth floor, a small room about 12 by 23 feet, dark, drab and damp. She found out later there were 32 rooms just like it on this floor alone. It was lit by a single fluorescent bar – her wages would have electricity costs docked – and the floor was bare concrete. Double and triple bunk beds made of metal took up every inch of wall space, leaving a narrow corridor down the centre of the room. She learned later that during peak periods, when the factory took on extra staff, twenty or more girls would pack in to sleep here, some squeezed two to a single bed. Several bunks had thin mattresses, others folded blankets. Some were occupied, their inhabitants silent behind sheets or torn plastic draped to provide a little privacy. Pictures from magazines were stuck to the cinderblock walls and possessions were stored in the bunk spaces: rolls of lavatory paper, transistors, plastic bags crammed with clothes, a couple of blouses hanging from a nail. Towels were bunched on wire hangers, toothbrushes and tubes of toothpaste stuck in mugs. Under the window, a grubby sink had a single tap. Beside it stood a mop and several cracked plastic buckets. The window was open so she could see iron grates outside, where wet clothing hung. There were three fans, and a single, communal desk. A notice was stuck to the wall, rules which another girl later read to her. There were many so she could remember only a few: No basking clothes in some river. No step on grass, offenders will be fined 50 yuan. No male or female staff going to the other gender's dormitory. The offender will be fired out.

Li Mei waited in a long queue of girls for the bathroom which two dozen people used to shower and wash their clothes. She was still there at midnight, when everyone in the village would have long been asleep, but the workers were only just off shift, too tired even to grumble as they waited for what seemed like hours to shower. Sometimes, the girl beside her said, there was no water for showers or even to brush your teeth, and the toilet was 'horrible'. Li Mei found the water (which like lavatory paper she was charged for) was almost cold and before she was finished, the next girl in line was banging on the door. It was almost 2 a.m. before the queuing stopped. By then she was finally in her lower-bunk bed, separated from the hard surface by a straw mat even thinner than the one she used at home.

Next morning she had no breakfast, for it was a meal she would have to buy and prepare herself – only management staff and group leaders had breakfast provided. It was difficult to get dressed and tidy with so many girls sharing the narrow space between the bunks. At 7.30 a.m., in factory uniform of blue blouse with a white collar over trousers with her ID card displayed (she would be fined 5 rmb if she did not wear it, two days' wages if it was lost), she followed her guide through passages lined with cardboard boxes. The air in the spraying and colouring department was filled with paint dust and smelled sourly of chemicals – acetone, ethylene, trichloride, benzene – and hurt her throat. The windows were fitted with heavy wire mesh, the exits locked to prevent pilfering. Noisy ventilators added to the din of the spraying machines so the team leader had to shout at Li Mei to be heard. She was given a blue chef's apron to wear and shown how to paint the eyes of the dolls with four pens of different sizes : fussy work, she thought, easy enough. But she had to paint one every 7.2 seconds – 4,000 a day. She was warned to check the chemical labels on the tins of paint and thinner she was to use, but not asked if she could read. One of the girls – some were only twelve or thirteen – told her no one understood the labels or even if they were correct, and some were labelled in English anyway. Li Mei's cotton mask and gloves were thin and by the end of the second day they were thick with paint particles and useless. She asked for new ones but was refused: they were replaced just once a week. Her hands became stained with the chemical paint which plain water would not remove. The girls showed her how to clean them with solvents which irritated her skin, and whose hazards they were ignorant of. During the first few days she found the overpowering heat combined with the smell of chemicals repulsive. She felt she was going to throw up and she had stomach aches and felt dizzy. Once she fainted: her section leader told her to have a rest, rub on some herbal ointment and go back to work.

The toy industry's response to bad conditions has been to go the route of establishing codes of practice and auditing them, despite the fact that there are strong arguments against dependence on such a system, both on principle and practical grounds. There have been so many different codes that some toy factories reputedly had to submit to as many as fifty monitoring visits in a year from different companies. The International Council of Toy Industries, the toy men's global trade association, bore this allegation in mind when in 2002, it agreed to launch CARE, a worldwide auditing process: under it there would be one audit system for the industry. It also overcame one of the other major criticisms of auditing: that companies monitored themselves. Auditing is now by professional groups. By late 2005, sixty-five US brands and over 200 worldwide had signed agreements that they would only accept products from factories confirmed as being in compliance with the code. At the same time, more than 400 Chinese factories entered the programme. Six independent audit firms were appointed.

Despite such efforts, many critics claim codes and monitoring can never do more than alleviate the sweatshop problem, and that the toy companies themselves know this and only push them for public relations reasons. Li Youhan, a corporate social responsibility specialist within China, is one such critic: he believes companies ultimately are really concerned about their sales in Europe and the US, and that codes and monitoirng are all about corporate image, with little real concern for the workers in China. The National Labor Committee's Charles Kernaghan believes codes can never be the answer; to him they are simply a dangerous 'privatization of human rights'. Large toy companies depend on the law for their own rights, he says: 'But they're saying to the people, "We'll keep the laws for our own trademarks and our logos but for human rights and work rights, we'll have private monitoring schemes."' He is convinced one reason the industry pushes monitoring is to try to head off 'enforceable laws backed by sanctions, which are as strong as the laws protecting their trademarks. They're going to circle the wagons and do everything possible to make sure they keep this thing in their private hands.'

Dr Stephen Frost, Hong Kong academic and Chinese labour expert, recalls that an Asia Monitor Resource Center researcher visiting a Chinese factory producing goods for a well-known multinational company noticed that in contrast to the warning and safety signs in Chinese that dotted the factory walls, there was a solitary sign in English – a copy of the company's workplace code of conduct. He asked why it was in English – a language workers could not read – if it was meant to tell workers of their rights. The manager agreed, but confessed that he had never really thought about it. To Frost this confirms that codes of conduct are not written for workers: 'They are written about workers, for an audience elsewhere – in shopping malls, on university campuses, or in cyberspace. Codes of conduct are not written by Chinese or Thai workers. Managers in Chicago or Los Angeles write them in a language that engages protest movements and consumer action groups. Codes are not the result of consultations with workers or freely elected representatives. They are the result of media campaigns that publicize wages and working conditions beyond the imaginations of most European and North American shoppers. They are the product of consumer threats and boycotts. They are not designed to transform Asian workplaces. They are designed to protect and promote brand names and markets.'

* * *

Li Mei sneezed constantly and her eyes streamed, spoiling her work. They moved her to the moulding department. She felt a blast of heat – she was told later it rose to 104° Fahrenheit – when the door was opened, and the air was fuzzy with fibrous dust and the smell of burning plastic. Here she was told to watch the other workers and then began to stamp out parts of plastic dolls with repetitive movements performed many times a minute, 3,000 times a day. Open the machine, put in the plastic, press the machine, take out the plastic. Gloves were issued but no one could wear them – it was unbearably hot and they made it too difficult to handle the tiny plastic parts: once the production line started, her hands and eyes could not stop for a minute.

Li Mei had to learn a lot of rules because she would be fined for any infraction. Her section leader – whose name, like those of all the managers, she had to memorize – told her she must not leave her work position at all during her shift. There was to be no chatting, joking, laughing or quarrelling. She must not disturb anyone's work, nap, or read a newspaper. She must not fail to punch her work card, nor must she punch in for another worker. She would lose two hours' wages for each minute she was late, and for half an hour's lateness she would lose a whole day's pay including overtime. No lingering after work, or dropping parts on the floor. For poor work she could be dismissed or fined to cover the spoiled part. So she worked carefully – and too slowly: she was fined two days' pay.

Like most migrant workers, Li Mei knew within a month that she was being exploited (almost all the working and living conditions she endures are unlawful). But at this factory, although workers have heard rumours of people at other factories mounting *public protests, even forming picket lines, they felt powerless.*

Li Mei soon had small wounds on her hands and elbows, burn marks on her uniform, her shoes, and socks. When they moved her to trimming the plastic toys with small sharp knives, she often cut herself. She made many mistakes at first because of her inexperience, and her team leader insisted she redo the work that same day, no matter how tired she was. She soon saw that other departments endured equally bad conditions: where they made the toy cars, the heat from the melting of zinc was almost beyond bearing, and accidents occurred because the floor was so slippery. The sound level there was considerably higher than in Li Mei's department, as workers inserted and removed moulds from the machines without a break, but they had no ear muffs to protect against hearing loss. When Li Mei was very tired she cut her hand – the machine she was using lacked basic safeguards – and it bled heavily, but the medical box was locked. Rather than pay in the medical clinic, she bound the wound up in a bit of cloth. Much worse things happened: workers in the die-casting and moulding departments lost fingers and even arms, while hole-making workers often had their hands punctured and crushed because they had no re-inforced gloves. (Workers in those departments were the only people to have industrial injuries insurance, although this, like old-age insurance which only the managerial staff are granted, is part of Chinese legislation for every worker.) Chinese Labour Law also demands yearly body check-ups to keep the workforce in good health and while some factories pay for these, others insist the workers themselves do so. Li Mei's factory charges 40 rmb ($4.83), more than three days' wages. The workers view the check-ups with *trepidation because management uses them to screen for and fire sick workers, 'advising' them to take a 'long vacation'. If, as regularly happens, hepatitis B is discovered – spread through sharp edges at work and overcrowded conditions – workers are fired without compensation.*

At 11.30 a.m. they break for lunch until 1.30 a.m. Li Mei waits in line in the canteen. She had been told on her first day that she would be fined for leaving food – an unimaginable idea then – but now she struggles to eat it. The food is cheap compared to a meal in a restaurant, but poor quality, maybe one dish of boiled pork leg with seaweed, two of vegetables – greens and some small pickle slices. Many people choose to buy food from stalls at the factory gates, even though the cost of food is already docked from their wages. Many of the girls don't really want to eat anyway because of working under such heat.

They go back to work from 1.30 p.m. to 5.30 p.m., and after another meal return to their workplaces from 6.30 p.m. to 11.30 p.m. They are given a coupon for a snack before starting forced overtime work to fulfil their quota. On a typical day this could be until 2 a.m., and at peak periods 4 a.m. There are twelve public, paid holidays each year in China, but the factory ignores them. (Her cousin's factory allows just six.) Li Mei learned that the only time she wouldn't have to work overtime at night was during the mid-autumn festival. It is typical practice for management to raise the production quota. Forty-five batches of toy pens might be the quota for an eight-hour shift and keep everyone at full stretch, but then it would be raised to 60 and again to 70, and the workers must stay as long as it takes to fulfil or face a fine. Sometimes they are so busy that even after leaving work at 4 a.m., they have to be on the early morning shift next day without *any break at all. Or they might work an overnight shift from 6 p.m. to 6 a.m. It is hard not to doze off in the hot workrooms, and for that they will be fined 30 to 40 rmb ($3.62 to $4.83). During peak periods, the girls have their lunch still sitting in their workstations, and then they can use the rest of the time to sleep there, too, slumped across the tables. They save the time it takes to walk to the dormitories – and avoid the risk of being fined for lateness.*

To avoid interruptions on the production line, access to bathrooms and drinking water is restricted to just one worker per section at a time. They are given an 'off-duty permit' and told to be very quick – there are fines for taking more than five minutes. Sometimes, when the production line is working fast and the girls ask for bathroom permission they are told, 'You can be off soon. Go later when you're off duty. Hurry through the work!'

The most obvious criticism of using company codes to regulate working conditions is the claim that, although they might bring about some improvements, they do not cure the problem. They are Band-Aids.

Mattel was not only early into audits, but compared with other toy companies has a sophisticated monitoring scheme and has been relatively transparent. Even here, though, activists point out sweatshop abuses have not been eliminated. In 2004, seven years after the code's implementation, the *Los Angeles Times* interviewed workers at thirteen factories in China, Indonesia and Mexico that make Mattel products. The headline summed up 'Sweat, Fear and Resignation Amid All the Toys. Despite Mattel's efforts to police factories, thousands of workers are suffering.'

At one factory, *Times* reporters found workers going three weeks without a day off, others whose overtime was forced. At another, workers sometimes laboured 24 hours straight at about 20 cents an hour. They endured poor ventilation, a lack of bathroom breaks, and feared beating if they complained. Near Shenzhen, workers recounted how they routinely worked 11 hours a day, six days a week; in Indonesia, a 21-year-old woman talked of friends and colleagues who had assembled Barbie dolls for 30 days straight without any time off; at a Mattel-owned factory in Guanyao, Hangzhou, 'workers are so fatigued that those who return early from lunch sleep at their spots on the assembly line, their heads resting on their hands.' Some workers at one plant received no pay at all after charges were subtracted for meals and rent.

During Li Mei's second month, there is an inspection by foreign businessmen and buyers. The factory has a procedure for these 'show tours' which they know of long beforehand. A 'Welcome' sign is posted at the gate and the factory, including the narrow corridors usually packed with flammable materials, is tidied and cleaned, medicine boxes unlocked. Dangerous chemicals are hidden, safety gloves and respiratory masks distributed. The cafeteria is cleaned, food (briefly) improves. Underage workers have to leave the factory grounds before the inspectors arrive, and some are even sent home. Others are told to go to the cinema. Girls in overcrowded dormitories are instructed to pack away their possessions, so it seems that fewer people are in occupation. The books are doctored: workers are told to sign both a real payslip and a false one when they collect their wages, fake payrolls showing higher wages are put in place, fake time cards display legal hours and overtime. For workers like Li Mei, contracts are produced and distributed before the inspectors arrive – and re-collected when they leave.

The workers are all very tense during the inspection. They have to learn by heart – just the way they did at school – a long list of answers to anticipated questions. 'Management tell us to lie to the auditors,' a man from the spraying department warns Li Mei.

Q. *How long is the work-week?*
A. *Five days a week.*
Q. *Can you choose not to work overtime during rush orders?*
A. *Yes. Just talk to the foreman or register with the Department of Personnel.*
Q. *Does the factory withhold your salary?*
A. *No.*
Q. *When you start, is there any deposit?*
A. *No.*
Q. *If you make a mistake at work, is there a penalty?*
A. *No. The team head and foreman will teach us with patience.*
Q. *How many people live in a dorm? Do you feel crowded? Is there enough light?*
A. *Ten people. It is not crowded. There is enough light.*

And afterwards, those who answered correctly – and no one chose not to, knowing they could be fired – received 50 rmb, several days' pay. (90 rmb = $10)

It is a perverse fact that just as auditing of factories has developed, so too has anti-auditing – factories have become more sophisticated and proficient at hiding the truth about conditions. A 24-year-old worker at the Shenzhen factory told the *Los Angeles Times*, 'Mattel has no way to know the truth about what really goes on here. Every time there is an inspection, the bosses tell us what lies to say.' Workers said that because Mattel inspected twice a year, managers promised extra pay if they lied that they worked only eight hours a day, six days a week. Leung Pak-nang, of the Hong Kong Christian Industrial Committee, describes local managers deceiving monitors with a second set of books and false time cards. 'Workers are warned that they'll lose their jobs if they talk.' Kelvin Ho Chun-Hung, a director at CSCC, an American social auditing firm, said, 'It gets more difficult for monitors to detect cheating. We know how to audit better, but the factories learn from us and then try to get around the audits.'

In one absolutely devastating look at monitoring, Dr Dara O'Rourke, an assistant professor at Massachusetts Institute of Technology, accompanied auditors from Pricewaterhouse Coopers on factory inspections in China and Korea and then assessed them. The company is the world's largest private monitor of labour practices, and its audits include those for major toy companies and for Disney and Wal-Mart. Dr O'Rourke reported, 'In these inspections, PwC auditors found minor violations of labor laws and codes of conduct. However, the auditors missed major labor practice issues. Auditors failed to note: hazardous chemical use and other serious health and safety problems; barriers to freedom of association and collective bargaining; violations of overtime laws; violations of wage laws; timecards that appeared to be falsified.' He noted, 'These omissions are due to problems in PwC's monitoring methods. PwC auditors gathered information primarily from managers rather than workers, depending largely on data provided by management. Worker interviews were problematic. All interviews were conducted inside the factories. PwC auditors had managers help them select workers to be interviewed, had the managers collect their personnel files, and had them bring the workers into the office for the interviews. The managers knew who was being interviewed, for how long, and on what issues.'

It might be argued that all that is wrong is how monitors go about their tasks, but later reports show continuing failures in auditing.

In yet another piece of research, this time involving 100 interviews with workers at nine Chinese toy factories in 2004, investigators found seven of the nine plants had been systematically cheating during audits. The organizations behind the report, Fair Trade Center and SwedWatch, said, 'Our survey shows serious problems. At five of the factories the workers work up to fourteen hours per day. At six of the factories, the workers do not even have one day off per week during peak season.'

It is a problem not restricted to toy factories. The *Financial Times* recently found that auditors were estimating that more than half of the factories they saw in China were falsifying time cards and documents to hide excessive hours, underpayment, and health and safety inadequacies. It means, said the newspaper, 'that some Western groups' assurances that they are abiding by China's labour laws and their own codes of conduct are based on faulty information.' Gary Beadell, managing director of Level Works, an auditing group, estimated that over 90 per cent of the factories he saw in China falsified at least some of their records.

It is not just that workers are forced to lie; many are afraid that if they tell the truth, they will be out of a job: American companies have cancelled contracts after factories have been exposed. This is a factor that, say critics, has also hampered campaigns against toy sweatshops. Although they are committed to expose and bring change, campaigners do not want to destroy jobs. Charles Kernaghan admits, 'You can't call for boycotts. It is true that in the global economy it is better to be exploited than to have no job at all.'

For campaigners, a defining moment took place in 2000 after a McDonald's toy supplier was exposed for using child labour. Because of this, the company ended its contract with City Toys, a premium toy supplier operating in Shenzhen, resulting in the closing down of four subsidiary plants of City Toys and the immediate lay-off of tens of thousands of workers without compensation. For that reason, organizations such as the Hong Kong Christian Industrial Committee which expose abuses, no longer identify individual factories. It may lessen the impact of their findings, but it does not throw migrants out of work.

One of the virtually insurmountable difficulties of monitoring is what the monitors do not see. There are thousands and thousands of subcontractors; a main supplier may be inspected, but workers elsewhere may actually be doing some or all of the job. It is a key feature of the toy business that only the companies themselves know where their toys are actually made. Even that is not strictly correct – because of sub-contracting, they may not know the truth. Those who buy in from distributors may draw in products from hundreds of different factories. A labour-rights staff member at one of the big-name companies confided to labour experts Anita Chan and Hong-zen Wang that standards at the company's major suppliers had improved under monitoring – but at subcontractors they had declined.

Toyman, one of the largest toy suppliers in Sweden,

imports 95 per cent of its goods from China. The managing director of the company, Stefan Risberg, admitted that he did not know very much about the working conditions under which their toys are manufactured: 'We have papers, which say that the workers live decently and that there is no child labour.' But it was impossible to check upon the suppliers' subcontracted factories, he maintained, estimating that each supplier used as many as fifteen to twenty of these.

When it comes to mass retailers like Wal-Mart and Target, who have their own toy ranges, the results of their own monitoring processes are not disclosed to any outsiders. Nor will they or any of the toy companies divulge the locations of their suppliers, arguing it is proprietary information.

All in all, two factors largely negate the real effectiveness of codes and monitoring as a way of ending abuses in China.

The first is the country's absolute, draconian ban on free association. Chinese law does not allow workers the rights to organize independently, to bargain collectively, and negotiate over working conditions. Only one trade union is legal, the All China Federation of Trade Unions, which is an arm of the Chinese Party-State. Although the ACFTU is putting effort into what it calls 'collective consultation', credibility is challenged by its reliance on the party and, more often than not, the employers, for its survival. Dissidents and work activists can be sent to labour camps for 're-education'.

Second is the seeming incompatibility between what the toy companies want from their suppliers – the lowest prices and the ability to produce in large volume at short notice, and at the same time working conditions that will not ruffle feathers in the West. The manager of a Dongguan factory told CSR Asia, 'We are under enormous stress. Customers place late orders, they change their orders part way through manufacturing, and they pay their bills late. At the same time they ask us to provide better training for our staff, better health and safety, and better accommodation. We just cannot do it all.'

By all accounts the squeeze is increasing. Big customers demand rock-bottom prices. In the words of the *Wall Street Journal*, 'It's the survival of the cheapest.' The *Financial Times*, like the *WSJ* hardly an anti-capitalist publication, notes, 'The pressure on Chinese factories, already the lowest-cost in the world, to supply goods even more cheaply is enormous.' Chan KaWai, associate director of the Hong Kong Christian Industrial Committee, estimates that prices demanded by international toy companies ordering from China fell 30 per cent in the three years to 2004.

Robin Munro, of the *China Labour Bulletin*, comments, 'Western consumers always expect prices from China to fall and the factory owners have nowhere to go but to squeeze the workforce.' At a training session for Chinese managers in Ningbo, Zhejiang province, one young manager received loud applause when he said, 'None of the foreign buyers are willing to pay for what we have to do to get certified.'

Frank Clarke, a spokesman for the American Toy Industry Association, admitted the pressure to the journal *Plastics News*: 'Retailers force prices down, it's relentless. It forces toy companies to manufacture as inexpensively as they can.'

Turnaround times constantly get shorter. One factory manager, I.Y. Sim, said that manufacturing time used to be ninety days but now 'the buyers only permit a two-week . . . time.' Another supplier, Tong

Hon Fu, said, 'Sometimes we get special demands, but we do not ask to get extra paid. The competition is very hard. If we don't accept it, other plants will receive the order.'

Toy companies, not surprisingly, see things from a different perspective. Isaac Larian, the entrepreneur behind Bratz, waxes lyrical. 'China is fantastic because you get cheap labour and they're ingenious, they're innovative. They make magic happen. Something that takes three months to do in Europe, they can do in Hong Kong or China in a week.'

The Chinese website Bingfeng Teahouse produced an interesting discussion. One visitor to a toy factory noted that the boss told him he liked Japanese buyers more than American buyers. A contributor named Elena added a message: 'Let me explain why the toy factory boss dislikes American buyers. They request better conditions for their workers but pay very low prices for the product, making it impossible for the factory boss to give better conditions to the workers as his margins are too low. Anyone who has worked with American companies such as Wal-Mart will know this. I call this hypocrisy on the part of the American buyers.'

The most hopeful portent for the Chinese toy workers may lie in something beginning to worry the industry. It may seem unbelievable in a country of 1.3 billion, but a shortage of workers has developed in areas like the Pearl River Delta. Today many factory gates carry Help Wanted signs that would have been rare a few years ago. 'We're seeing the end of the golden period of extremely low-cost labour in China,' said Hong Liang, an expert on labor costs at Goldman Sachs. 'There are plenty of workers, but the supply of un-educated workers is shrinking.'

Even the Chinese authorities accept that among the reasons for this are the very bad conditions in labour-intensive industries such as toys. One result has been to push up wages and, in some cases, force factories to improve conditions. In Shantou, Guangdong, Wei Peibin, a Barbie doll exporter, increased pay by 10 per cent in 2005 in an attempt to recruit workers. Brian Ho, a labour observer, says that in Guangdong in 2006 'there seems to be evidence now that labour conditions are improving due to shortages.' To attract workers, some companies even advertise, 'We promise we will not owe you wages.'

Could this be an indication of a better future? It may not be that simple. First, some factories blame their labour shortages on Western company auditors and local labour officials making them curb enforced excessive overtime, meaning that their workers cannot earn as much. Shortage of labour also raises the spectre of more child labour, by increasing the pressure on factory managers not to look too closely at IDs claiming applicants are over the legal age of sixteen. Observers claim this is happening already. A Chinese government survey in 2005 admitted to finding child labour most prevalent in industries which included toy manufacture. That same year the *South China Morning Post* reported that about 300 children were working under abusive conditions at a Guangdong toy factory. The factory owner was reported to have said he had been forced to ignore the minimum age because of the worker shortage.

Earlier, an official with the provincial labour bureau in Shenzhen, who spoke to *United Press International* on condition of anonymity, said factories hire children because they can be paid less and worked much harder than older, more experienced workers, who are likely to complain over low wages. The official said when government officers or foreign business executives come to inspect the factories, the managers are tipped off beforehand, and underage workers are sent home. 'It's a game to them, when the bosses come to check the factories they make everything look good for the inspection,' the official said. 'But after they leave it's back to business as usual.'

Significantly, higher factory costs because of higher wages may simply encourage a flow of work to cheaper plants elsewhere. Yangzhou, southern Jiangsu province, is a centre of stuffed-plush-toy production; some of the 600 factories there are already moving to other, less industrialized provinces where labour is cheaper. Some may move to other countries, as many are convinced the scale of China's share of world production may not continue indefinitely. However, this reduction is unlikely to happen quickly or dramatically – if at all. Robert Eckert, Mattel's CEO, made it clear in 2005 that he thought Chinese production would continue to be very high in the toy business despite increased costs: 'I suspect that the entire industry will be in China for at least the mid-term.'

To face the fact there is a very dark side to toy production is not to deny that Chinese toy factories are part of an economic boom that has saved millions from terrible poverty. Nor that, although sweatshops still exist and much of the production remains unskilled, there has been real movement up the value chain into areas like hi-tech. Quality control, mid-level management skills, and the infrastructure have all improved. Microsoft has research labs in China, and Bill Gates enthuses, 'The talent of the people there is unbelievable.' What is unique about China is that for the first time there is a poor country that can compete on the world stage with both low-wage manufacture and in making products like high-end circuit boards.

Western companies have been saved by outsourcing. For most of its history, Hornby produced its world-famous trains and Scalectric cars on its own premises in the UK. Today the plant remains, but forlorn and empty. The company, however, survives and thrives. In the mid nineties production shifted to China. Hornby decided not to cut the retail price, says Frank Martin, CEO, but to use the saving to build in more quality and detail and to develop more product: 'In the 1990s there might have been one new Hornby loco-motive in five years; nowadays we'd be looking to do at least two new each year. There might be one new Scalectric car brand each year, now we're looking at least twelve.' Before the move, says Martin, Hornby's profitability was being eroded because of competition from the 90 per cent of companies that had already moved to the Far East: 'Obviously it was very regrettable that you've got to make people redundant and reduce your workforce, but we still employ about 130 people in the UK and we've retained all the key skills. All of our product development, design, engineering, quality-standard-setting, sales, marketing, distribution – the highest-skilled high-sophistication-type jobs – are all retained in the UK.'

This is all a long way, though, from accepting that bad conditions are the alternative to no work at all. A Consensus Statement by Individual Faculty Members and Students of the Massachusetts Institute of Technology in 2001 put it well: 'While accepting that a bad job might be better than nothing, we should con-tinue to fight the abuse of human lives . . . If we justify abuse under the premise that is better than the worst alternative, we create a slippery slope leading down to the complete devaluation of human life.' Or as *New York Times* columnist Bob Herbert, a vocal critic of sweatshop abuse, wrote, 'What's next, employees who'll work for a bowl of gruel?'

With her tiny pay and all her debts – including what she owes her parents for borrowing on her behalf – Li Mei cannot save. The brutal routine, the unbearable hours and constant stress and pressure to meet excessively high daily production goals, the poor food and fatigue, drain her of hope. And only hope kept her going. She cannot resign from the factory but must apply for 'voluntary automatic leave'. This means she would be severing the 'work contract' at her own request. (When she said she had not signed such a contract, no one seemed to hear.) As punishment for this act – managers put leaving down to disloyalty and ungratefulness – she must forfeit one and a half months' wages. Without those wages, she does not have enough for the fare home.

Li Mei says, 'I'm tired to death and I don't earn much. It makes everything meaningless.' She had travelled hundreds of miles to reach the factory where her horizons have shrunk to her workplace and the dormitory. She and her family, like her fellow workers, are all caught in the same poverty trap. The desperate struggle of her parents to survive sent her away from home, the factory conditions of minimum subsistence keep her too exhausted and too indebted to return there. All she can do is go on. 'When we are working at the factory we in a way belong to the factory.'

It is unrealistic and credulous to expect that Chinese factories will voluntarily improve conditions for their workers under present circumstances. The toy industry claims codes and auditing are the answer, but that does not relieve the pressures on the factories from the companies within the industry – pressures that almost force managers to act illegally. Chinese Labour Law is in place. It is admirable, laying down minimum wages, reasonable hours, humane conditions, and protective practices. Workers have begun to protest increasingly for its enactment. But despite fine words from the authorities, empowerment remains weak, particularly in the smaller factories.

The crux of the problem of sweatshops is simple and it is this. The companies who order, the factories who supply, the local authorities who should enforce the law all have a common interest. They want cheap goods delivered on tight schedules, so that they can all thrive. The companies get their toys at the right prices and when they need them; the factory owners make money (even at low prices, if wages are small); the officials get a thriving local business community, with all that means in revenue and taxes – they adhere to the practical party message of Development Before All Else. And there is an old Chinese proverb: the mountains are high, and the Emperor is far away.

With 80 per cent made in China, we have little choice when it comes to the country of origin for the toys we buy. As a couple with a loaded trolley in a Wal-Mart in Torrance, California, in early December remarked to me, 'They're probably made under awful conditions. But what do you do? Accept it – or leave the kids with nothing?'

It's a distressing comment. The difficult truth is that we Western consumers must stop deluding ourselves. We cannot any longer demand ultra-cheap toys and expect at the same time to enjoy clear consciences. To think that we can is as naive as starting to believe in Santa Claus again.

AFTERWORD

Toys are created for children and given out of love – they are an infinitely valuable part of childhood. The best toys celebrate it, enrich it with emotion and memory.

But far too many do not. Increasingly toys are designed and then sold in ways that even five years ago would have been unthinkable. Sex, always a selling tool, is now aimed firmly at tween girls. Violence, often extreme, is targeted at boys. Toys preach sex and violence not only through themselves but via the massive spin-off superstructure with which they are so deliberately entwined – the clothes, music, film, electronics. Raunchy, suggestive, blatant, even cruel – the images here often seem more suited to an adult club than a playground.

Instead of enhancing and improving the childhood of our impressionable young, the toy business of today too often deliberately undermines it. That major part of it which constitutes the mass market seems to care little about the industry's heritage or responsibility, its place in society or its obligations to that society. Once, we could look with confidence to this industry to provide nurture along with pleasure. Not any more. Now, its major objective is to maximize sales and profits.

Acquisitiveness is constantly manipulated. Insecurities are played upon, the short attention span of youth stimulated for marketing gain. Our children are encouraged to become prematurely knowing and sexually aware – the very traits we abhor in other, more dangerous contexts, when we scream about abuse. These days, as Eric Gibson of the *Wall Street Journal* observes, 'we seem to do everything we can to rush our children into the adult world on the (erroneous) theory that the sooner they get there the better.' And it is all being done in front of our eyes, in pursuit of corporate profit. The toy industry is not alone in this, of course – but who once would have believed it would not only be deeply involved but often right at the forefront?

Even Hasbro, an old family-led firm with a long tradition of social responsibility and service to children, took a look at the success of Bratz and found it too tempting to disregard. Speaking to students at the Tuck School of Business at Dartmouth, Alan Hassenfeld, Hasbro's chairman, discussed the importance of corporate culture, ethics and morals. 'Don't only set the culture,' he said, 'live by it . . . Lead by example, not by words alone.' That was in 2005. A year later Hasbro announced its new dolls for six- to nine-year-olds for Christmas 2006 – Pussycat Dolls, modelled on the pop group that began as a risqué burlesque club act in peek-a-boo underwear. The company's general manager for marketing conceded the dolls might be a bit edgy for Hasbro consumers, 'but we're trying to add an aspect of realism.' That 'aspect' meant micro skirts, long boots and breasts (with tie-ins to Estée Lauder cosmetics and a nightclub at Caesar's Palace, Las Vegas). Hasbro was forced to change its decision as a result of a deluge of protests. The fact remained, however, that the company had planned to launch the dolls in the first place.

The obvious answer, of course, is that it is up to us. The remedy is in our own hands. We as parents are not forced to buy, no matter how great the pressures, the need to demonstrate love or to keep the kids quiet. This is what industry and marketing apologists tell us. And of course there is truth in it – we do use toys to buy absolution for the guilt of our perpetual busyness, in an attempt to provide a substitute for our love and our absences. But, in reality, being aware that it is not compulsory to buy the latest must-have toy is not a real or total answer. The deluge, the pressure, the constant day-in-day-out marketing bombardment on our kids is too great, too insidious for them and for us to withstand. The battle is too one-sided: we would have to be superhuman not to succumb at least part of the time. And the toy and marketing industries know this – and capitalize on it. They know their onslaught is so great that most of us can do little but fight a losing rearguard action.

Only a century ago children in the West, as elsewhere, were regarded and treated as miniature adults. They dressed, ate, and in many cases worked and lived just as their parents did. Today we believe that the ideal childhood should be one of imaginative play and innocence; that it is a precious and protected time. This is a very recent and very valuable concept. We must make sure it survives us.

BIBLIOGRAPHY

BOOKS

Asakawa, Gil and Leland Rucker, *The Toy Book*, Alfred Knopf, 1991

Brown, Kenneth D., *The British Toy Business, A History Since 1700*, Hambledon Press, London, 1996

Byrne, Chris, *Toys: Celebrating 100 Years of the Power of Play*, Toy Industry Association, New York, 2003

Chan, Anita, 'Culture of Survival: Lives of Migrant Workers Through the Prism of Private Letters', in Perry Link, Richard Madsen and Paul Pickowicz, eds, *Popular Thought in Post-Socialist China*, Boulder: Rowman & Littlefield, 2001

Cross, Gary, *Kids' Stuff: Toys and the Changing World of American Childhood*, Harvard University Press, 1997

De Graff, John, David Wann and Thomas H. Naylor, *Affluenza: The All-Consuming Epidemic*, Berrett-Koehler, San Francisco, 2001

Del Vecchio, Gene, *Creating Ever-Cool, A Marketer's Guide to a Kid's Heart*, Pelican Publishing, Louisiana, 1997

FAO Schwarz, The Original Toy Story, commemorative magazine published by *Playthings* magazine, New York, 2002

Fatsis, Stefan, *Word Freak: Heartbreak, Triumph, Genius, and Obsession in the World of Competitive Scrabble Players*, Penguin, 2001

Fennick, Janine, *The Collectible Barbie Doll*, second edition, Courage Books, Philadelphia, 1999

Fishman, Charles, *The Wal-Mart Effect: How the World's Most Powerful Company Really Works – and How It's Transforming the American Economy*, Penguin, New York, 2006

Fraser, Antonia, *A History of Toys*, Hamlyn, London, 1972

Handler, Ruth and Jacqueline Shannon, *Dream Doll: The Ruth Handler Story*, Longmeadow Press, 1994

Hirsh-Pasek, Kathy, *Einstein Never Used Flash Cards: How Our Children Really Learn and Why They Need to Play More and Memorize Less*, Rodale Books, 2004

Hong Kong Christian Industrial Committee, *How Hasbro, McDonald's, Mattel & Disney Manufacture Their Toys*, HKCIC, Hong Kong, 2001

Johnson, M. Eric, 'Learning from Toys. Lessons in Managing Supply Chain Risk from the Toy Industry', *California Management Review*, Spring 2001

Kaye, Marvin, *A Toy is Born*, Stein and Day, 1973

Kline, Stephen, *Out of the Garden: Toys, TV and Children's Culture in the Age of Marketing*, Verso Books, 1993

Koopman, Anne, *Charles P. Lazarus, The Titan of Toys R Us*, Garrett Educational Corporation, Oklahoma, 1992

Levy, Richard C. and Ronald O. Weingartner, *The Toy and Game Inventor's Handbook*, Alpha Books, 2003

Linn, Susan, *Consuming Kids: The Hostile Takeover of Childhood*, Anchor Books, 2005

Lord, M. G., *Forever Barbie: The Unauthorized Biography of a Real Doll*, Morrow, 1994

Luke, Tim, *Miller's American Insider's Guide to Toys & Games*, Octopus, London, 2002

McDonough, Yona Zeldis (editor), *The Barbie Chronicles*, Touchstone, Simon & Schuster, 1999

McNeal, James U., *Kids as Customers: A Handbook of Marketing to Children*, Lexington Books, 1992

McNeal, James U., *The Kids Market: Myths and Realities*, Paramount Market Publishing, 1999

McReavy, Anthony, *The Toy Story: The Life and Times of Inventor Frank Hornby*, Ebury Press, 2002

Miller, G. Wayne, *Toy Wars*, Times Books, 1998

O'Brien, Richard, *The Story of American Toys*, Abbeville Press, New York, 1990

Orbanes, Philip E., *The Game Makers: The Story of Parker Brothers*, Harvard Business School Press, 2004

Pecora, Norma Odom, *The Business of Children's Entertainment*, The Guilford Press, New York, 1998

Schneider, Cy, *Children's Television, The Art, The Business and How it Works*, NTC/Contemporary Publishing, 1989

Spock, Dr Benjamin, *Baby and Child Care*, Pocket Books, 1961

Stern, Sydney Ladensohn and Ted Schoenhaus, *Toyland: The High-Stakes Game of the Toy Industry*, Contemporary Books, 1990

Tinsman, Brian, *The Game Inventor's Guidebook*, Krause Publications, Iola, WI, 2002

Tosa, Marco, *Barbie: Four Decades of Fashion, Fantasy, and Fun*, Harry N. Abrams, New York, 1998

Toy Stories, *100 Years of Fun*, an anthology published by *Playthings* magazine, December 2002

Walsh, Tim, *The Playmakers: Amazing Origins of Timeless Toys*, Keys Publishing, Florida, 2004

Westenhouser, Kitturah B., *The Story of Barbie*, Collector Books, Kentucky, 1994

Whittaker, Nicholas, *Toys Were Us*, Orion Books, London, 2001

REPORTS

American Psychological Association, *Report of the APA Task Force on Advertising and Children*, February 2004

Annual Reports: Mattel, Hasbro, Lego, Jakks Pacific, Bandai, Brio, Tomy, Toys R Us. All for years 2002–2005

Bjurling, Kristina, *Easy to Manage – A Report on the Chinese Toy Workers and the Responsibility of the Corporations,* Fair Trade Center and Swedwatch, Sweden, May 2005

British Toy and Hobby Association, *Toy Factories: Sweat Shops or Role Models?,* Conference Proceedings, October 2001

Chan, Anita and Hong-zen Wang, *Raising Labor Standards, Corporate Social Responsibility and Missing Links – Vietnam and China Compared.* Paper presented at the conference 'The Labor of Reform: Employment, Workers' Rights, and Labor Law in China', at the University of Michigan, March 2003

Federal Trade Commission, *In the Matter of Toys R Us,* Opinion of the Commission, Public Record Version, 1998

Frost, Stephen, *Labour Standards in China, the Business and Investment Challenge,* A research paper, Association for Sustainable and Responsible Investment in Asia, Hong Kong, December 2002

Harris Nesbitt annual analysts' reports on the toy industry, years 2003, 2004, 2005, Harris Nesbitt Corp, New York

Hurst, Rosey, Hilary Murdoch and Daniella Gould, *Changing Over Time: Tackling Supply Chain Labour Issues Through Business Practice,* The Impactt Overtime Project, September 2005

International Confederation of Free Trade Unions, *Whose Miracle? How China's workers are paying the price for its economic boom,* Brussels, December 2005

Kernaghan, Charles, *Made in China: Behind the Label*, National Labor Committee, New York, March 1998

Kernaghan, Charles, *Made in China: The Role of US Companies in Denying Human and Worker Rights*, National Labor Committee, New York, May 2000

Learning from Mattel, Tuck School of Business at Dartmouth, Paper no.1-0072, Hanover, NH, 2002

Lum, Thomas, *Workplace Codes of Conduct in China and Related Labor Conditions*, Report for Congress, Washington, DC, April 2003

Mattel Inc, *Vendor Operations in Asia*, Tuck School of Business at Dartmouth, Paper no. 1-0013, Hanover, NH, 2002

Mattel Corporate Social Responsibility Reports, Mattel Inc, El Segundo, California

National Labor Committee, New York, *Toys of Misery*, February 2002

O'Rourke, Dara, *Monitoring the Monitors: A Critique of PricewaterhouseCoopers Labor Monitoring*, September 2000, unpublished paper

Playthings annual *Industry Almanac*, 101st edition, December 2003, and 102nd edition, December 2004, published by *Playthings* magazine, New York

Senate Democratic Policy Committee Hearing: Do China's Abusive Labor Practices Encourage Outsourcing and Drive Down American Wages?. March 2004

The Toy Industry in China: Undermining Workers' Rights and Rule of Law, China Labor Watch, September 2005

Toy Industries of Europe, Facts and Figures, TIE, Brussels, 2004

Toy Industry Association annual reports, 2004 and 2005, TIA, New York

Toys of Misery, Joint Report by China Labor Watch and National Labor Committee, New York, February 2004

Toys of Misery: Made in China, National Labor Committee, New York, February 2002

US Department of State, Country Reports for years 2003–2005 on Human Rights Practices: China, Washington DC

Wal-Mart: Sweatshop Toys Made in China, China Labor Watch and National Labor Committee, New York, December 2005

Wintenby, Frida, *Monitoring Compliance to Codes of Corporate Social Responsibility in China*, Department of Work Science, Gothenburg University, 2004

Wong, May and Stephen Frost, *Monitoring Mattel: Codes of Conduct, Workers and Toys in Southern China*, Asia Monitor Resource Center, Hong Kong, December 2000

Workplace Codes of Conduct in China and Related Labor Conditions, Report for Congress, The Library of Congress, April 2003

OTHER

The History of Toys and Games. A two-hour special on the History Channel, 20–21 December 2004.

PUBLICATIONS

Brandweek
China Labour Bulletin
CSR Asia Weekly
Hong Kong Trade Development Council Newsletter
International Council of Toy Industries Newsletter
KidScreen
Marketing to Kids Newsletter, Oceanside, California
Playthings
The Toy Book
Toy Directory Monthly
Toy Wishes
Toy News (UK)
Toys 'n' Playthings (UK)

ACKNOWLEDGEMENTS

It is not only products that live and die fast in the toy industry– so do jobs. The positions of people given in the book are as at the time of interview.

Nearly 200 people were interviewed at length. It would be impossible to thank individually everyone whose co-operation made this book possible. They will know who I mean and, I hope, realize how grateful I am. But there are some I must single out for special thanks.

Alan Hassenfeld, chairman of Hasbro, gave me the benefit of his unparalleled experience of a volatile industry. As did Fred Kroll, sixty-five years a toy man, who sadly died before the publication of this book. An original to the last, he had reached the age of eighty-two and had not long returned from toy selling (and scuba diving!) in Hong Kong and Australia. Stan Clutton, a senior vice-president at Fisher-Price, conveyed all that was best about the business. Sean McGowan, research analyst at investment and corporate bankers Harris Nesbitt, allowed me to observe toy executives pitching to Wall Street, and provided invaluable background and guidance on the whole business of toys. Sheldon Hirsch, CEO of Summit Media, lived up to his reputation of knowing more about toy advertising than anyone else in the US. Judy Ellis and Jennifer Lizzio, chair and assistant chair at the Toy Design Departments of the Fashion Institute of Technology, New York, and Otis College of Art, Los Angeles, respectively, shared with me their special perspectives of the industry.

A number of specialist observers, notably Maria Weiskott, editorial director of *Playthings*, Jim Silver, editor-in-chief of *Toy Wishes*, Brent Hopkins of the *Los Angeles Daily News*, and Jon Salisbury, long-time publisher of toy-industry periodicals and host of industry events in Europe and the US, unstintingly shared with me their years of insider knowledge and insight. As did Roland Earl, deputy director general of the British Toy and Hobby Association, Keith Elmer, and Andy Ralph.

At the Free Press, my editor Marty Beiser has been an inspiration and a pillar of strength on what proved to be a longer road than either of us had envisaged. I am immensely grateful to my agents, Emma Parry in New York and Bill Hamilton in London, who have been constantly and unfailingly generous with their encouragement, their expertise – and their time.

My very deepest thanks go to that wonderful institution for all writers, the Authors' Foundation. I am also immensely grateful to the London Library. In Hong Kong and China so many people were deeply involved, but I must mention particularly Chan Yan ('Chine') and Tim Pringle.

On a personal level, I thank several individuals whose interest and constant input meant so much, especially my old friends and fellow authors Raymond Hawkey and Peter Evans. David and Rosemary Cairns, Willard and Laura Balthazar, Geoff and Lisa Beldon, and Dr Allan and Christine Calder were endlessly sympathetic and patient. In New York and Los

Angeles, Susan Dudley Allen and Lorraine C. Winchester provided many kindnesses and much help. For many years, on this and other books Sybil Bedford gave warmth and encouragement, and I will truly miss her.

As always, this book would not have been written without Marcelle; I owe her more than I can ever express. And, of course, there are our children, Rachael, Charlotte and Dan, who made it clear throughout the writing of this book that they care as much about toys and childhood as I do.

SOURCES

CHAPTER ONE

Page 23. Jay Foreman quoted, 'It's up to all'. *Los Angeles Daily News*, 9 February 2006

Page 45. Bryan Ellis on broken families. *Evening Standard*, 28 January 2003

CHAPTER TWO

Page 59. 'I love ants'. Tim Walsh, *The Playmakers*

Page 62. Tim Coffey points out. *Desert News*, Salt Lake City, Utah, 16 June 2004

CHAPTER THREE

Page 78. There are many accounts of the early days of Trivial Pursuit. The most detailed is by William J. Thomas in *What's Up Niagara*, March 1985

Page 82. McNulty, 'The first time I saw'. discovergames.com

Page 82. *Wall Street Journal*, 21 November 2006

Page 87–8. Pedro Caceres quoted. *The Manufacturer*, 29 January 2004

Page 93. Phil Jackson quoted. *Business Week*, 24 November 2003

Page 93. Cranium CHIFF test. *Seattle Times*, 28 February 2004

Page 97. For the full fascinating story of Butts see Stefan Fatsis's book *Word Freak*

Page 101. Lew Herndon quoted. *Playthings*, 1 May 2001

Page 102. Whit Alexander quoted. *Northwest Indiana Times*, 26 November 1999

Page 103. Richard Tait quoted. *Seattle Post-Intelligencer*, 31 October 2003

Page 103. Game makers raised $30 million. Ibid.

CHAPTER FOUR

Page 105. Barbie sales, profits estimates. Bob Goldsborough, analyst, Ariel Capital Management, Chicago, and Anthony Gikas, senior research analyst, Piper Jaffray & Co.

Page 106. More Barbie dolls than people. Claim by financier Michael Milken after investing $200 million in Mattel during one of the company's problem periods

Page 107. Spies with telescopes. *Toyland*, Contemporary Books

Page 108. Top-selling toy figures. As at 11 March 2004, quoted *Toy News*, April 2004

Page 109. 'It's too late for Mattel'. *Keeping Ken News*, 2 March 2003

Page 109. 'Mattel's boss comes'. *The Times*, London, 4 December 2004

Page 113. 'You get hooked'. *Fortune Small Business*, 18 April 2003

Page 114. Barbie's position in a room. *Baseline*, 4 August 2005

Page 116. Pregnant Midge. *USA Today*, 24 December 2002

Page 117. Singing Baby Bouncy sales. *License! Europe*, 1 October 2003

Page 117. Started when Wal-Mart. Ibid.

Page 117. Bryant walked into. *The Guardian*, 6 October 2004

Page 118. Suggested by Carter Bryant. *The Times*, London, 4 December 2004

Page 119. Tweens $1.7 billion. *CBS Marketplace*, 9 January 2005

Page 121. 'Our mothers, they replied'. *KidScreen*, 1 February 2003

Page 123. Hasbro dropped the pink. *Toy Wars*

Page 125. Down to 70 per cent. Jim Silver, publisher *Toy Book*

Page 125. Nick Austin quoted. *Surrey Advertiser*, 10 December 2004

Page 126. 'dressed suspiciously'. *Business Week Online*, 13 December 2002

Page 128. Barbie licensed goods. Estimate Jim Silver

Page 131. 'Mattel is behaving like'. *Financial Times*, 27 March 2004

Page 132. Logan Bromer quoted. *Cornell Daily Sun*, 19 April 2005

Page 133. Lauren Beckham Falcone quoted. *Boston Herald*, 30 June 2004

Page 133. Patricia Leavy quoted. Associated Press, 22 November 2003

Page 133. Dr Sheena Hankin quoted. *Daily Telegraph*, London, 26 December 2003

Page 133. Fashion Institute of Technology students shocked. *Record*, New Jersey, 23 November 2002

Page 134. 'Kids are little rebels'. Ibid.

Page 134. Jewish Barbie dolls Associated Press, 10 September 2003

Page 134. Dr Abla Ibrahiem quoted. *Cairo Journal*, 2 June 1999

Page 135. Iranian dolls priced at. BBC World Service, 5 March 2002

Page 135. Fulla doll. *St Petersburg Times*, Florida, 15 May 2005

Page 135. Religious Jewish doll. *Totally Jewish*, 12 March 2001

Page 136. Modest Barbie clothing. *Jewish Journal of Greater Los Angeles*, 7 December 2001

Page 136. Barbie Grants A Wish Weekend. *Wall Street Journal*, 9 January 1998

Page 137. Barbie collector Paul David. Ibid.

Page 137. Mattel pursues libelous. Ibid.

Page 137. Barbie detractors emerged early. *Forever Barbie*

Page 138. Big Dyke Barbie. *Globe and Mail*, Toronto, 25 April 1997

Page 139. Tom Forsythe case. *The Times*, London, 29 June 2004

Page 139. Mattel sues MCA. Townsend and Townsend and Crew attorneys, 1 August 2003

Page 140. Simba Toys court ruling. *Deutsche Welle World*, 12 December 2004

Page 140. Barbie's Shop case. *The Calgary Sun*, 18 September 2004

Page 140. $10,000 in legal fees. *Calgary Herald*, 21 July 2005

Page 141. Jill Barad – 'protect Barbie'. *Los Angeles Times*, 10 May 1997

Page 141. Mattel agreement. *Miller's Magazine*. Ibid.

Page 141. *Barbie Gets Sad Too* film. *Humanist*, America, May–June 2002

Page 141. Steven K. Smith replies to Mattel. PhD Dissertation, Dr Michael Strangelove, University of Ottawa, 1998

Page 142. Thomas P. Conley on Larian. *Business Week*, 2 May 2005

CHAPTER FIVE

Page 149. Joe Eckroth quoted. *CIO Magazine*, 15 May 2002

Page 151. By the mid 1950s. *American Insider's Guide to Toys & Games*

Page 153. Richard Hastings quoted. *Business Week*, 24 November 2003

Page 153. Norman Walker, year of 'seismic change'. *Toy News*, January 2005

Page 157. Topper Toys, Mattel rivalry. *Sports Illustrated*, Fall 1970

Page 158. Licensed product 25 to 30 per cent sales. *Barron's*, 2 February 2005

Page 164. Andrew Berton, gaps in marketplace. Patent Café Website, 25 October 1999

Page 165. Robert Glickman quoted, 'How much'. Associated Press, 6 November 2005

Page 168. Brahm Segal quoted on Lego. *New York Times*, 2 February 2005

Page 172. Toys thrown out survey. CBBC *Newsround*, 18 May 2005

Page 172. Fred Paprin quoted. *Publishers Weekly*, 18 October 2004

Page 173. Jim Madonna quoted. *International Herald Tribune,* 2 April 2005

Page 174. Tom Conley quoted, 'special kind of person'. *TD Monthly*, October 2005

Page 176. Robotic doll will enquire. *The Sun-Herald*, Australia, 6 March 2005

CHAPTER SIX

Page 179. Sells more each year. Charles Fishman, *The Wal-Mart Effect*

Page 180. 30 per cent of the market. The top five toy retailers in 2006 were Wal-Mart 30 per cent, Target

15, Toys R Us 14, Kmart 4 and KB Toys 1. Harris Nesbitt estimates

Page 180. John Taylor quote. *Tribune News*, Knight Ridder newspapers, 9 March 2003

Page 180. Wal-Mart visits. *KidScreen*, 1 November 2003

Page 181. Price sheet for Wal-Mart. *Washington Post*, 31 May 2004

Page 181. Dennis McAlpine quote. *New York Daily News*, 1 December 2003

Page 182. Storefronts lost. Harris Nesbitt

Page 184. 'The predominance of Toys R Us'. *Toyland*

Page 184. Over $1 million in free goods. FTC document

Page 186. Withheld over $540,000. Opinion of the FTC, Public Record Version

Page 187. Rick Jackson shared his worries. *The Bloom Report*, August 2004

Page 188. Private-label toy figures. Harris Nesbitt estimates

Page 190. Nearly a third of all toys. *New York Times*, 16 August 2001

Page 190. Biggest in world. *Marketing*, 15 September 2004

Page 190. Cracker Jack figures. History of Snacks and Food, The Great Idea Finder website

Page 191. Wendy's study. *Newsweek*, 12 December 1988

Page 192. Insiders joked. *Nation's Restaurant News*, 28 June 1999

Page 192. Happy Meals a fifth business. *Wall Street Journal*, 3 March 2003

Page 192. 'One has to wonder'. Rick Munarriz, *The Motley Fool*, 20 August 2004

Page 193. Meetings to canvass opinion. *Toy News*, March 2004

Page 194. David Niggli quoted. *Playthings*, January 2005

Page 196. Kathleen McHugh quoted. *Virginian-Pilot*, Norfolk, Virginia, 30 December 2004

Page 197. The Little House, Baton Rouge. *Business Week*, 24 November 2004

Page 201. 'When the big-box retailers'. *Berkshire Eagle*, Pittsfield, MA, 24 February 2005

Page 201. 'We don't sell Big Macs'. *Seattle Post-Intelligencer*, 7 February 2004

Page 201. Learning Tree, Kansas. *KidScreen*, 1 February 2004

Page 201. Tree Top Toys dropped. *Washington Post*, 31 May 2004

Page 202. Joe Diaz quoted. *Playthings*, January 2004

CHAPTER SEVEN

Page 216. Larry Hama quoted. yojoe.com interview, December 1997

Page 217. Children's advertising rose. Ipsos-ASI, advertising pre-testing company, 2004

Page 217. Top four companies spent. *Toys and Games in the USA*, Euromonitor International, September 2005

Page 218. Advertising men have qualms. *Campaign*, 18 July 1997

Page 219. Best colour for commercials. *The Toy and Game Inventor's Handbook*

Page 219. ABC, Mattel deal. *Forever Barbie*

Page 219. Total ad spend $1 million. Stephen Kline

Page 220. Mattel now spent. *Forever Barbie*

Page 220. Regis Brown quoted. *Variety*, 10 April 2000

Page 221. Within four years, Lego. *Business Week*, 6 October 2004

Page 221. Barbie video sales. Ibid.

Page 222. Al Kahn quoted. *Animation World Magazine*, 18 February 2005

Page 222. Ian Downes quoted. *Toy News*, January 2003

Page 223. Yellow-neck duck vetoed. *Wall Street Journal*, 27 January 2006

Page 223. Ben Ferguson quoted. *Publishers Weekly*, 18 October 2004

Page 224. Al Kahn quoted. *Christian Science Monitor*, 31 March 2003

Page 226. Zero to Three defended. *Boston Globe*, 22 March 2006

Page 227. Little Robots programme. *The Guardian*, 23 July 2003

Page 227. *Dr Who* revived. *Daily Telegraph*, 3 April 2005

Page 227. Advertisement for *Bob the Builder*. *Toy News*, May 2005

Page 227. Jocelyn Stevenson quoted. *The Independent*, 13 June 2005

Page 229. *Yu-Gi-Oh* on the Net. *Wall Street Journal*, 7 October 2002

Page 230. Intelliseek analysed blogger posts. *Boston Herald*, 17 July 2005

Page 230. Top Internet destinations. Nielsen/Net Ratings

Page 231. NeoPets, time on site. Nielsen/Net Ratings 2004 figure

Page 232. Mattel software on CD-ROMS. salon.com, 15 June 2000

Page 235. Half commercials toy advertisements. *Journal of Developmental and Behavioral Pediatrics*, 2001

Page 236. Kathryn Malvisi quoted. *Sunday Times*, 29 December 2002

Page 240. Leo Zahn quoted. Ghostbusters Net Website, 19 July 1999

Page 241. Sean Brierley quoted. BBC, 23 November 1999

Page 241. Cy Schneider, special meaning. *Children's Television, The Art, The Business and How it Works*, 1989

Page 242. Leo Burnett document. *Kidscope*, Leo Burnett, London, Summer 1999

Page 242. John Geraci quoted. *CBS Market Watch*, 12 May 2004

Page 243. 'You want that nag factor'. *Chicago Sun–Times*, 31 October 2001

Page 243. Cheryl Idell, importance nagging. *National Review*, 7 July 2004

Page 244. Larian on nagging. *The Times*, London, 4 December 2004

Page 244. Professor Kathy Hirsch-Pasek quoted. *The Arizona Republic*, 7 December 2005

Page 245. Learning category sales figures. NPD tracking group

Page 246. Chartered Institute of Marketing research. *Sunday Times*, 29 December 2002

Page 246. Harris Interactive survey. *CBS Market Watch*, 12 May 2004

Page 248. European advertising bans. *Wall Street Journal*, 29 March 2004

CHAPTER EIGHT

Page 254. Number of migrant workers. Report in the official government Xinhua News Agency, 18 January 2006

Page 254. 8,000 toy factories. China Chamber of Commerce for Import and Export of Light Industrial Products and Arts-Crafts, February 2006

Page 257. 'Of the $9.99 retail price'. Asian Monitor Resource Center figures, reported Inter Press Service, 22 December 2002

Page 257. Direct labour costs for fifty toys. *How Hasbro, McDonald's, Mattel and Disney Manufacture their Toys*, Hong Kong Christian Industrial Committee, December 2001

Pages 258 et seq. Composite story of a migrant toy worker. Main reports consulted were:

Anita Chan: *The Culture of Survival*

China Workers Need Your Help – China Labor Watch 2001

Easy to Manage – A Report on the Chinese Toy Workers and the Responsibility of the Corporations, Fair Trade Center and Swedwatch, Sweden, May 2005

How Hasbro, McDonald's, Mattel and Disney Manufacture Their Toys – Hong Kong Christian Industrial Committee 2001

Made in China, National Labor Committee 2000

Spiegel On-Line, November 2005

Sweatshop Toys Made in China, China Labor Watch/National Labor Committee 2005

Toys of Misery, National Labor Committee, February 2002

Toys of Misery, National Labor Committee/China Labor Watch 2004

What's in a Sweatshop, China Labor Bulletin October 2002

Reports in: *CNN Money* 2005; *International Herald Tribune*, May 2002

Page 262. 'No one wants to invest', *Human Rights for Workers Bulletin*, 19 December 1997

Page 262. Mattel's CEO earned. *The Nation*, 30 December 1996

Page 263. Toy Industry Association statement. Reuters, 10 February 2002

Page 263. Tom Conley quoted. *TD Monthly*, September 2005

Page 264. Well under half the legal minimum. *Easy to Manage – A Report on the Chinese Toy Workers and the Responsibility of the Corporations*, Sweden, May 2005

Page 264. Han Zhili quoted. In Tim Pringle, *Labour Unrest in China – A Labour Movement in the Making*

Page 264. Robin Munro quoted. *China Labour Bulletin*, 2 November 2004

Page 264. Zhang Ye quoted. *China Business Review*, May–June 2002

Page 264. Migrant's death from overwork. *Chongqing Morning Post*, 24 August 2006

Page 265. Bosses kept back 100 billion. *Far Eastern Economic Review*, 22 January 2004

Page 268. Li Youhan quoted. *CSR Asia Weekly*, 5 October 2005

Page 269. Stephen Frost quoted. *Carnegie Council on Ethics and International Affairs Journal*, Fall 2000

Page 273. Mattel workers interviewed. *Los Angeles Times*, 26 November 2004

Page 276. Kelvin Ho Chun-Hung quoted. *South China Morning Post,* 31 January 2005

Page 276. Pricewaterhouse Coopers inspections. Dara O'Rourke, *Monitoring the Monitors*, 28 September 2000

Page 277. Cheating audits at plants. *Easy to Manage – A Report on the Chinese Toy Workers and the Responsibility of the Corporations*, Sweden, May 2005

Page 277. 90 per cent falsify records. *Financial Times*, 22 April 2005

Page 278. Impossible to check subcontractors. *Easy to Manage – A report on the Chinese Toy Workers and the Responsibility of the Corporations*, Sweden, May 2005

Page 280. Factory under enormous stress. *Financial Times*, 22 April 2005

Page 280. Robin Munro quoted. *The Observer*, London, 5 December 2004

Page 280. Training session for managers. *Straits Times*, Singapore, 17 July 2004

Page 280. Frank Clarke quoted. *Plastics News*, 19 December 2005

Page 281. Suppliers on buyer demands. *Easy to Manage – A Report on the Chinese Toy Workers and the Responsibility of the Corporations*, Sweden, May, 2005

Page 281. Website discussion group. Bingfeng Teahouse postings, 25 April and 3 May 2005

Page 281. End of golden period. *New York Times*, 3 April 2006

Page 282. Barbie exporter increased pay. *The Peninsula*, Qatar, 27 August 2005

Page 282. Companies promise not to owe. Xinhua news agency, February 2006

Page 282. Chinese government survey on child labour. *CSR Weekly*, 9 November 2005

Page 282. Children under abusive conditions. *South China Morning Post*, 15 July 2005

Page 282. Labour official quoted on child workers. *United Press International*, 26 February 2002

Page 283. Robert Eckert quoted. Mattel second quarter conference call, 2005

Page 283. Bill Gates quoted. BBC, 19 February 2004

INDEX

Abbott, Eleanor 96–7
Abbott, Scott 77–8, 79–81, 82
ABC bricks 204
ABC Television 219
Abidin, Fawaz 135
advergaming 231–4
advertising, toy 51, 111,
  219–20
advergaming 231–4; animation
  and 214–16; birth of 218–20;
  cost of 36; effectiveness
  217–18, 246–50; faster
  paced 240–1; female
  targeted 239–40; growth in
  215–17; history of 36;
  Internet 11, 220, 229, 230–3;
  male targeted 239, 240;
  preschool 225–7, 246–50;
  regulation 213–17, 246–8;
  rules 211–16; spending on
  215–17; television
  commercials 12, 36, 51–4,
  211–17, 225–7, 228–32,
  237–41, 246–50; Tickle Me

Elmo 51–4; toy led
  programming 211–28;
  Transformers 211–16
Advertising Age 216
Advertising Handbook, The
  241
agents 58, 68–9, 95
Air Pro Hockey 186
Alexander, Whit 102–3
Alien Eggs 164–5
All China Federation of Trade
  Unions 279
All Things Equal 100
Amazing Allysen 31
Amazon.com 103
American Academy of
  Pediatrics 225, 246, 249
American Girl 194–6
American Greetings 160, 161
American Psychological
  Association 241, 246
American Speciality Toy
  Retailers 196
American Student List 229

American toy industry:
  domination of 10, 39–40,
  147–9; financial value of 10,
  39–40; history of 34–8, 147,
  150–3; large retailers,
  domination of 10, 22, 39,
  178–87; large toy
  companies, domination of
  10–11, 39–40, 152–3, 162–4;
  manufacturers 11, 40–1;
  New York Toy Fair,
  importance to 24–33; small
  retailers 177–8, 193, 194–8,
  203–10; small toy
  companies 40, 65, 164–5,
  200; *see also* toy industry
Angel, Rob 97
Anjar 70
Ant Farm, the 55, 59
AOL-Time Warner 158
Applause 236
Aqua 139
Aquapets 188
Arakawa, Minoru 141–2
Arcadia Investment Corp 180
Arco 153
Ariagno, Federica 248
Arons, Russell 127
Asia Foundation 264
Asia Monitor Resource Center
  269
Auerbach, Stevanne ('Dr Toy')
  32, 42
Aunty Hilary's Toys and
  Books, Tucson 197
Austin, Nick 125
Ayers Concepts 90

Babbler 249

Baby Alive 31
Baby Born 62
Baby Einstein 245
Baby Jesus doll 158
Bacal, Joe 211, 213, 215,
  235–6, 244
backgammon 84
Barbie 17, 31, 44, 55, 63
  adaptability of 114–16;
  advertising campaigns 106,
  113, 126; American Beauty
  Queen 123; 'Anti-Barbie
  Club' 138; banned 134–5;
  Barbie Liberation Movement
  138; Barbie loves Benetton
  132; birth of 109–12; Bratz,
  rivalry with 25, 106, 108–9,
  122, 125–6, 128, 142;
  change in appearance
  115–16, 120; Collectors'
  Club 136; Day to Night 113;
  Dyke 138; Exorcist 138;
  Family Tree 116; Jewish
  dolls 135; Ken and 111–15,
  139, 243; lambasted 137–9;
  licences 126, 128–31;
  manufacture 111–12;
  marketing and research 112,
  114, 119–21, 126–7; My
  Scene 26, 126, 230; pink
  colour 120, 123, 189;
  Princess and the Pauper
  horse 163; problems with
  105–8; Really Works
  Appliances 70; rivals 25,
  108–9, 122, 125, 126, 128,
  142; secrecy and security
  139–41; sexualized image of
  132–8; Slumber Party 138;

Sweatshop 138; Trailer Trash 138; videos 122, 220–1
Barbie Gets Sad Too 141
Bar Code Battler 157
Barnes & Noble 82, 103
Barney 28, 44
Batman 159
Battleship 89
BattleX 231
BBC 225, 227
Beadell, Gary 277
Beanie Babies 11, 28, 54, 56, 191, 196, 198, 200
Beanstalk Group 159
Becker, Jim 70, 92
Beckett, Geoff 29
Bendon 223
Benetton 132
Berko, David 69
Bernstein, Bob 191
Berton, Andrew 164
Beyblades 220
Big Time Toys 164
Billund 167
Bingfeng Teahouse 281
Binney, Alice 60
Binney, Edwin 54, 60, 150
Bionicle 168, 220
Birnkrant, Mel 57, 58
Bloch, Phillip 115n
Bloom, Philip 33, 39, 187
Blues Clues 250
Blumen, Frank 32
Bob the Builder 31, 168, 220, 227, 250
Boohbah 225
Bounce Around Tigger 58
Bousquette, Matthew W. 127

Bowling, Mike 58
Brainy Baby 245
Brams, Dick 190
Bratz Fashion Dolls 148, 173, 244, 281
Barbie, rivalry with 25, 106, 108–9, 121, 122, 125, 126, 128, 142; creation of 117–18; licensing 128, 141–2, 173, 192; sexualized image of 132–5; success of 125, 141–3, 288; toy-led programming 220; Wal-Mart and 181
Break the Safe 93
Breyer 201, 202, 205
Brierley, Sean 241
Brio 44, 201, 204, 205
British Toy and Hobby Foundation 45
Bromer, Logan 132
Brown, Buster 158
Brown, Regis 220
Brunot, James 98
Bryant, Carter 117–18
Build A Bear 194, 195–6
Bulls Eye Ball 91
bungee balls 32
Burger King 192, 225
Business Week 41, 106n, 113, 126, 142, 223
Butt Ugly Martians 158
Butts, Alfred 97–9
Buzz Lightyear 17, 192, 250

Cabbage Patch Doll 23, 29, 39, 47, 54, 56–7, 61, 62–3, 155, 223, 261
Caceres, Pedro 87–8

Campaign 218
Canadian Toy Show 80
Candy Land 30, 54, 96–7, 223
Cap Toys 68, 153
CARE 268
Care Bears 31, 62
Cat in the Hat 240
Cavity Sam 84
Cha, Rosa 129
Chan, Anita 278
Charmkits 157
Charness, Wayne 189
Charren, Peggy 226
Chartered Institute of
   Marketing (UK) 246
Chebache 95
Checkered Game of Life 86
checkers 85
chess 84
Chicago International Toy and
   Game Fair 93
Chicago Sun-Times 243
Chicco 261
Chieftain Products 81
child:
   preschool 225–8, 234–5,
   248–50; psychology and toy
   marketing 18, 61, 130–2,
   227–8, 230–2, 235–7, 241–6;
   sense of play 9, 12, 171
Child World 185, 187
Children's Advertising
   Review, The (CARU) 247
Children's Market Services
   Inc. 192
Children's Online Privacy
   Protection Rule 231
Children's Programme, The
   247

Children's Television
   Workshop 51
China 37, 40, 43
   Bainan Toy Factory 258;
   child labour 282; costs of
   factory production 12, 18,
   20, 218, 256–7; Dongguan
   255, 258–9, 280; factory
   codes and auditing 267–8,
   273–4, 276–7, 279–80, 286;
   factory fires 261–2; Hasbro
   and 87–8; labour laws
   263–5, 285–6; migrant
   workers 12, 253–4, 265;
   number of factories 254;
   Pearl River Delta 252–4,
   281; Shenzhen 255, 256,
   258, 261, 274, 275, 278, 282;
   shift of production to 87–8,
   147, 169; speed of
   production 26; toy industry
   response to bad factory
   conditions in 262–4, 267–9,
   273–4, 275–6, 278, 279–81;
   Wal-Mart and 254, 276, 279,
   281, 286; working
   conditions in toy factories
   12, 258–85; Yangzhou 283
China Business Review, The
   263
China Labour Bulletin 264,
   280
Chinese Chess 48
Christensen, Martin 42
Christiansen, Ole Kirk 166,
   169n
Christmas 23, 41, 238
Chun-Hung, Kelvin Ho 276
Chunky Farm 201

Churchill, Winston 100
Circus World 33
City Toys 278
Clark, Maxine 196
Clarke, Frank 280
Clicker, Joe 56
Cluedo 30, 83, 97, 101
Clutton, Stan 38, 49, 50–1, 57, 63–4
Coffey, Tim 62
Coleco 28, 89, 155
Colorforms 55
Comcast 226
Commercial Alert 226
Conley, Thomas P. 142, 174, 263
Corbett, Jim 29
Corgi 152
Cornell University 241
Corolle dolls 203
Costco 201
Couzin, Mary 77, 93, 94, 100
Cowen, Joshua Lionel 54, 150
Cracker Jack 190
Cranium 93, 102–3
Crayola Crayons 9, 54, 60, 150, 232–3
Crumlish, Christian 136
CSCC 276
CSR Asia 280

D'Arcy Masius Benton & Bowles Communications 51
Daviau, Rob 83, 93
David, Paul 136
Dawn Dolls 157
D.E. Shaw Group 22
Destination 96
Diaz, Joe 202

DIC Entertainment 161
Dichter, Dr Ernest 243
Dickson, Richard 126, 128–31. 134
Digi Makeover 31
Dinky 175
Discovery channel 202
Disney 158, 181, 219, 230, 233, 245, 276
Dole, Kevin 237, 238, 239
Dora the Explorer 18, 159
Doubleday store 71
Downes, Ian 222
Dr Who 227
DSSAgent 232
Dubren, Ron 46–54, 56
Due, Allan M. 242
Duncan, Donald 72
Duplo 167

Early Leaning Centre 189
Easy Bake Oven 30, 55
Eckert, Robert A. 41, 148, 156, 211, 251, 283
Eckroth, Joe 149
educational toys 32, 197, 244–6
Edward Scissorhands 240
Ellis, Bryan 45
Elmer, Keith 24, 182, 206, 249
EnterZone 136
Erector Set 17, 54, 150, 201
Erickson, Erick 74–5, 160
Etch-a-Sketch 17, 54, 55, 232, 254
European Union 153, 170, 247, 248
Excel Development Group 164
Eyler, John 15, 185

Fairytale Fashions 203
Fair Trade Centre 277
Falcone, Lauren Beckham 133
FAO Schwarz 15–17, 22, 182,
    185, 193–4
Fashion Institute of
    Technology 133
fast food restaurant toys 190–3
Fatsis, Stefan 98–9
Federal Communications
    Commission 217, 247
Federal Trade Commission
    186, 229
Feely, Patrick S. 148
Ferguson, Ben 223
Financial Times 277, 280
Finding Nemo 192
Fisher-Price 9, 34–5, 37, 38,
    44, 55, 63–5, 152, 158, 235,
    261
Flavas 127–8
Flores, Pedro 71–2
Fly Pen, the 31
Folkmanis dragon puppet 178
Food Standard's Agency (UK)
    193
Foreman, Jay 23
*Forever Barbie: The
    Unauthorized Biography of
    a Real Doll* (Lord) 111
Forsythe, Tom 139
Fortune 112, 148
4Kids Entertainment 221, 222,
    224, 228
Fox 222
Friedman, Neil 52
Frisbee 55, 58, 72
Frito Lay 190
Frost, Dr Stephen 269

Fu, Tong Hon 281
Fuhrer, David 58
Fulla 135
Funky Pumpkin 239, 240
Funosophy Inc 188
Fur Real Pets 44
Furby 18, 23, 32, 54

Gabriel Games 49, 70
Galdin, Debbie 232
games
    co-branding 89; failure rate
    of 83; history of 83–6;
    invention of 78–81, 84–5,
    101–3; inventors and 78–9,
    80–1; licensed products 89;
    marketing 82–3, 89;
    resilience of 100; testing
    93–4
Garcia, Monica 136
Garfinkel, Simson 232
Gates, Bill 283
General Mills 89
Geraci, John 242
Germany 40, 150
Gibson, Eric 288
Gietz, Ken 200
Gietz, Michele 200
G.I. Joe 54, 55, 57–8, 70,
    138–9, 215, 219, 254
Gilbert, Dr A. C. 54, 150
Gimbels' 59
Girls Intelligence Agency
    233–4
Girson, Jonny 201
Glass, Marvin 72–6
Glickman, Joel 165
Glickman, Robert 165
Global Toys 34

Goldberg, Genna 63
Goldberg, Rube 73
Goldfarb, Eddy 61, 73
Goldman Sachs 281
Gon, Lee Hae 30
Gorfinkle, Anne 224
Gotti Jr, John 54
Gotz 205
Graf, Tim 95
Greenman, Nat 36
Griffin Bacal 213, 215, 233
Griffin, Tom 211, 213, 215
Grossfeld, Norman 228
Grossman, Danny 188
Grossman, Martin 164–5
Gruber, William 58
Gruelle, Johnny 59–60
Gruelle, Marcella 59–60
Grymes, Debi 197
Gund 173–4
Gutfleisch, Helmut 30

Hama, Larry 216
Hamleys 194n
Hancuff-Sellers, Susan 201
Handler, Barbara 110, 111
Handler, Elliot 110, 113
Handler, Ken 111
Handler, Ruth 110–12, 123,
    143, 219
Hands on Toys 202
Haney, Chris 77–8, 79–81, 82
Haney, John 79–80
Hankin, Dr Sheena 133
Hansa 31
Harner, Mel 236
Harris Interactive 242, 246
Harrop, Froma 133
Harry Potter 32–3, 159, 168

Harvard Medical School 241
Harwell, Sam 164
Hasbro 21, 36, 77, 261, 288–9
    advertising 211–17; anti-
    competition lawsuits 186;
    core brands 161; domination
    of market 39, 40, 65–6,
    85–6, 147, 152; evolution
    into 'lifestyle company' 173;
    failed ideas 157; games 83,
    84, 85–6, 90–1, 98, 244;
    inventors and 47, 57, 64, 65;
    licensing deals, domination
    of 158–9; manufacturing and
    assembly centre, East
    Longmeadow 87–8;
    marketing 228, 233–5;
    Mattel, rivalry with 123;
    orders 199; Pawntucket
    headquarters 87, 211; public
    relations 88; research and
    development 233–4; role in
    toy fairs 21, 23, 43; Sindy
    and 123; takeovers 85–7,
    89–90; Toys R Us,
    relationship with 188, 189
Hassenfeld, Alan:
    on business culture 288; on
    complexity of toy business
    164; on 'core brands' 161;
    on retailers 37–8; on toy
    fairs 21, 23–4, 42; on
    widening age range of toy
    market 176
Hassenfeld, Merrill 36
Hassenfeld, Stephen 212, 219
Hastings, Richard 153
Hellboy 31
He-Man 192, 220

Henley, Ian 172n
Henry J. Kaiser Family
    Foundation 226–7, 246
Herbert, Bob 285
Herndon, Lew 101
Hershey, Brian 229
Hesel, David 203–10
'Hip-Hop: The Game' 29
Hirsch, Sheldon 163, 185,
    211, 236
Hirsch-Pasek, Professor Kathy
    244
Hirtle, Mike 84, 89–90, 91–2,
    94, 100
HIT Entertainment 226, 227
Ho, Brian 282
Hodgson, Peter 71
Hokey Pokey Elmo 182, 185
Hollywood Reporter 141
Holy Folks 31
Hong Kong 43, 197, 255, 257,
    281
    Christian Industrial
    Committee 257, 276, 278,
    280; Coalition for the Safe
    Production of Toys 262; Toy
    Fair 26, 43, 122
Horn Abbot 80, 81, 82, 102
Hornby 55, 175, 284
Hornby, Frank 55, 175
Hot Wheels 10, 23, 55, 63,
    157, 182, 192, 216, 220, 238
*How the Grinch Stole
    Christmas* (Dr Seuss) 159
Howling Monkeys 96
Hughes, Gregory 29
Hula Hoops 55
Hungry Hungry Hippos 36,
    54, 91

Hyman, Greg 50, 56
Hyper Racer 158

Ibrahiem, Dr Abla 134
Ideals Toys 37, 99, 112, 158
Idell, Cheryl 243
Incredible Hulk, The 32, 159
Initiative 231
Intelliseek 230
International Council of Toys
    Industries 262, 268
*International Journal of Eating
    Disorders* 137
inventors 17, 46–76
    agents as 69; amateurs 47–8,
    68–9, 95; toy fairs and
    28–30; entrepreneurs and
    68–72; examples of 28–30,
    46–9, 56–61, 68–9; first
    great age of 54–5; games and
    83, 94–5; independent
    outsiders 54; number of
    American 47–8; patents and
    66–7; problems 62–3, 69;
    professional 92–3; rewards
    28–9, 56–8, 74, 94–5; risks
    57–8, 61–2; royalties 57–8,
    66, 95; toy companies,
    relationship with 28–9, 36,
    47, 63–5; triggers for 58–9
Iran 135
Irwin, Dr Stacey O. 225
Irwin Toys 37, 70
ITV 223

Jackson, Phil 93
Jackson, Rick 187
Jacob J. Javits Conference
    Center 24, 27–8, 32

Jaffe, Jack 89
Jakks Pacific 23, 63, 158
James, Betty 59
James, Richard 58–9
Japan 176
Jem 123, 124
Jensen, Julia 116, 124, 127, 131
Jewish dolls 134–5
John, Deborah Roedder 236
Johnny Eagle rifle 157
Johnny Service Body Shop 157
Johnson, Charlotte 111
Johnson, M. Eric 199
Jolly, Tom 94
Jupiter 232
Just Group 220
J.W. Spears Company 85

Kadar Industrial Toy Company 261
Kahn, Al 221, 222, 224
Kaiser Family Foundation Report 226–7, 246
Kalinske, Tom 148
KaWai, Chan 280
KB Toys 37, 182, 187, 208
Kearns, Ann 158
Kenner Products 33, 37, 66–7, 89, 153, 160, 261
Kernaghan, Charles 268, 278
KGOY 10, 118
Kiddie City 185, 187
Kids R Us 249
Kidshop 233
Kipling, James 66–7
Kiscom 57
Kislevitz, Adam 55

Kmart 37, 142, 208
Knerr, Richard 72
K'Nex 153, 165
Knudstorp, Jorge Vig 169
Kohner Brothers 36, 37
Koosh balls 61
Kremer, Tom 99
Kroll, Fred 34–8, 46, 66, 91, 151
Kurnit, Paul 233

Larian, Farhad 141
Larian, Isaac 108, 116
  character 109, 121, 141;
  creation of Bratz 117–18,
  122; goads Mattel 109, 126,
  128; marketing Bratz 122,
  125–6, 244; on Chinese toy
  manufacturing 281; on MGA
  173; on sexualized image of
  Bratz 134; on success of
  Bratz 142–3; on toy business
  148; protects Bratz copyright
  141
Larian, Yasmin 118
Lazarus, Charles 34, 183–4
LeapFrog 56, 148, 170–1, 173, 188, 189
LeapPad 56, 170–1
Learning Express 202
Learning Tree, The 201
Leavey, Patricia 133
Legends of Abraham 96
Lego 17, 30, 43, 163, 166–70,
  178, 188, 189, 190, 205, 208,
  220, 221, 227, 238
Legoland Park 167, 169
Leo Burnett 242
Level Works 277

Levine, Milton 59
Levy, Richard 57
Lew, Ronald 139
Lexiko 98
Liang, Hong 281
Liar Liar Pants on Fire 30
licensing deals 56–8, 62, 66–7,
    70
    agents and 57; birth of
    cartoon character deals 174;
    double license 67; extending
    brands through 44, 62–3,
    158–61; increase in 62,
    158–61; movie 44, 62, 66,
    221–2 see also under
    individual movie title;
    rewards of 158; TV
    programme 213, 215 see
    also under individual title
Lightspeed Research 229
Lilli Doll 111, 123
Lincoln Logs 54, 58
Lionel Trains 54, 150, 176
Little House, Baton Rouge,
    The 197
Little Mermaid 123
Little People 44, 55
Little Robots 227
Little Tikes Company 187
London Toy Fair 27, 43
Loomis, Bernie 33, 160
Looney Tunes 50
Loonie Lynx 36
Lord, M.G. 111, 122
Lorimar-Telepictures 216
Los Angeles Times 273, 275
Los Angeles Toy District 149
Louis Marx and Company
    220

Lowe, Edwin 89, 99
Lucas, George 141, 222

M&C Toy Centre Ltd, Hong
    Kong 25
Macdonald, Julien 131
MacDonald, Sue 230
Macy's 53, 98
Madame Alexander doll 178,
    192
Madonna, Jim 173–4
Magic Mouse Toys 201
Magic Touch Ponies 121
Maguire, Bruce 52–3
Malvisi, Kathryn 236
'Mansion of Happiness' 86
manufacturers, toy 11–13,
    41–2, 87, 111; see also
    China
marketing, branding and
    promotion 11–13, 83–4
    advergaming 231–4;
    advertising and 211–20;
    Barbie 112, 114, 119–21,
    126–7; buzz 199, 233;
    change and growth in
    211–17; child psychology
    and 18, 61, 130–2, 228–30,
    235, 241–6; consumer
    generated 233; covert data
    collection 11, 228–37;
    creating shortages 199–200;
    cross branding 83–4; fad toy,
    concentration on 171–2;
    games 83–4; 'going
    upstream' 221; history of
    34–8, 150–3, 154–7, 211–17;
    Internet 11, 229–32;
    orchestrated word of mouth

233; packaging 16, 84; secrecy, security and 75, 136; sex and violence, use of 10, 132–3, 240, 287–8; stealth 233; 'sweating the brand' 79; toy led programming 211–28; Transformers 211–16; viral 232–4; younger groups, targeting of 11, 130, 131–4, 222–4

Marry, Date or Dump? 96
Martin, Frank 175, 284
Marvel Entertainment 159
Marvin's Magic 33
Marx, Louis 37, 123, 150–1, 220
Matchbox 10, 37, 55, 60, 192
Matson, Harold 110
Mattel:
  acquisitions 63, 195; advertising 106, 212–20; Barbie, defends image of 134, 139–41; Barbie, importance of within 105–6, 110–13, 124–5; Barbie, problems with 105–8, 119–20; birth of 110; brands 127; bureaucracy 163; domination of 39, 40, 66, 89, 147, 152, 156, 186; factories 257, 262, 273–4, 275–6; failures 127–8; FOB selling and 197; fortress mentality 106; games 89, 92–3, 98, 101; Hasbro takeover, attempted 153; headquarters 106–7; interactive 232; inventors and 47, 66; K'Nex,

passes on 165; Lego plant and 167; licenses, handling of 128–31, 158–9; 'lifestyle company', evolution into a 128, 173; management team 106–8, 113, 114–16, 119–20, 127; marketing 233–4; MGA Entertainment, rivalry with 106, 108–9, 117–18, 121, 128, 136, 142; product promotions 241; profits 194, 257; research/intelligence machine 92, 114, 118–19, 125, 231; retailers, relationship with 163, 184, 188; role in toy fairs 23, 43; secrecy, lawsuits and product protection 26, 106–7, 117, 136–7, 139–40; test centre 114; TV advertising 216, 219, 230–1
May Department Stores 196
MCA Records 139–40
McAlpine, Dennis 181
McCann-Erickson 248
McDonald's 141, 190–3, 225, 231, 278
McFarlane Toys 187
McGowan, Sean 146, 155, 156, 164, 174
McHugh, Kathleen 196
McNally, Michael 220
McNeal, Professor James 234–5
McNulty, Kevin 81–2
McVicker, Joe 59
Meccano 55, 175
Mega Bloks 168–9
Megazords 31

Mei, Li 258–61, 265–7, 270–3, 274–5, 285
Melin, Arthur 'Spud' 72
Mellow, Steve 231
Messina, Mario 249
Metaframe 152
Meyer, Burt 75
MGA Entertainment 25, 109, 116, 117, 128, 136, 141, 142–3, 173, 181
Mickey Mouse 158
Mickey Mouse Club 219
Microgames of America 116
Microsoft 231, 283
Milken, Michael 170
Miller, Barbara 140
Miller, Dan 140
Miller's Magazine 140
Milton Bradley and Company 86–9, 98, 153
Miss America 123
Miss Seventeen 122
M.I.T. (Massachusetts Institute of Technology) 137, 167, 276, 284
Mobell, Sidney 85
Moehl, Bob 43, 51–4, 239, 248
Monogram Models 152
Monopoly 17, 39, 54, 83–4, 85–6, 89, 91–2, 94, 208
Monsters Inc. 191
Morris, Mark 88, 93
Morrison, Walter Frederick 72
Mousetrap 54, 73–4, 89
Mr Machine 73, 112
Mr Potato Head 17, 54, 55, 189, 219
MTV 126
Muffin the Mule 228

Munro, Alan 240
Munro, Robin 264, 280
Muppets 44
Murder 97
Murtha, Gene 50, 51
Muslim dolls 135
My Dream Baby 117
My Little Pony 223, 236
Mystical Toys 201

National Association of Broadcasters (NAB) 213, 215
National Economic Research Institute 265
National Games Week 101
National Geographic 202
National Labor Committee 263, 268
NeoPets 190, 231
Nerf Ball 54, 55, 70
Neurosmith 245, 249
New Boy 135
New York International Toy Fair 18–33, 52, 70, 71, 75, 81, 95, 103, 111, 115n, 132, 174, 204, 215
New York Times 47, 285
Nickelodeon 158, 192
Niggli, David 194
Nike 30
Ninja Turtles 39
Nintendo Corp 116, 141, 231
No Sweat 96
Noodle Kidoodle 193
Nordstrom 141
NPD Group 84
Nuremberg Toy Fair 42–3, 203, 204

Obb, The 55
Odell, Jack 60
O'Donnell, Rosie 53
O'Hare, Bucky 157
Operation 54, 84, 89
Orenstein, Henry 157
O'Rourke, Dr Dara 276
Othello 54, 92

Pace Club 186
PacMan 79
Pajeau, Charles 54
Pak-nang, Leung 276
Paprin, Fred 172–3
Pardee, Scott 95
Parker Brothers 38, 39, 85–6,
   87, 89, 98, 152
Patriot Challenge 96
PBS 225–6
Pedigree Toys 123
Peibin, Wei 282
Pictionary 54, 83, 97, 102
plastic 151–2, 152n, 167
play, child's sense of 9, 12, 171
Play-Doh 9, 17, 56, 59, 161–2,
   220
Playmates Toys 159, 161
Playmobil 205, 208
Playskool 152
PlayStation 100
Playthings 24, 162
Pluto Platter 72
Pokemon 54, 148, 222
Poland 40
Polise, Helen 239, 240
Polly Peck 230
Poses, Eric 100
Pound Puppies 58
Power Rangers 31

Powers, Pamela 201
Pox 234
Pratt, Anthony 97
Pratt, Louise 205
preschool children 50
   marketing to 222–6;
   programming 223–5
Pressman Toy Corporation 35
Pressman, Jack 35
Pretend and Play 31
Pricewaterhouse Coopers 276–7
psychology and toy marketing
   18, 61, 131–4, 228–9, 235–7,
   241–6
Pussycat Dolls 288–9

Radica Games 148
Radio Flyer Inc 25
Raggedy Ann 59–60
Rahimi, Masoumeh 105, 135
Ravensburger 205
RC2 Corporation 148
RDS 231
Rehtmeyer, Carol 62, 95
repeat buying 12
Rescue Heroes 250
retailers, toy
   closures 22, 182, 186–7;
   dominance of large 15–17,
   22, 28, 39–40, 179–89;
   inventors bypass 189–90,
   196–200; pricing 65, 181–3,
   187–8, 201; small and
   specialized 24, 28, 177–8,
   196–7, 200–3, 203–10; toy
   companies and 181, 184; *see
   also* under individual
   company name
Right Start Inc. 193

Riley, James Whitcomb 59
Risberg, Stefan 279
Risk 208
Roberts, Xavier 28, 56, 61
Rokenbok 201
Ross, Ivy 107–8, 116, 119–21,
    123–4, 127
Rowland, Pleasant 194–5
Rubik, Erno 58, 99
Rubik's Cube 29, 39, 54, 99
Rubin, Arnie 22
Rubinson, Aram 183
Rupp, Edward 239, 240
Ruskin, Gary 226

Salisbury, Jon 43, 157, 189
Sam's Club 202
Samoa Joe 30
Sandreuter, Regina 204
Scalectric 284
ScandalMonger 95
Scene It? 101
Scheman, Marty 50–2
Schneider, Cy 124n, 241
Schwarz, Frederick August
    Otto 193
Schwarz, Stephen 56, 61–2,
    65, 157, 211, 215
Scrabble 48, 54, 77–8, 82–3,
    87, 89, 97–8, 102, 208
Searles, Mike 249
Sears 112
Segal, Brahm 168
Selchow and Righter 81–2, 89,
    98
Selecta Sprielzug 209
Sesame Street 50, 51, 56, 224,
    226, 248
Sesame Workshop 158, 226

Shackelford, Judy 113
Shalek 241
Shalek, Nancy 241
Shapiro, Lisa 173
Shimmi 135
Shockinis 30
Shockwave 231
Siegel, Seth 159
Silly Putty 54, 58, 70–1
Silver, Jim 26, 149, 172–3,
    177, 189
Sim, I.Y. 280–1
Simba Toys 140
Simon 54
Simon and Schuster 98
Sindy 124
Sing and Snore Ernie 63
Singing Bouncy Baby 116–17
Sinnett, Barbara 201
Skeleton Warriors 159
Slinky 9, 59
Smith, C. Harold 54, 60, 150
Smith, Leslie 60
Smith, Rodney 60
Smith, Steven K. 141
Snakes and Ladders 85
Snoopy Sniffer 34–5, 37
Sock'em Boppers 164
Sony 231, 233
Spears 85, 89, 152
Spelling Beez 29
Spengler, Tom 231
Spiderman 32, 159
Spielberg, Steven 176, 221
SpinMaster 68–9, 173, 181
Spock, Dr Benjamin 12
SpongeBob SquarePants 158,
    159, 192, 240
SSA Public Relations 229

Star Wars 33, 66, 89, 141, 159, 161, 168, 178, 215, 222
Starz, Diva 230
Steffi Love 140
Steiff bears 201, 203
Steinem, Gloria 133
Stevenson Brothers 205
Stevenson, Jocelyn 227
Stillinger, Scott 60–1
Stompers 61
Strangelove, Dr Michael 136
Strauss, Jack 98
Strawberry Shortcake 62, 160
Stretch Armstrong 67–8
Student Marketing Group 229
Summit 236
Sunshine Symphony 245
Super Balloon 70
Super Swimmer 164
SwedWatch 277

Tait, Richard 102–3
Take Four 96
Talicor Games 101
Tamagotchi 32
Target 37, 79, 182, 202, 279
Tashjian, Joy 221
Taylor, Jody 148
Taylor, John 180
Teen Nick 126
Teletubbies 225, 249
television
  advertising *see* advertising;
  non-commercial
  broadcasting, impact of toys
  on 224–7; product licensing
  and *see* licensing; toy led
  programming 211–28
Temple University 244

Tenschen, Dick 199
Thomas the Tank Engine 201, 202, 220
Thompson, Dan 96
Thundercats 216
Tibbs, Dan 30
Tickle Me Elmo 23, 47, 49–54, 56, 63–4, 182, 224
Tickle Me Taz 50, 51
Tickles the Chimp 50
Tinker Toys 55, 152
Toad Wars 157
Toddler Tabitha 117
Tonka Corporation 55, 59, 89, 152
Toobers 202
Toon Town Online 230
Topper Toys 157
Totally Spies 223
Toy Building, International 53, 81
toy buyers 27–8
Toy Center, New York
  International 24–6, 32, 35, 172
toy companies
  advertising *see* advertising;
  domination of large 11, 43,
  88–90, 152–3, 159; failed
  152–3, 157; inventors and
  28–9, 36, 47, 63–5;
  manufacturing *see* China;
  manufacturers; marketing
  see marketing, branding and
  promotion; retailers,
  relationship with 180–1,
  201; speciality 44, 58–61,
  164–5, 201; toy fairs and 23,
  42–4; *see also* under
  individual company name

toy fairs 18–33, 42–4, 52, 70, 71, 76, 80, 81, 93, 95, 103, 132, 151, 174, 203, 204, 215; *see also* under individual fair location

toy guy, real 13, 33–40

toy industry
adult market 175–6; changing nature of 22, 38–9, 152–3, 172–4; competitiveness of 10–11, 30, 146–8, 152–3; corporate domination 10, 38–9, 146; current problems 153–7; failures 157–8; financial value of 10, 16; 'hit' mentality 41; hot toy and 53–4, 154–5, 160, 188; lifestyle entertainment business 12, 172–3, 223; prices and costs 22, 63, 65–6, 149, 181–4, 195, 206–9, 257; rewards for success 10–12, 39, 57, 71, 113–14, 128; risk factors 13, 57–8, 156; seasonality of 23, 33, 41, 149, 154; secrecy of 23n, 26, 75, 124, 129–30, 136–41; shrinking 10, 147, 152–3, 174; uniqueness 148–9, 174–5; *see also* American toy industry

Toy Industry Association 22, 29, 47, 142, 150, 174, 247, 263, 280

Toy News 41

Toy Retailers Association (UK) 198n

Toy Shop of Concord 177–8, 193, 203–10

toyshops *see* retailers, toy

Toy Story 59, 191

Toy Wishes 26

toy makers *see* toy companies and manufacturers, toy

Toys Manufacturers Association of America 150

Toys R Us 33–4, 253

Bratz and 122; buyers 207; customer relations 208; domination of 37, 39, 152, 179, 194, 205; games 189; K'Nex and 165; New York store 15–17; pricing 169; problems 183, 185–7, 188; ruins competitors 185–6; Tickle Me Elmo and 52; toy makers snub 28; Wal-Mart, rivalry with 22, 180, 183; warehouse clubs and 186

Trading Cards 101

Transformers 214–16, 217, 220, 221, 242

Treantafelles, Paula 118

Tree Top Toys 201

Trivial Pursuit 54, 58, 77–83, 84, 101

Trott, Donald 180

Tucker, Nicholas 244

Turco 152

Tweenies 225

tweens 119, 125, 127, 133, 229

Twinkleberries 148

Twister 30, 54, 57, 89, 101, 163

Tyco Toys 47, 50, 51–2, 54, 63, 123, 152, 261

Ty Inc. 199, 200

Uberplay 100
Uncle Freddie's Toy Factory 34
United Press International 282
Upstarts! 102
US-China Business Council 263
US Marine Corp 'Toys for Tots' 187
US toy industry *see* American toy industry

Varadi, Ben 68–9
Verdi, Robert 133
video games 44, 100, 103
View-Master 54, 58
Vivid Imaginations 123, 125
Vtech 173

Waddington 89, 97
Walker, Norman 43–4, 153
Wall Street Journal 118, 136, 145, 179, 256, 280, 288
Wal-Mart 22, 52, 54, 116, 117, 164, 202, 208
  Chinese manufacturing and 180, 254, 276, 279, 286; effect upon toy business of 22, 37, 39, 79, 116, 153, 179–82, 207; price slashing 180–2, 185, 187, 194, 208; size of 179; smaller retailers and 202; toy companies, relationship with 188, 189; toy fairs, involvement in 43; toy makers' snub 28
W. & S.B. Ives of Salem 86
Wang, Hong-zen 278
Warner Bros 231

Warner, H. Ty 11, 28, 56, 198–200
Webb, John 29
Weenies 57
Weiskott, Maria 24
Wendy's 191
Werner, Ed 80
Western Initiative Media Worldwide 243
Weston, Stan 57–8
WGBH 226
Whad' Ya Know? 96
Whalley, Anderson 140
Wham-O 72
Where'd You Get That? 200
Whiz Novelties 35
Who Wants To Be A Millionaire? 102
Wild Planet Toys 188, 190
Wildflower Group 172
Winnie the Pooh 44, 63, 168
Wiz-War 94
Woo, Charlie 145, 149
Wood, Anne 225
Wood, Michael 171
Worldpop 229
WPP 229
Wright, James 70–1
Wright, John Lloyd 54, 58

Xixiang, Yang 264

Yahtzee 54, 89, 100
Yakity-Yak Talking Teeth 54, 60
Ye, Zhang 264
Yoder, Ron 32
Youhan, Li 268
Young Media 223

Young, Jeremy 100
Young, Neil 176
Youngsters 206
yo-yo 71–2, 151
Yu-Gi-Oh 32, 199n, 222, 229

Zahn, Leo 240
Zany Brainy 182, 193

Zapf Creations 27, 62
Zero to Three 226
Zhili Handicraft Factory 261
Zhili, Han 264
Zicklin School of Business 262
ZipZaps 190
Ziv, Sy 33–4, 184
Zots 202

WHAT CAN I DO?
Lisa Harrow

Are you hoping to change the world?

In this handy little Yellow Pages of ethical choices, Lisa
Harrow shows you how small changes to the way you
live can make a difference. Whether you're concerned
about pesticides in food, toxic substances in your home,
poisons in children's play equipment, polluted waterways,
or, most alarmingly, water supplies drying out, this
guide to eco-friendly internet sites will give you ideas,
information, inspiration and the tools you need to make
the world a better, healthier and greener place.

If you have a green shopping bag, a compost heap or a
recycling bin you are already helping to protect the Earth.
What Can I Do? will open your eyes to other changes you
can make to protect yourself, your family, and our world,
without completely altering your way of life.

'A comprehensive and annotated guide . . . a remarkable
little book. Buy it. And use it'
Professor Lord Robert May, Oxford University

'I have seen the dying coral in the South Pacific, in the
Caribbean and in the Sea of Cortez. I have tasted the smog
in Los Angeles and Manila, and I have seen buildings
crumbling into the streets rotted by pollution in Mexico
City. I have witnessed the monumental waste of resources
all over the world, and the governments' inertia or simple
indifference. Now Lisa Harrow has given us a handbook
to help each of us make a personal start on doing our
bit to preserve the planet for future generations'
Patrick Stewart

9781905811045

eden project books

JIHAD VS. MCWORLD
Terrorism's Challenge to Democracy
Benjamin R. Barber

'A BOLD INVITATION TO DEBATE THE BROAD
CONTOURS AND FUTURE OF SOCIETY'
New York Times

Jihad vs. McWorld is an essential text for anyone
who wants to understand the challenges facing us after
the tragic events of September 11 and in light of the
current conflict in the Middle East. In this groundbreaking
and timely study, Benjamin R. Barber offers a penetrating
analysis of the central conflict of our times: consumerist
capitalism versus religious and tribal fundamentalism.
These diametrically opposed but intertwined forces
are tearing apart – and bringing together – the world
as we know it, undermining democracy and the
nation-state on which it depends.

On one hand, capitalism is rapidly dissolving the social
and economic barriers between nations, transforming
the world's diverse populations into a blandly uniform
market. On the other hand, ethnic, religious and racial
hatreds are fragmenting this political landscape into
smaller and smaller tribal units. Barber explores the
powerful and paradoxical interdependence of these
forces and suggests a game plan to enable the survival
of civic society and the core values of democracy.

'WRITTEN WITH AN EXCEPTIONAL COMBINATION
OF ERUDITION, INTELLIGENCE AND EMPATHY . . .
[*JIHAD VS. MCWORLD*] MAY HELP TO ILLUMINATE
THE PRESENT IN A TIME OF DIZZYING
TRANSFORMATIONS'
Los Angeles Times Book Review

9780552151290

CORGI BOOKS

THE MYSTERY OF CAPITAL
Hernando de Soto

'ONE OF THE FEW NEW AND GENUINELY PROMISING
APPROACHES TO OVERCOMING POVERTY TO
COME ALONG IN A LONG TIME'
Francis Fukuyama, author of *The End of History*

Why does capitalism triumph in the West but fail almost
everywhere else? Elegantly, and with rare clarity, Hernando
de Soto revolutionizes our understanding of what capital
is and why it does not benefit five-sixths of mankind.
He also proposes a solution: enabling the poor to turn
the vast assets they possess into wealth.

'A REVOLUTIONARY BOOK . . . IF THE CRITERION
IS A CAPACITY NOT ONLY TO CHANGE PERMANENTLY
THE WAY WE LOOK AT THE WORLD, BUT ALSO TO
CHANGE THE WORLD ITSELF, THEN THERE ARE GOOD
GROUNDS FOR THINKING THAT THIS BOOK IS SURELY
A CONTENDER . . . THRILLINGLY SUBVERSIVE'
Donald Macintyre, *Independent*

'FEW PEOPLE IN BRITAIN HAVE HEARD OF HERNANDO
DE SOTO . . . BUT *THE MYSTERY OF CAPITAL* HAS
ALREADY LED THE COGNOSCENTI TO PUT HIM
IN THE PANTHEON OF GREAT PROGRESSIVE
INTELLECTUALS OF OUR AGE'
Mark Leonard, *New Statesman*

'ASTONISHING . . . MAKES A BOLD, NEW
ARGUMENT ABOUT PROPERTY'
Matt Ridley, *Daily Telegraph*

'A VERY GREAT BOOK . . . POWERFUL AND
COMPLETELY CONVINCING'
Ronald Coase, Nobel Laureate in Economics

'A CRUCIAL CONTRIBUTION. A NEW PROPOSAL FOR
CHANGE THAT IS VALID FOR THE WHOLE WORLD'
Javier Perez de Cuellar, former Secretary-General of the
United Nations

9780552999236

BLACK SWAN

RUBBISH!
Richard Girling

We can no longer cope with our waste. Every hour in the UK we throw away enough rubbish to fill the Albert Hall – a statistic quoted so often that perhaps we've stopped imagining what it means. And every year the flow accelerates.

This is the story of our rubbish – from the first human bowel movement to the littering of outer space. With a handkerchief to his nose, Girling picks through our fridge mountain, our crumbling sewers, trading waste, packaging waste, hazardous industrial waste . . . it is a mucky saga of carelessness, greed and opportunism, wasted opportunity and official bungling. But *Rubbish!* is also a plea for us to consider other kinds of waste: the trashing of our landscape, the unstoppable floods of junk that clog our mailboxes, litter the skies and foul the airwaves . . .

Rubbish! may not be a conventional battle cry but this is unmistakably a call to arms – not just for the three 'R's – reduce, re-use, recycle – but for us to fight for new ideas, brave initiative rather than reliance on old systems that are crumbling before our eyes.

'THIS DEEPLY RESEARCHED, HEARTFELT BOOK WILL MAKE YOU BY TURNS DEPRESSED, ANGRY AND INSPIRED TO ACT'
Sunday Times

'BE SCARED. BE VERY SCARED. BUT BE SURE TO READ THIS BOOK'
Ben Elton

9781903919446

eden project books